Literary
San Francisco

Literary San Francisco

A Pictorial History from Its Beginnings to the Present Day

by Lawrence Ferlinghetti and Nancy J. Peters

CITY LIGHTS BOOKS
and
HARPER & ROW, PUBLISHERS, San Francisco
Cambridge, Hagerstown, Philadelphia, New York,
London, Mexico City, São Paulo, Sydney

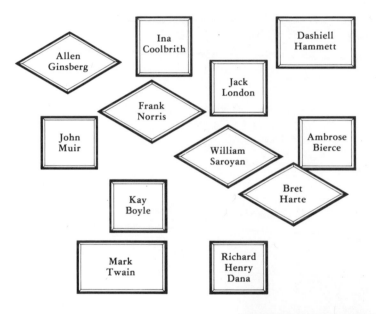

On the front

FIRST EDITION

Designed by Donna Davis

Library of Congress Cataloging in Publication Data

Peters, Nancy Joyce.
Literary San Francisco.

Bibliography: p. 237
Includes index.
1. American literature—California—San Francisco—Pictorial works. 2. San Francisco—History—Pictorial works. 3. Authors, American—California—San Francisco—Portraits. I. Ferlinghetti, Lawrence, joint author. II. Title.
PS285.S3P4 810'.8'0979461 79-3598
ISBN 0-06-250325-1

80 81 82 83 84 10 9 8 7 6 5 4 3 2 1

Contents

Acknowledgments/vii

Introduction/ix

Part One: Beginnings (Costanoan Indians through 1910)/1
Nancy J. Peters

Part Two: The Twentieth Century/121
Lawrence Ferlinghetti

Afterword/235

Bibliography/237

Photo Credits/247

Index/249

Acknowledgments

The authors thank the following organizations and their staff members: Bancroft Library, University of California, Berkeley (James D. Hart); California Section, State Library, Sacramento (Kenneth I. Pettitt); San Francisco Public Library (Gladys Hansen, Johanna Goldschmid); Oakland Public Library; Doe Library and Library Reprographic Services, University of California, Berkeley; California Historical Society; Society of California Pioneers; John Howell-Books; Holmes Book Company; KPFA (Vera S. Hopkins); ILWU Library (Carol Schwartz); New Glide Publications (Ruth Gottstein); Chinese Cultural Center; African-American Historical Society of San Francisco; City Publishing Company (Francis Ford Coppola); City Lights Bookstore; Harper and Row, San Francisco.

Special thanks for additional assistance from Oscar Lewis, Ruth Witt-Diamant, Henri Lenoir, Bob Sharrard, Raymond Foye, Joe Wolberg, Paula Lillevand, Judy Stone, Louise Kertesz, Michael Horowitz, Gui de Angulo, Carolyn Cassady, Harry Lawton, Patrick Sweeney, Bob Levy, Pamela Mosher, Neeli Cherkovski, Stephen Schwartz, David Reno, Mickey Friedman, Vincent Zukowski, Kai-yu Hsu, Paul de Fremery, and Ruthanne Lum McCunn.

Nancy J. Peters would like to acknowledge in particular these sources for Part I: *San Francisco's Literary Frontier* and *The Seacoast of Bohemia* by Franklin Walker, *The Story of the Files* by Ella Sterling Cummins Mighels, the many publications pertaining to the city's literary history by James D. Hart, and the extensive manuscript and picture collections at the Bancroft Library. She is especially grateful to research assistant Raymond Foye, Philip Lamantia, and James D. Hart, who read Part I and made useful suggestions. Errors and interpretations are her own. Lawrence Ferlinghetti thanks the authors in Part II and others who sent information, pictures, and documents. Further sources for both parts are listed at the end of the book.

Introduction

I

I grew up in New York with the firm view that nothing west of the Hudson really existed. And in that New Yorker's demented map of America, there was a high island sticking up at the far western edge of the great American slough: San Francisco. I came to it as to an island (one of those literary carpetbaggers who rode west in the early 1950s) arriving by overland train and ferry from Oakland. It looked like an island, vaguely Mediterranean, with its white buildings, a little like Tunis from the sea, not really a part of America. That was the illusion. It was very much the place where the West ended, the place where the frontier was first civilized.

The idea of an isolated San Francisco persists: as late as 1971 the Oakland Museum thought it something still to be refuted, with a historical exhibition called "California is not an island . . ."— a quote from a Father Kino in 1708. Still, we would hope this book to be no provincial effusion. For this is no Athens of the West, as some snob dubbed it. Nor is it a northern Florence to the Rome that is Los Angeles. Troy would be closer, and there are those who think

there is some wooden horse here and are forever sending out scouts, political and literary, to discover what will next burst out of it. And perhaps Helen will yet be freed.

II

Eighty or ninety years ago, when all the machines began to hum (almost, as it seemed, in unison), San Francisco was still the only city on the West Coast. Even earlier, in 1851, when John Babsone Soule (not Horace Greeley) coined the phrase "Go west, young man" he could only have had San Francisco in mind. Los Angeles was still a pastoral place of Spanish angels and Seattle a lumberjack port. By 1854, San Francisco had a polyglot population of Americans, Spaniards, French, Italians, Germans, Austrians, Chinese, British, Irish, and Australians mixed with blacks and Amerindians, with thirty-seven resident foreign consuls to serve them. There were twelve daily papers in several languages, more magazines than in London, and theaters in English, French, Spanish, German, and Chinese. This roaring town (which Daniel Webster had called a "wretched whaling station") consumed more coffee, tea, champagne, and cigars than Boston and boasted that New York dresses better than Paris, and San Francisco dresses better than New York. (It was never a cowboy town—derbies outnumbered Stetsons and sombreros.) There were almost as many hotel rooms, boarding-houses, pensions, cafés, saloons, dance halls, whorehouses, restaurants, and theaters as there were single-family houses.

It was not a family town, hardly a bourgeois society. The 1862 census reported thirty thousand men and only five thousand women. Mark Twain, who arrived in 1863, is supposed to have said, "The miner came in '49, the whore in '51, they rolled upon the barroom floor—then came the Native Son." A historian of the 1850s reported,

> On any occasion of public excitement, there is gathered together a multitude, which cannot be paralleled in any other place, of stalwart, bearded men, most of whom are in the early prime of life, fine, healthy, handsome fellows. The variety and confusion of tongues and personal characteristics, the evident physical strength, reckless bravery, and intelligence of the crowd, makes a *tout ensemble* that is very awful to contemplate . . . armed, as at all times most of them secretly are, with revolvers and bowie-knives . . . these youthful giants are the working spirits of San Francisco, that have given it a world-wide reputation for good and evil.

Until 1869 (when the Golden Spike was driven and the railroad blasted through to end the West's isolation), San Francisco was the literary capital of a huge frontier territory, with a young culture built neither on American Puritan or European petty bourgeois models nor on the old agrarian farming base. It was a wide open frontier culture with possibilities for a future ideal society such as had never existed.

But the Golden Spike nailed down much more than a rail. It nailed down an iron direction for that new world in which, up to that time, at every rutted crossroads, on every unfenced range, all possibilities, from anarchism to vigilante fascism, still existed. It nailed the future to the past. It nailed the new western world to the industrial civilization of North America and Europe. The railroad, spreading its tentacles over the West, became that octopus Frank Norris novelized, and it sowed the iron sperm of that industrial monster which rules life today.

By 1871—when the Paris Commune was proclaiming its own version of a new society—the old bourgeois values of family, propriety, property, law & order, were already becoming entrenched in San Francisco. It was no accident that the dominant style of San Francisco architecture was Victorian. It was no whim that made "Don't call it Frisco" the fashionable maxim in Nob Hill mansions looking down on Barbary Coast sailors and hustlers who called it as they saw it and played it as it lay. The Bohemian Club, started in 1872 as a men's club for free-swinging journalists, artistic wits, and part-time poets, gradually became a symbol of what was happening—the *embourgeoisement* of society—becoming in our century an enclave of merchants and bankers, high politicians, military and professional men with some artistic leanings and the politics of the Trilateral Commission, the beating heart (western division) of our military-industrial perplex.

III

It is slightly astounding that no survey of San Francisco literary history in the twentieth century has ever been published. This book is obviously an eccentric shot at it, full of our own predilections and prejudices—for how else to cover the creation of a metropolis from sand dunes and gold dust in 130 years, short of creating a "history factory" like H. H. Bancroft's? The scope of the book is limited to literary life in the San Francisco area, although literary people in picturesque provincial colonies like Carmel, Big Sur, or Bolinas have been mentioned under our breath. And the life of the theater here has also been excluded; that would take a separate book. Lastly, we should say this is not a "guide," listing all the literary presses and exact locations of birthplaces, literary plaques, and monuments in the City—that too would take a separate volume.

Naturally there are limits to the photographic essay—the thoughts of the people in the pictures seldom come through. The photos are but the surface-image of the live beings, all that remains beyond their recorded words. Behind the image, the truth vanishes. We can only guess what was really going on "behind the scenes" in each mirror of time caught here, each a window on the past, with the eternal freshness of a mirror. Were they thinking eternal truths or insipid platitudes? Probably some of each. Who among them really changed the world? They could only change it by changing the way the world saw itself. In these pictures, we see the part of them that watched the world. Some liked what they saw; others decidedly didn't. Some tried to change it; some were totally consumed by their own private dramas. A few were activist, a few insurgent. Look at them and make up your own interpretation, as we have. After all, history is mostly a fiction made of the memory of sound and fury.

Writing history is a poetic endeavor, akin to astronomy, or its opposite. Looking through the wrong end of the telescope, scanning the past, we see the gesturing figures disappearing over the horizon, into the great night of time. Still, the great voices echo above the hubbub, and do not fade away.

—LAWRENCE FERLINGHETTI

TELEGRAPH HILL

Part One: Beginnings
(Costanoan Indians through 1910)

CALIFORNIA IMAGINED. "Know ye that on the right hand of the Indies there is an island called California, very near to the Terrestrial Paradise which is peopled with black women without any men among them, because they were accustomed to live after the fashion of the Amazons. They were of strong and hardy bodies, of ardent courage and great power. In this island called California, because of the great ruggedness of the country and the innumerable wild beasts that lived in it, there were many griffins such as were found in no other part of the world." So California was first imagined. This is from Garcí Ordóñez de Montalvo's prose adventure, *Las Sergas de Esplandián* (*The Exploits of Esplandian*), written in the late fifteenth century, many years before the Spanish voyagers encountered it on the plane of reality and marked it on charts as an island. That fictional land had no base metals, only gold and precious stones. The California women, led by Queen Calafía and armed with weapons of pure gold, besieged Constantinople with the griffins as a spectacular air force. They were fierce in combat, slew Christians and Moslems alike, and brought men back to their island.

When he translated Vasco de Lobeira's *Amadís de Gaula* (*Amadis of Gaul*) from Portuguese into Spanish, Montalvo attached his own tale to the sprawling romance of knight errantry, wildly popular in the sixteenth century. Today it is remembered as the book that inspired Cervantes's hero to take the name "Don Quixote de la Mancha" and embark on his immortal adventures. In fact, when the barber and the curate sort through Quixote's books in an attempt to root out the chivalric fantasies that afflicted their friend with madness, they spare *Amadís de Gaula*, "for it was the best of all the books of this kind"; however, Montalvo's story about Esplandián, "the legitimate son of Amadís," was the first to be tossed on the fire.

Magical islands, Amazons, fabulous beasts, and treasures were part of an ancient literary heritage; and early navigators fully expected to find the marvelous on their voyages. In 1493, Columbus reported learning of an island of women warriors on his way to the Indies. Later he claimed he had sailed in the vicinity of the Terrestrial Paradise, the literal Garden of Eden. It is almost certain that the California episode of

Montalvo's tale was inserted into his book as a direct result of Columbus's account. The European imagination was ignited by the possibility that the strange things dreamed in myth, the Bible, and other ancient books were about to be uncovered in the mysterious oceans and continents that had suddenly come into being.

MORE FANTASTIC THAN FICTION. The Spaniards had already come upon genuine wonders in the civilizations of South America. When he heard an Indian legend about Ciguatan, an island of women to the north of Mexico, Hernando Cortés sped expeditions in that direction. An "island of gold and pearls" was reported by Fortún Jimenez in 1533. Maps of 1540 show "California" emerging out of unfamiliar seas, and it was hoped that fabulous riches would similarly emerge. Overland parties ventured into forbidding regions; and seamen like Juan Rodríguez Cabrillo (1542), Sebastián Rodríguez Cermeño (1595), and Sebastián Vizcaíno (1602–1603) surveyed the coast in frail galleons. Their ships' logs, diaries, and letters make up an early expository literature of dangerous encounters, astonishing landscapes and peoples, disaster, and death.

Exploration came to a halt in the seventeenth century. It wasn't until the astute Viceroy Antonio María Bucareli noted English and Russian encroachments on the Pacific coast that measures were taken to extend control over California. Gaspar de Portolá headed an expedition (1769–1770) overland to find the "excellent harbor" recommended by Vizcaíno on the last venture north. Letters and diaries tell a story of illness and near-starvation during the harrowing journey, which was a bitter disappointment to Portolá because he was unable to find the exact locations described. Portolá thought it "of no importance," but Sergeant José Ortega had stumbled upon "a great inland sea," San Francisco Bay; and before long, plans were made for occupation.

Expedition journals record how a few years later Juan Bautista de Anza headed out with two hundred forty settlers— a few friars, their servants, and soldiers with families who had previously been "submerged in poverty in Sinaloa." When they reached Monterey, a few stayed; the rest continued on to a place described as "desolating the heart with unutterable gloom," today the city of San Francisco. in 1776, the year the thirteen Atlantic colonies won their independence from England, the Mission of Saint Francis de Assís, or Dolores, was established on the barren dunes, a forlorn outpost of the Spanish empire. Father Francisco Palóu, "in the name of our sovereign amid many a cannon volley from land and sea and fusillades by the soldiers," consecrated the Presidio on September 17, "the day being the festival of the Imprinting of the Stigmata of our Seraphic Father Saint Francis."

Having resolved "to note down what-ever has happened and may happen in this new Vineyard of the Lord," Fran-cisco Palóu (c. 1722–c. 1789) became San Francisco's first writer. He and Junípero Serra had been inmates of the same religious house in La Palma, Mallorca. They came to America together and shared the rugged task of frontier conquest Palóu records in his biography of Serra, *Relación Histórica de la Vida y Apostólicas Tareas del Venerable Padre Fray Junípero Serra*, published in Mexico City in 1787. In promoting his friend for beatification, Palóu so embroidered upon Serra's real achieve-ments—distorting facts, slandering secular explorers, and supplying miracles—that this part of his book may be said to qualify as imaginative literature. Certainly his portrayal of the tough conquistador has perpetuated him as a falsely saccha-rine figure. But in all other respects, Palóu was a sharp observer and prodigious writer; his monumental chronicles (*Notícias de la Nueva California*), not limited to his nine-year stay in San Francisco, stand as the definitive record of the period.

"The Vision of Anza" by Walter Francis

Fr. Francisco Palóu

V. R. DEL V. P. F. JUNIPERO SERRA

This frontispiece of the original edition of Palóu's *Life of Junípero Serra*, the earliest Californian book, has the macabre feeling of Goya's "black paintings."

"In the beginning, the world was covered with water except for the top of a mountain peak (Diablo). Coyote stood there alone. One day he saw a feather floating on the water, drifting towards him. Suddenly it arose. It turned into Eagle and flew to join him. Eagle and Coyote were alone but soon Hummingbird came. They were surrounded by water, so Eagle, carrying Hummingbird and Coyote, flew to the Sierra de Gabilan. When the water receded, Eagle sent Coyote down the mountain to see if the world was dry yet. He told him to look in the river bed. Coyote found a beautiful young woman lying there. He married her and made her swallow a wood louse, and she gave birth to the first human beings."
— late recollection of a Costanoan myth

𝒞OYOTE VANISHES. Although Montalvo's griffins survive in the California condor, *pseudogryphus californianus,* the black Amazons failed to materialize, and the gold discovery was far in the future. Yet for thousands of years, a large population with a traditional oral literature had been living "very near to the Terrestrial Paradise." Of the approximately two hundred fifty thousand California Indians, an estimated seven thousand lived on the San Francisco Peninsula. The Costanoans (Spanish *costaños*, coastal dwellers) were comprised of several liguistically associated groups—Ohlones, Ahwastes, Romonans, Tulomos, and Altatmos—that moved around within the region's tribal watersheds. They ate the venison, birds, acorns,

berries, fish, and shellfish abundant in the Bay Area; and they had an efficient technology. Authoritarian rule, work for its own sake, and oppressive religion were unknown to them before the Europeans arrived. They were a reasonably peaceable, egalitarian people who feasted, gambled, and danced and sang to the sun, to redwood trees, and to the spirits of the Bay. Louis Choris, the Russian-born artist who visited the Mission and the Presidio in 1816, saw the Costanoans as he has depicted them in these drawings.

The missions were to convert Indians, integrating them as peon labor into Spanish feudalism. The presidios, like Roman frontier forts, were to control the natives and protect settlements from aggressors. The Indians proved not to be pagan Innocents waiting to be subjected to Christ and Crown and soon revolted against cruel discipline, sexual repression, and hard agricultural labor on rocky soil. The missions extinguished a centuries-old economic and social life. Stripped of their language and identity, deprived of freedom, rounded up by soldiers and kept under guard, the tribes at the Mission of Saint Francis, like other California Indians, died from European diseases and despair.

The Franciscans, at least, regarded them as human, if inferior, beings. After secularization of the missions (1834), in spite of courageous resistance, native Americans were robbed of their land and murdered by ruthless Anglo-American settlers and merchants. In 1850, the U.S. Indian agent was able to find in San Francisco a single Indian survivor, who told him, "I am all that is left of my people. I am alone."

So thorough was the destruction of this ancient people, "dancing on the brink of the world," as a lyric line from one of their dance songs describes them, that almost nothing of their poetic vision survived—only a few fragments of coyote tales and this song, sung by Wood Rat when animals used human speech.

Ka istun xaluyaxe	I dream jump
Ka mas ictunine	I dream of you
werenaKai	rabbit
TceicaKai	jackrabbit
ekenaKai	quail

$\mathcal{R}$OMANTIC INCURSIONS. Sir Francis Drake, plundering ships and cities to "anoy the King of Spain," stopped at Drake's Bay and points south in 1579. Chaplain Francis Fletcher, who wrote the narrative record of the *Golden Hind*'s voyage, was the first of many authors to complain of the area's summer weather: "Wee were not without some danger by reason of the many extreme gusts and flawes that beate vpon vs, which if they ceased and were still at any time, immediately vpon their intermission there followed most uile, thicke and stynking fogges."

But it wasn't until the late eighteenth century, when conflicts among expanding colonial empires were well under way, that Europeans were drawn to California. Spain had made the first claim but had only a rudimentary hold on the sparsely populated territory. The Russians were moving down the coast, harvesting seals and otters; the English, French, and Americans were hunting the mythical Northwest Passage. In 1806, Georg Heinrich Langsdorff sailed to the Spanish settlement in San Francisco with Nicolai Rezanov, hoping to secure supplies for the struggling Russian colony in Sitka. Langsdorff's *Voyages and Travels in Various Parts of the World* provided a romantic theme for generations of future writers.

Though the Spanish were suspicious of Russian intentions, the Presidio offered hospitality; and during their stay, Rezanov and the beautiful daughter of the commandant, fifteen-year-old Concepción Argüello, for reasons of state and of the heart, vowed to be wed. Rezanov set off to report to the Tsar and secure papal approval for the marriage, but he never returned. Concepción waited faithfully, then abandoned hope and entered a Dominican convent. Almost forty years later she learned Rezanov had died in the snows of Siberia before ever reaching home. Bret Harte, Gertrude Atherton, and M. G. Vallejo's granddaughter, Francisca McGettigan, wrote versions of the story; and on his 1972 trip to San Francisco, the Russian poet Andre Voznesensky researched an epic poem about the tragic lovers.

Three detailed diaries of the ship *Rurik*, which made an extended stop in the area (1816), furnish an extraordinary record of life at the Mission and Presidio; one by Otto von Kotzebue, ship's captain and son of Goethe's reactionary detractor; another by Louis Choris, the young artist whose beautiful drawings and paintings provide a rare visual record; the third by Adelbert von Chamisso, ship's naturalist and botanist, better known as a romantic poet, creator of the legendary *Peter Schlemihl*, who sold his shadow to the devil.

This engraving of the San Francisco Presidio as it looked when Rezanov courted Doña Concepción was made from a drawing by an unidentified artist on that expedition.

Franz Geritz '27

$\mathcal{F}$IESTAS, MANIFESTOS, PRONUNCIA-
MIENTOS. Isolation, problems of subsistence, and a limited population made an unfavorable climate for secular writing. The provincial cattle economy, flooded after 1810 with an abundance of land grants, led to the dominance of vast feudal estates. Residents of the *ranchos* and Presidio soldiers excelled in song, music, and dance at resplendent fiestas and in an oral rather than a written literature. Wandering bards traveled the land, and early settlers in the Bay Area shared the rich story-telling tradition of the South: romantic ballads and tales of legendary figures—perhaps of the unregenerate scoundrel Señor Juan Urdemales, the worst man who ever lived, or of La Llorona, the Mexican Medea whose sobs still haunt the night, warning the hearer of impending doom.

After Mexican independence from Spain (1821), native-born *Californios*, restless under the yoke of remote Mexico City, wanted home rule and control over trade and resented the use of California as a dumping ground for criminals. Mission land designated for Indians was grabbed by powerful private owners. Frequent political upheavals in Mexico, a dislocated economy, and shifting class relations provoked a politically oriented literature in the form of oratory, pronunciamientos, and inflammatory manifestos. Comic songs and scurrilous lampoons instead of swords were weapons in duels. *Decimas*, ten-line stanzas of vituperative verse with the power of malediction, were scrawled on walls. Local political preoccupations limited poetry to a narrow topical level, leading Mariano Guadalupe Vallejo to lament, "The country was ridden with poetasters."

"In California," noted Vallejo, "there were many poetical geniuses, but they lacked the opportunity to cultivate the spirit of the muses." The Church main-

Mariano Guadalupe Vallejo

tained stringent rules against unorthodox reading and did not encourage innovative writing. When he was a young officer at the Presidio in 1831, Vallejo bought a box of books from the supply ship *Leonor*. His purchases included forbidden works by Rousseau and Voltaire, and he was temporarily excommunicated. This episode did not deter him, for he was an avid reader and book collector. After Lieutenant Vallejo moved north permanently to his giant land-grant *ranchos*, he founded a printing press (1837), wrote poetry and a five-volume *História*, and built up the largest library in California. His memoirs reveal that when his Casa Grande burned down in 1867, he lost some twelve thousand volumes.

$\mathcal{E}$YES WEST. Captain James Cook's narrative of exotic travel revealed that huge profits could be made by selling skins to China, bringing so many traders to the West Coast that by 1820 seals and otters were almost extinct. The first English visitor to San Francisco (1792), Captain George Vancouver, described an impoverished settlement neglected by Spain in *A Voyage of Discovery*. This weakness did not go unnoticed by rising American imperialism, for even before the break with England, the revolutionists had an ambitious eye on the West. Philip Freneau, Poet of the American Revolution, was formulating the common dream of empire in *The Rising Glory of America* as Thomas Jefferson envisioned a massive highway from coast to coast and predicted in 1787 that within forty years all territory west of the Mississippi would be occupied by yeoman farmers.

About the time Andrew Jackson was trying to buy San Francisco Bay from Mexico for $500,000, the first important American literary figure sailed through the Golden Gate. Recovering from an eye ailment, Richard Henry Dana (1815–1882), a nineteen-year-old rusticated from Harvard for rebelliousness, shipped out on one of the hide and tallow vessels that had replaced the Yankee sealers in the Pacific. Dana wrote, "It was in the winter of 1835–1836 that the ship *Alert*, in the prosecution of her voyage for hides on the remote and almost unknown coast of California, floated into the vast solitude of the Bay of San Francisco. All around us was the stillness of nature. . . . Over a region far beyond our sight there were no other human habitations, except that an enterprising Yankee, years in advance of his time, had put up, on the rising ground above the landing, a shanty of rough boards, where he carried on a very small retail trade between the hide ships and the Indians."

Dana admired the "hundreds and hundreds of red deer" on the green hills in sight of Angel Island, where he and other crewmen collected a year's supply of wood. *Two Years Before the Mast*, Dana's book about life at sea and in the Mexican territory, was intended to "present the life of a common sailor at sea as it really is—the light and the dark together." "Housed on the wild sea, with wild usages": Dana chose these words to preface his book, which he hoped would ameliorate the brutal treatment suffered by seamen and secure justice for them. *Two Years Before the Mast* was an immediate popular success; it permanently influenced the literature of the sea and has never been out of print since its publication in 1840 by Harper's, which, to Dana's furious regret, bought it outright for only $250, denying him any royalties.

After graduating from Harvard, Dana entered law practice in 1840, specializing in international admiralty law and taking many maritime cases. His *The Seaman's Friend* (1841) was a standard manual of the law at sea. A founder of the Free Soil Party, he was deeply involved, too, in the antislavery movement, giving legal assistance without charge to slaves captured under the Fugitive Slave Law.

The voice of the sea called him to further travels; on a trip around the world, he returned to California, steaming into San Francisco Bay on August 13, 1859. "We bore round the point towards the old anchoring-ground of the hide ships, and there, covering the sand hills and the valleys, stretching from the water's edge to the base of the great hills, and from the old presidio to the mission, flickering all over with the lamps of its streets and houses, lay a city of one hundred thousand inhabitants."

13

CONJUNCTION OF DESTINIES. Through-out the 1840s, wagon trains flowed across the continent. The 1837 depression sent Yankee traders and land speculators, mountain men and southern farmers out West, spurred by panegyrics describing a paradise waiting to be taken from anarchic, feeble Mexico. William Gilpin, an expansionist friend of President Jackson, articulated the policy of Manifest Destiny (1845): "The untransacted destiny of the American people is to subdue the continent . . . to rush over this vast field to the Pacific Ocean . . . to confirm the destiny of the human race . . . to regenerate the superannuated nations." Congressman Buncombe's metaphor was less eloquent, but the message was unmistakably the same: "Sir, sir, we want *elbow-room*—the continent—the *whole* continent, and nothing *but* the *continent*! And we will *have* it! Then shall Uncle Sam, placing his hat upon the Canadas, rest his right arm on the Oregon and California coast, his left on the eastern sea-board, and whittle away the British power, while reposing his leg, like a freeman, upon Cape Horn!"

Walt Whitman, placing his faith in democracy and prosperity as they operated through an aggressive foreign policy and laissez-faire, gave literary expression to the theme of Manifest Destiny as he sang of brotherhood moving west to connect the earth's nations, of empire and American dominion over land and sea. "I chant the new empire, grander than before," he sang, in praise of the American who "colonizes the Pacific." Providing the context for awakened national ambitions, these beliefs rationalized America's first war of conquest, the annexation of Texas (1845), and the Mexican cession of the rest of the Southwest, including California (1848).

Alfred Robinson saw it all. He had come as a twenty-two-year-old trader to California in 1829 and married into the fabulous de la Guerra family, his gala wedding recounted by Dana in *Two Years Before the Mast*. Robinson's book, *Life in California Before the Conquest* (1846), published anonymously, is a major source of information about the waning Spanish culture. He made some accurate predictions: factories, massive trade with the Far East, the Panama Canal, gold and silver deposits in the California mountains needing only skilled miners to extract them, a huge emigration West, and a populous San Francisco.

Joseph Smith had been planting the Stakes of Zion in a westerly direction ever since the revelation of the golden tablets in Palmyra, New York. The Mormons were singing, "The upper California, oh, that's the land for me/ It lies between the mountains and the great Pacific Sea/ The Saints can be supported there; and taste the sweets of liberty." After Smith was cut down in his jail cell by the Carthage mob (1844), Brigham Young decided to get the saints out of the United States and into California but got no further than the Great Salt Lake in Utah. His colleague, Sam Brannan, however, sailed with a printing press and 238 pioneers into San Francisco harbor on July 31, 1846. To his disappointment, Captain James Montgomery had replaced the Mexican flag with the American and occupied the Pueblo less than a month before.

Brannan made the best of things; as it happened, he made a fortune. But first he set up his press and published San Francisco's first newspaper, the *California Star* (1847). The following year a special promotional edition

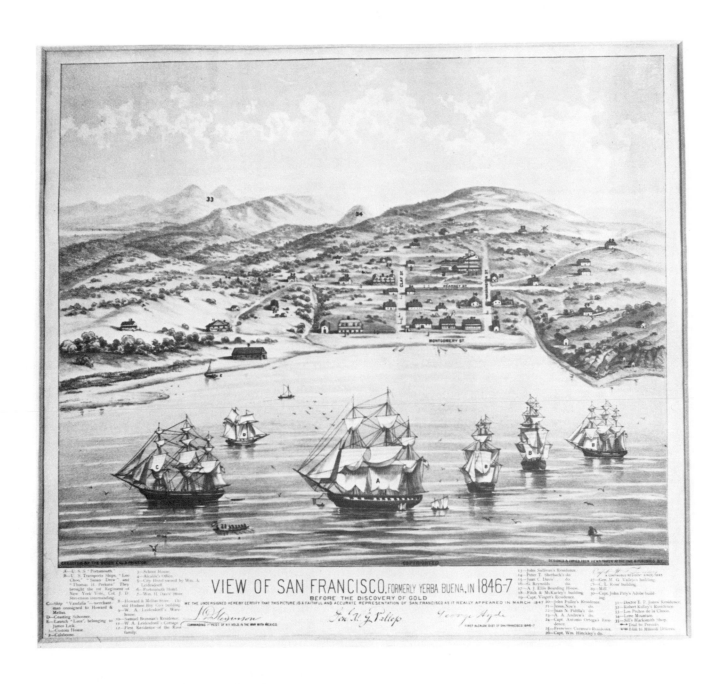

VIEW OF SAN FRANCISCO, FORMERLY YERBA BUENA, IN 1846-7
BEFORE THE DISCOVERY OF GOLD

carried the sensational news that James Marshall had discovered gold at Sutter's Fort; and when the *New York Herald* picked up the story in August 1848, the great gold rush was on.

"A Ball in the Mines" by J. D. Borthwick

$\mathcal{G}$ OLD. They came by the thousands, from all social classes and from every continent. Historian Hubert Howe Bancroft wrote, "It was no pilgrim band; not an expedition for dominance or territory, nor was it a missionary enterprise, nor a theoretical republic. It was a stampede of the nations, a hurried gathering in a magnificent wilderness for purposes of immediate gain by mining for gold." The unique circumstances of the gold rush provoked an immense quantity of writing and a world of curious readers. Among professional men of letters who wrote books about it, young Bayard Taylor, assigned to California by the *New York Tribune*, gave an attractive account of gold rush events in

a series of letters to his paper that formed the basis of his *Eldorado; or Adventures in the Path of Empire*. Many diarists left realistic, intimate, and often moving records of their experiences: Elisha Perkins Douglass (*Gold Rush Diary*), William Shaw (*Golden Dreams and Waking Realities*), Sarah Royce (*A Frontier Lady*), and J. D. Borthwick (*Three Years in California*). Scottish-born artist Borthwick enlivened his book with his own illustrations.

Some gold seekers arrived by wagon and horse across the plains; the Argonauts sailed around the Horn or across the Pacific or ventured by boat, canoe, and on foot across the menacing terrain of Panama and Nicaragua. Fiction couldn't hold a candle to this reality.

16

Heinrich Schliemann dug California gold before he uncovered treasure of another kind in Troy (*First Voyage in America*). Jacob Babcock Stillman's *Seeking the Golden Fleece* discloses typical and memorable catastrophes: swindling, profiteering, greed, illness, brutality, filth, hurricanes, shipwreck and starvation. Back East, Thoreau was disgusted, comparing the gold rush to a shameful scramble for pennies tossed by God: "Going to California. It is only 3,000 miles nearer to hell."

Through a peculiar conjunction of destinies, the discovery of gold coincided with the long Irish potato famine, starvation in China, and the devastated 1848 revolutions in Europe, bringing thousands from France, Germany, China, Ireland, England, Italy, Hungary. Every country was quick to publish books on how to make a fortune in California. Alexandre Dumas, père, wrote *Un Gil Blas en Californie* in the form of a memoir by a young Frenchman who panned for gold amid the emerald firs but saw a better future in commerce. In order to get rid of republicans and other political undesirables, the French government enlisted Dumas, fils, to run a lottery; four thousand winners were shipped off to California.

Edwin Bryant, *alcalde* in 1847, wrote *What I Saw in California* (1848), a straightforward account of his cross-country trips and conditions in the pueblo when it had a population of only a few hundred. With the discovery of gold, the publishers had to rush a new edition into print to meet the sudden demand, appending maps and gold mining tips. It was translated into many foreign languages and frequently reprinted, and it paved the way for a new genre, the California guidebook.

Oddly, the first gold rush "novel" was written by a man who had never been to California but had trained for the law in the offices of Richard Henry Dana. George Washington Peck, named for the president who purportedly never told a lie, wrote under the name Cantell A. Bigly. The title of his book, *Aurifodina; or Adventures in the Gold Region* (Ore for dinner), was a hint of the zany puns to come; for instance, heroines called Prittacritta, Rosachika, and Briteiziz; and a hero greeted by blonde natives with a cordial "*Eau de Dieu!*"

Miner,   Wall, how der du! put down your trunk
          Your journey makes you puff
          You've travelled hard, I like your spunk.
          Say! have you been up t'the 'Bluff'?
Elephant, I reckon, yes...have you?
Miner,   "Yes Sir...ee" I've been there tu,
Elephant, What saw you there? No Gold I swear!
          To get it from the Sand; you can't,
Miner,   I saw one chap when you was there,
Elephant, Who?
Miner,   I saw the "ELEPHANT."

$\int$ EEING THE ELEPHANT. Thousands of letter sheets, a combination broadside and postcard, were produced by San Francisco's artists, writers, and printers. Lithographs and wood engravings, many accompanied by verses like this delightful depiction of "seeing the elephant" or by vignettes of mining life like the letters of Louise Clappe ("Dame Shirley"), illustrated local scenes and news events. Others described the city's perpetual attractions—earthquakes, fires, assassinations and so on. Senders could simply sign their names or add a message to friends and family at home.

Like her friend Emily Dickinson, Louise (Amelia Knapp Smith) Clapp[e] (1819–1906) went to Amherst Academy and grew up during the first stirrings of New England's literary renaissance. Unlike the great poet, however, she said,

"I am a regular nomad in my passion for wandering." She had always hoped to go to the far West; so she married Dr. Fayette Clappe, who was bound for the Feather River mines to "see the elephant."

This expression originated on the East Coast, where in 1796 a live elephant was first displayed, to the amazement of Americans. To boast that one had enjoyed this novel experience was to be an initiate, a worldly person. The sardonic application of the term in the gold rush to mining life meant to have seen it all and come away with no illusions. "We have lived through so much excitement for the last three weeks, dear M," wrote Mrs. Clappe, "that I almost shrink from relating the gloomy events which have marked their flight. But if I leave out the darker shades of our mountain life, the picture will be incomplete. In the short space of 24 days, we have had murders, fearful accidents, bloody deaths, a mob, whippings, a hanging, an attempted suicide, and a duel."

This summary of events at Rich Bar is taken from Louise Clappe's perceptive, witty letters to her sister. She first issued these examples of "epistolary art" as letter sheets under the pseudonym Dame Shirley. In 1854 they were reprinted in the *Pioneer*. In *California . . . ,* Josiah Royce wrote of them, "a marvelously skillful and undoubtedly truthful history, infinitely more helpful to us than the perverse romanticism of a thousand such tales as Mr. Bret Harte's, tales that, as the world knows, were not the result of any personal experience of really primitive conditions." In fact, the central incidents of Harte's "The Outcasts of Poker Flat" and "The Luck of Roaring Camp" can be found in Mrs. Clappe's letters. Frogs must have been companions to many a miner, for Dame Shirley mentions a tame frog in a bar, a frog that was to have a celebrated cousin in Calaveras County.

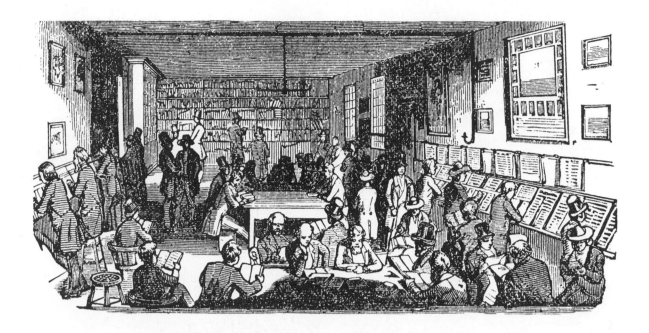

$\mathcal{B}$OOK BOOM. A multinational population, surprisingly literate, traded used books in the streets. Circulating libraries sprang up in unexpected quarters. Miners in the mountain diggings lined their rude cabins with books and formed reading clubs. In 1849, San Francisco's first two bookstores, the Pioneer Bookstore in the old City Hotel building and J. H. Still's Newsroom and Periodical Depot in Portsmouth Plaza, were founded.

The first book published in the city, *California As It Is, And As It May Be; or A Guide to the Gold Region*, was issued in 1849 by future mayor Washington Bartlett, at 8 Clay Street. Although he deplored the scarcity of women and detested the climate, the author, Felix P. Wierzbicki, M.D., encouraged his readers to come: "If people were willing to take it easy, they would, ninety-nine times out of a hundred, even like it." In addition to practical information on navigating the bay and getting along in the new city and at the mines, he dispensed a little genteel medical advice, recommending in particular abstinence from coffee, tea, and mercury.

Even before the gold rush, the *California Star* had been advertising Harper's Family Library. By 1850, there were five bookstores in town; by 1852, Cook and LeCount's shop had a stock of a hundred thousand volumes; and by 1856, the number of bookstores had increased to forty. Consignments of books were exported from New York, a nine-month passage around the Cape, and others came directly from Europe in the original French, German, Spanish, and Italian. People read the classics (Shakespeare, Pope, and Byron), the moderns (Dickens, Scott, Dumas, Sand, Stowe, and Cooper), and the mass market books (wild westerns and dime novels).

Pictured here is the library located in the men's temperance hotel, What Cheer House, opened in the early 1850s by Robert Woodward. Its low prices made it the city's most popular boardinghouse; in the mid-1860s, it boasted a thousand rooms and served three thousand meals a day. The unemployed Henry George spent a fateful winter here, where he read Adam Smith's *Wealth of Nations* and began pondering economics.

George Horatio Derby

tedium, fruitless labor, and loneliness but also reveled in euphoric release from social constraints. Out of this experience, western humor was born, full of roistering, barracks camaraderie, practical jokes, hoaxes, boasting, and tales of fantastic exploits.

The most original and daring of the pioneer jokesters was George Horatio Derby (1823–1861), who began his career at West Point. In his autobiography Mark Twain recalled that General Ulysses S. Grant told him about the time a professor gave the cadets the following problem: " 'Given, that a thousand men are besieging a fortress whose equipment of men, provisions, etc. are so and so—it is a military axiom that at the end of 45 days the fort will surrender. Now young men, if any of you were in command of such a fortress, how would you proceed?' Derby held up his hand in token that he had an answer for that question. He said, 'I would march out, let the enemy in, and at the end of 45 days I would change places with him.' "

This was a hint of the long line of outrageous hoaxes he was to perpetrate on the army, publishers, politicians, and just about everybody. Derby seems to have had only a nodding acquaintance with his superego; though this is doubtless required of military men, few have conducted their campaigns with Derby's imagination and comic gift. He was a legend in his time, a scandal, and an inspiration to his rough and ready contemporaries.

After rococo escapades in various parts, he became a leader of a group of writers who assembled at Barry and Patten's Saloon in San Francisco and contributed to the *Pioneer* under the names "Squibob" and "John Phoenix." His drawings, burlesques, and other antic writings were published posthumously as *The Squibob Papers* and *Phoenixiana.*

*T*HE GOLD RUSH was an anomaly—a rupture in Victorian decorum. Men were on a riotous holiday, displaced among unaccustomed hazards. "They were no brood of mad adventurers," wrote H. H. Bancroft, but had a "tendency to gratify present desires at the expense of the future. . . . Human nature turned loose in an unfenced field cuts queer capers. . . ." Like men at war, they endured

$\mathcal{K}$NOWN AS the Cyrano de Bergerac of California because of his large nose, forty-niner Alonzo Delano (1802?– 1874) found the road to riches a rocky one and sympathized with others who had suffered privation and disappointment. Delano wanted to tell the ironic stories of half-starved miners living in a land of gold and finding only dross, of miners plagued with homesickness, scurvy, and the bloody flux. These were men aptly described in song as "living dead in Californ-ee!"

In San Francisco in the early 1850s, he set himself up as a vegetable dealer on the waterfront and began writing prose sketches under the name "Old Block," referring to his method of writing: "When I had written my first article, weeks afterward, my pen-knife caught my eye— whittling followed in the train of thought —chips, and then the musty old saying, current in my boyhood of, 'Chips of an Old Block'; and so I carried out the association of ideas . . . meaning one who had had experience." Franklin Walker notes in *San Francisco's Literary Frontier* that Delano's articles in the *Pacific News* caught on at once, for "in them he described the greenhorn, the miner, the trader, the gambler and other Western types with just the right combination of realism, homely philosophy, pathos, and humor."

Collections of his humorous ruminations, *Pen-Knife Sketches, or Chips of the Old Block* (1853) and *Old Block's Sketch Book* (1856), charmingly illustrated by pioneer artist Charles C. Nahl, were local best-sellers. Delano's *Life on the Plains and Among the Diggings* (1854) is an engaging account of his travels, whimsical adventures, and mining days. Scenes from his Chaplinesque comedy, *A Live Woman in the Mines* (miners eating their shoes, the novelty of ladies), reappeared in Chaplin's *The Gold Rush* in a similar spirit.

After one of the many San Francisco fires "cooked his cabbages," he left his produce stall on Long Wharf, moved to the greener pastures of Grass Valley, and became a banker and developer of quartz mines.

$\mathcal{M}$OST VERSATILE of the early literary men, J. Ross Browne (1821–1875) worked on Atlantic whalers and Ohio riverboats; traveled in Africa, China, Iceland, and the South Seas; was an authority on mining engineering, an Indian agent, a foreign correspondent, and a legislative clerk. He wrote adventure fiction, satire, social commentary, and travel books, illustrating many of them himself. When he wasn't wandering, he lived at "Pagoda Hill," an eccentric family home he built in Oakland.

His *Etchings of a Whaling Cruise* (1846) preceded *Moby Dick* and was admired by Melville, who wrote a review of it, commenting on the attractive possibilities of a book about whaling life. Because many early Californians came directly from abroad, international ties encouraged foreign departments in newspapers and a market for travel books. Mark Twain modeled *Innocents Abroad* on Browne's satire, *Yusef* (1853), a comic, irreverent portrayal of traveling Americans. Browne's *Crusoe's Island . . . with Sketches of Adventures in California and Washoe* (1864) anticipated Twain's *Roughing It*. Twain drew much from Browne's humorous storytelling style and his iconoclastic probes of hypocrisy, bigotry, and the absurdities of governments and religions. After Twain had become a national literary hero, Browne once dryly remarked on his appropriations, "He made plenty of money on his books, some of it on mine."

Son of an Irish writer jailed for seditious libel and inciting revolt against English tyranny, Browne was alert to California-style injustice. As gadfly to the Indian bureau, he reiterated that "their [Indian] history in California is a melancholy record of neglect and cruelty" and urged the government to admit it encouraged genocide. He wrote with Swiftian irony: "Unacquainted with our enlightened institutions, they could not understand why they should be murdered, robbed, hunted down in this way, without any other pretense or provocation than the color of their skin and the habits of life to which they have been accustomed . . . the idea, strange as it may appear, never occurred to them that they were suffering for the great cause of civilization, which, in the natural course of things, must exterminate Indians."

Browne's lithograph from *Crusoe's Island*, "Protecting the Settlers," illustrated an event he described with heavy sarcasm: "Armed parties went into the *rancherias* in open day, when no evil was apprehended, and shot the Indians down—weak, harmless, and defenseless as they were—without distinction of age or sex; shot down women with sucking babes at their breasts; killed or crippled the naked children that were running about; and after they had achieved this brave exploit, appealed to the state government for aid."

Browne championed human rights everywhere, insisting that all people

"Protecting the Settlers"

were of the same blood. During the anti-Chinese hysteria of the 1870s in San Francisco, he wrote appreciations of China, which he visited; and his articles on Chinese culture for the local papers denounced the "popular fallacy" of racism.

*J*OHN ROLLIN RIDGE (1827–1867) was born on the prosperous Georgia plantation owned by his grandfather, Major Ridge, a Cherokee tribal chief. Ridge's father, educated in New England, married the white daughter of a Connecticut school principal, and the young couple moved to the family estate. The Cherokees disagreed about what action to take when the U.S. government broke its treaties guaranteeing Indian rights to hereditary lands being stolen by white settlers. The Ridges believed it futile to attempt a victory by military means and advised accepting government proposals for resettlement. After the tragic migration to the undesirable lands of the new western Indian Territory, an angry rival faction led by John Ross massacred the Ridges in 1839. John Rollin survived; late in his life, following the tactics of his family, he joined the Cherokee delegation to Washington to demand Indian rights (1866). Ridge is also pictured at the far left (on next page).

However, Ridge did not forget seeing his father stabbed to death. He wrote in a letter to his cousin, "There is a deep-seated principle of Revenge in me which will never be satisfied until it reaches its object." After killing a man in self-defense in the Indian Territory, Ridge gave up trying single-handedly to avenge the murder of his father, and he went to California in 1850, still gunning for the last four living assassins.

Ridge trekked through California, prospected for gold, and contributed essays and rhapsodic nature poems to the *Hesperian* and the *Golden Era* under the name "Yellow Bird," the English translation of his Cherokee name.

The anarchic growth of San Francisco condensed historical processes in an extremely rapid and violent way. "In 1856," wrote William Brewer in *Up and Down California*, "it was terrible—its fame for murder and robbery and violence spread over the world. . . . Robbers were policemen and murderers were judges. The most prominent citizens were shot in the streets." A great many non-Anglos, too, were killed by "hoodlums" in a period known for arson, mining methods that destroyed rivers and land, and the codification of laws excluding Chinese, blacks, Mexicans, and other minorities from equal justice, and laws depriving *Californios* of their homes in violation of the Treaty of Guadalupe Hidalgo.

In 1856, Yellow Bird created one of the West's most durable legends in the story of a passionate outlaw, a blood-thirsty Robin Hood well suited to the raw frontier. *The Life and Adventures of Joaquin Murieta, the Celebrated California Bandit* (1854), issued as a pamphlet illustrated dramatically by Charles Christian Nahl (whose famed painting of a wild-eyed Murieta aboard a fiery steed is pictured here), caught the popular imagination. Ridge's tale was to travel around the world, undergoing a multitude of revisions, the exploits of Murieta appearing in state histories, films, articles, and poems throughout America, Spain, France, Mexico, and Chile.

The story was based in fact. A $5000 reward was offered for a bandit, possibly named Joaquin. Exploiting an emotional

situation and seeing an easy way to make $5000, the vicious ranger Harry Love shot down the first likely Mexicans he could find, bringing back the head of the presumed Joaquin and the severed hand of his comrade, Three-Fingered Jack, which were preserved in alcohol and put on public display.

Ridge constructed a fictional past for Joaquin, borrowing incidents from mining camp lore, and he detailed the savage wrongs the bandit suffered at the hands of Anglos. Murieta left behind him "the important lesson that there is nothing so dangerous in its consequences as injustice to individuals—whether it arises from prejudice of color or from any other source; that a wrong done to one man is a wrong to society and to the world," Ridge wrote, his own principle of revenge inscribed in the contagious story of a wronged man dealing out justice and planning a revolution against the gringos.

The Golden Era.

"WESTWARD THE STAR OF EMPIRE TAKES ITS WAY"

BROOKS & LAWRENCE, PUBLISHERS, No. 543 CLAY STREET.

SAN FRANCISCO, CALIFORNIA, SUNDAY, DECEMBER 7, 1862.

VOL. XI.--NO. 1.

[Original.]

"FOREVERMORE."

BY P. JUNIOR.

We sleep, and eat, and drink,
Speak, act and think—
And then—ah! *then* what do we do?
Can you tell me, or can I you
What *then* becomes of Christian? Pagan? Jew?
When after sleeping, eating, drinking;
After speaking, acting, thinking;
After all the worry and the shame;
After all the gold and fame;
After life! O brother man! we stand
Within the clutch of Azrael's hand—
What *then* will come to you and I?
And still the stars are in the sky,
And still the billows foam ashore;
The earth is firm beneath man's tread:
Will these be thus, when I am dead?
Forevermore?

How may I find the real?
What signs reveal
The cryptic dwelling of my fate?
How question the predestinate?
How silence doubts, which alternate
With credence in analysis
That promises eternal bliss,
Or endless ministry in hell,
As one may evil do, or well?
What is the meaning of this breath
That links the opposites of life and death?
Why do I hear? and see? and feel?
Why am I flesh? and God ideal?
What is the sum of Wisdom's store?
One answer only, comes to me,
Whispered alike by Earth, and sky, and sea—
Forevermore!

And thus since Fate denies
To human eyes,
The vision of the mystery
That lays beyond Earth, Air and Sea;
And gives us but credulity;
Why then, in life, should it be wrong
To slay the *doubts* and *fears* that throng
About a *proofless* code of Right?
To turn from this eternal night
Which hides Creation's strange intent?
What is the riddle that these priests invent?
Why do their teachings reap but gold?
O brother man! the world is old,
But never yet has Science found;
Never yet could man expound;
The mighty enigmatic law,
Which gives intelligence with breath;
Which taken intelligence with death—
Forevermore.

And so, let bigots rave.
The noble, brave,
The beautiful, the sweet, the true,
While yet we live, we'll not the less pursue,
Because a motley, mongrel crew
Build altars to Hypocrisy and Cant;
Because we hear their vulgar rant.
I'll gaze into my darling's eyes
To find therein a paradise;
And while she crimsons at my kiss,
She'll crown me with a heavenly bliss—
That so intense will be, my memory
Will mirror joy eternally;
And folded in her arms I'll lie,
Lulled by the music of her sigh—
To all oblivion of vexatious creeds,
Of all Philosophy's imperious needs,
Content to wake—that o'er and o'er
Sweet rosy lips my lips may press,
To nestle in her soft caress
Forevermore.

K.G.C.

OR,

THE MYSTERIOUS KNIGHT.

A ROMANCE OF THE GREAT REBELLION.

BY G. B. DENSMORE.

CHAPTER XXXV.—MEETING AND PARTING.

Victorine was disarmed by the dignity with which her victim bore his misfortunes. She crept back to the room in which Warren was lying with a feeling of self-abasement. How contemptible seemed this craving for revenge now when it was gratified.

The room was darkened by the order of the physician. A single lamp upon a table at the foot of the bed cast a feeble and gloomy light over the apartment, just sufficient to reveal the outline of a face or figure. A man was standing by the bedside as she appeared at the door, but he stepped softly back, not turning his face toward her, and as she advanced he withdrew. She leaned over the bed and bent her face to the lip of her insensible friend. He breathed, but his breath came so faintly, his face was so still and white, his lips so cold, that she thought each moment would be the last.

"What a boon it is to die!" she murmured. "Oh, my friend! kind heart! noble man! would

Extended upon the floor in front of the door in the inner room was the form of a man, with his pistol beside him, still grasped in his hand.

flowing hair that covered her shoulders. Then he stepped back again as if he would go away without a word, but at that moment she raised her head, and her face turned toward him.

A screen shut from that part of the room all but a faint reflection of light, but she knew who stood beside her. She moved back slowly as spirits glide into darkness, and her face whose color had not changed through the stormy scenes of that night became white as the face of a corpse.

"Louise," said the man, extending his hands, "do you fear me?"

She stopped, arrested at the sound of her name spoken in that familiar tone. Gone for the moment were the years that had past since she last heard it, and, grasping the outstretched hand she sank on her knees at his feet.

"Not to me, Louise," he said, raising her in his arms, "I forgave you years ago."

"You forgave me," she repeated, "when you thought I had died."

"Then and before, but perhaps it was not till I knew you were living and heard your history that I ceased to feel resentment."

She raised her head and a half happy look drove the wearied and care-worn expression from her face.

"I thank Heaven," she whispered, "that I lived till this night."

"And I," he answered, "for you have lived to redeem yourself. "Our daughter, Louise, may now embrace her mother."

"Thank you; it is the one favor I would have asked. Oh! Mr. Graham! I hope God will reward your kindness."

"And you, Louise, I trust God will reward your integrity. How many whom we call pure, thrown upon the world as you were, would have lived as you have. But you must have suffered very much, my poor child."

"Yes, but most of all because I felt that I was despised by those whom I most loved."

"I understand you now," he said, in a sweet grave tone. "Our friend here has related your history as you told it to him."

"And you believe me?" she asked eagerly, and in the glimmering darkness her face as she raised it tenderly was lighted with ineffable happiness.

"I believe you with my whole heart and soul. I believe you so entirely, that I give our child to you to educate, and instruct in her woman's duty."

"Oh, you are too kind. I thank you, oh, I thank you for having said those words, but I dare not accept."

"Dare not?"

"What would the world say, Ralph? the world which never forgives the errors of a woman?"

"The world is at school, my friend, and we whom experience has made wise, should teach it a lesson."

"It is an old dull scholar and very hard to learn when teachings clash with its prejudices."

"Have you found it so?"

"I have found it so. For seven years, from twenty to twenty-seven, I have lived alone and lived purely, yet I dare not take my only child to my home."

"But I dare place her in your home and trust her entirely to you. It is a proof I can give to the world that I have faith in your integrity."

"You are very kind, Ralph, but it must not be. Living with me, some of the shame that will ever surround me would fall upon her. No, I thank you, Heaven knows how sincerely, but it is better that she does not know her mother is still living. Go, now; I have seen you and felt your hand clasp mine in forgiveness, and am happy. Go, Ralph, and God be with you."

"And you, Louise, where will you go?"

"I do not know."

"You will tell me, when you do know?"

"No."

"Louise!"

"But in all this I see no reason why you should deny yourself the consolation of friendship?

"No, but not yours, Ralph. Good-by."

He saw her move slowly away, her face half turned toward him. In the brighter light that fell across the doorway he saw her queenly form revealed distinctly for a moment, saw her sad but still beautiful face as she turned for a farewell look, and then she disappeared.

CHAPTER XXXVI.—EXPLANATIONS.

A few brief explanations may be necessary to account for the occurrence of the events just related.

It will be remembered that Warren had written to request the presence of Mr. Graham at G—— on the morning he sent to Baltimore for Victorine. Fully aware of the peril of his enterprise and of the danger to which Victorine would be exposed in the event of his defeat or death, he desired to procure for her the protection of some one powerful enough to shield her from the enmity of her husband and his friends.

Apart from this he justly believed that an interview with Mr. Graham, and an assurance of forgiveness for the past, would restore in some measure her self-respect and peace of mind. He arrived at G—— later in the night than he intended, and Mr Graham was impatiently waiting when Victorine and Simon drove up to the door of the hotel and were accosted by Mr. De Grey.

Mr. Graham had not then been informed that his former wife was living, as the abrupt departure of Victorine for Baltimore had prevented his meeting with Simon as Warren had promised. When Victorine disappeared with De Grey, he approached and accosted her servant. Having been advised by Warren of his purpose of procuring an interview between Victorine and Graham, Simon did not hesitate to inform his former master who the lady really was.

His surprise was profound, but when he learned that her life, since her supposed death had been free from sin, his generous and noble heart was moved with compassion.

Shortly after, Warren himself appeared. He had given the officers in command of the men the necessary directions to have all in readiness to proceed, when the time should come, upon the main object of the expedition.

He now related to Graham the history of Victorine as he had received it, her connection with the Knights, its object, and the danger which threatened her. While conversing, they had been walking through the streets to avoid observation. It was now midnight. The streets were silent, dark and deserted save by members of the Council as one by one they repaired to the hall in which their meeting was to be held.

At this stage of his narrative, they were interrupted by Simon. His intelligence upset all Warren's plans and caused, as we have seen, his complete defeat.

the opposite wing of the building. Taking advantage of a moment when the sentinel's back was towards him, he issued from his hiding-place and followed. He soon discovered in which room he was, and listening, heard his voice and another which he recognised to be a lady's. He heard enough of their conversation to learn that the lady's name was Gertrude, and that her consent was given to an immediate marriage.

Warren was surprised and indignant when he received this information. Believing that he had furnished Gertrude with indubitable evidence of the fact of Victorine being the wife of De Grey, he was at utter loss to account for her conduct. In the first bitterness of disappointment he thought he would let her go the way she had chosen, but to this Graham would not consent. Beside, De Grey was absent from the council, and if the marriage took place might not attend at all. After a brief consultation it was decided to secure him first, as quietly as possible, then promptly arrest the others. How he was defeated is already known. But Simon's first thought was for the safety of his mistress. When he saw Warren fall he glided out of the room and went to the part of the hotel in which she was confined. The sentinel was walking to and fro in the passage but, attracted by the report of a pistol and a few minutes later by the rush of men into the hotel, he came forward near the main staircase, listened a minute, then retraced his steps. The mulatto grasped his pistol by the barrel, and followed with a stealthy step till he approached the door, then with a single blow knocked him senseless at his feet. A minute sufficed to break open the door, and another to inform Victorine of what had taken place. The confusion which prevailed in the hotel favored her escape. She hurriedly wrote the little note the President afterward found upon the table, but fearful that De Grey might enter the apartment alone, she withheld the accusation afterward produced till it could be given into the hands of the President. The darkness of the night enabled her to conceal herself, and Simon, who was informed of all her plans, undertook the safe delivery of the letter.

The very care which Warren had taken through all his investigations to preserve the utmost secrecy, rendered his defeat the more complete. Had the officer in immediate command of the expedition been fully in his confidence, he might have succeeded in part. As it was he knew not what to do or which way to turn.

CHAPTER XXXVII.—DISCOVERY.

It was three o'clock when the President, accompanied by the other Members of the Council, left De Grey to return to Washington. The train in which they had come was in readiness, and an hour later they drew near their place of destination. During their journey, the events of the night as may be supposed formed the subject of conversation. They comprehended they

listened. Within all was silent. He opened the door noiselessly. Extended upon the floor in front of the door of the inner room was the form of a man, with his pistol beside him, still grasped in his hand.

Motioning to his followers to remain where they were, he advanced into the room. The man did not move. He went up and stood beside him. The rascal was sleeping.

The President knelt upon one knee, drew his handkerchief from his pocket, then signaled to his men to come forward. In a minute the three men were beside the sleeping sentinel. The President then covered his mouth with his handkerchief, one man grasped his wrists, another his feet. He awoke to find himself gagged and in a grasp of iron.

To bind his hands and feet, fasten the gag in his mouth, was the work of an instant. Then, helpless and useless as if still sleeping, he was removed from the door he had so poorly guarded.

The Chief now turned off the gas, then stepped before the inner door and tapped gently.

He heard the steps of a man crossing the room, and beckoning his men beside him, drew his pistol and waited.

"Who's there?" asked a gruff voice.

He knocked again, gently as before.

The bolt turned in the lock, the Chief stepped one side standing in darkness.

The door opened. A man's face appeared, just visible by the light reflected from the other room.

"Hist! Not a word, not a breath!" said the chief, and he softly placed the muzzle of his pistol against the man's temple.

For a time the command was literally obeyed. The man neither spoked, nor moved, nor breathed. The touch of the cold steel seemed to congeal his blood.

"You are a sensible fellow," said the President still holding the weapon against the man's head, while his assistants grasped his arms and drew him into the ante-room. "Here, sit down, and whatever else you may think of, don't forget that the first sound you make will compel me to kill you."

And the President stood over the unfortunate man while the others bound him and placed him beside his associate.

He then went to the door and looked within. A single glance assured him that there was no one there to dispute possession.

No person, but the safe containing the papers it was so necessary for him to have, stood in one corner, apparently as solid and impenetrable as a block of iron.

Apparently, but the key taken from Warren's neck, guided by a skilful hand, unlocked its iron wall and left its priceless treasures at the mercy of its captor.

He stationed one man at the outer door, the other beside the prostrate sentinels, then shut himself in the office.

He glanced over the mass of papers displayed before him. There were numerous bundles which did not concern him, and them he carefully laid aside. At last he came to those in which he was interested.

He seated himself by the table and examined them leisurely. At first he was moved as much by curiosity as by a serious apprehension that any definite information had been obtained in regard to their plans.

But soon his look became more eager, his eye gleamed and his face was like snow. He pressed his hand to his forehead and that man of iron trembled like a frightened child.

There before him was a complete list of the names the Council had selected the night before as the men they could safely advance into the confidence of the in-coming Administration—men whose connection with the Order he thought known only to himself and associates. There were others also holding high positions in the National Government, whose names were added to the list.

last that he had found all that had a bearing upon the Order, he gathered them together carefully, placed them in the grate, lighted a taper from the gas and set them afire.

The blue blaze glimmered round the edge, grew warmer and brighter as they fed on this dainty food, flashed up bravely for a minute, and died away.

A few white fleecy ashes crumbled on the grate, and that was all.

The Knight watched them till the last spark had expired then turned away with a sigh of relief. He was saved. Two hours before he had seen the life flicker on the face of his daring enemy, and go out as the blaze had died in the grate.

He placed the other papers within the safe, locked it and laid the key on the mantel. A moment later and he would have left the room, but a footstep, as of a heavy person treading softly, crossed the adjoining apartment; the door opened slightly and disclosed a familiar face.

The face came and went like a flash; the door closed, but too late. The Knight sprang forward, forced his way and stood face to face with Col. Jones.

For two or three minutes they stood gazing at each other, the eyes of the chief blazing with unutterable scorn, while the other blanched and shivered in abject fear. Then the former, disdaining words, stepped forward and laid his hand heavily on the Colonel's shoulder.

"Come," he said, moving towards the outer door.

"Where?" gasped the unfortunate Colonel.

"Silence, wretch! Come with me."

The Colonel struggled and drew back. He read his doom in the threatening brow and gleaming eye of his superior.

The latter surveyed him a moment in silence.

"Colonel Jones," he said, at length, "you have betrayed us. You must answer to me or the Council. Choose.

"Hear me," said the prisoner; "I am not guilty; I have not betrayed you."

"You are here and Warren—do you know where he is?"

"Dead, I hope," he answered bitterly.

"He is dead; now tell me how it happens that you are here and he in your place.

"In my place."

"Last evening this daring man was present at our meeting. How came he with the password?"

"I do not know."

"Very well; if you know nothing, the sooner you are out of the way the better.

The Chief closed the door of the room. His face, so calm, yet determined, signaled his dreadful purpose.

"You refuse to confess?" he said.

"No; replied the Colonel more resolutely, but I have conditions."

"Oh! you are in a position to make terms!"

"I can tell what I know or die with the secret."

"The secret! What secret?"

"Sir! you are powerful! if you promise to spare my life—"

"Impossible! our laws are imperative."

"Very well. I know nothing."

The chief reflected a moment. It was quite possible that others beside Warren were engaged in the same work and that Col. Jones knew who they were.

"Go on," he said;" "if I promise to spare your life—"

"I will tell how this has happened."

"I promise; we are alone and no one need know what passes between us."

Colonel Jones now related how he was entrapped by Warren, substantially as it is known to the reader.

The President was satisfied that Warren had no trusted associate, otherwise the recital was of little value.

"I will keep my promise," he said, "but you must come with me."

"Where?"

"I will conduct you myself. Recollect it was your life I promised to spare."

He looked at his victim significantly and smiled.

"Have no fear, my friend," he said softly. "You shall live. Come, it is nearly morning."

The Colonel followed shudderingly. The smile and soft tone conveyed a threat the more dreaded because so vague.

CHAPTER XXXVIII.—THE SURGEON.

A strong desire to see her fallen champion had induced Victorine to return to the hotel, after the departure of the Council, but she knew that it would not be safe to remain. Her confession, while it worked the ruin of her hus-

$\mathscr{G}$ OLDEN DAWN OF LITERARY JOURNALS. California became a state in 1850, but because the overland telegraph did not make its effect felt on journalism for another decade, news came irregularly to isolated San Francisco. All the papers had more space for local affairs, editorials, and literary material, giving them a provincial flavor and a vigorous originality. "Full of intelligence, fun, news, and incidents," as it announced itself, the *Golden Era* (1852–1893) was the king of the early literary journals. Begun by J. Macdonough Foard, twenty-one, and Rollin M. Daggett, nineteen, the informal weekly in newspaper format was a smashing success from its first issue in 1852. Daggett hiked through the mountain diggings selling subscriptions to the miners at $5 a year, and circulation skyrocketed. The early *Golden Era*, the "*vade mecum* of the mining camps," was a mix of old news, gossip, opinions, articles reprinted from the encyclopedia and elsewhere, and poetry and sketches by local writers signing themselves with noms de plume such as "Jeems Pipes of Pipesville," "Riding Hood," and "Comet Quirls."

Unique features, such as a correspondents' column that answered readers' queries and supplied odd bits of trivia, endeared it to frontiersmen. It published whatever lines of rude verse a miner or pioneer wife might be inspired to send; some received encouragement, others, sparkling admonishments. The better poetry appeared on the front page in the "Poets Corner" along with serialized "sensation" novels. Parodies of acclaimed authors and a fair proportion of comic horseplay gave a firm foundation to San Francisco's long tradition of jocular journalism.

The *Pioneer* (1854–1856), the first literary monthly, was modeled on *Knickerbocker Magazine* and aimed "to avoid heavy twaddle and to seek to entertain." It was heavy with learned essays lightened occasionally by sketches and verse. Its creator, Ferdinand Ewer, a Harvard man, became notorious for a spiritualist hoax and for alarming personal oscillations between bizarre high church and roaring atheism.

Hutchings's California Magazine (1856–1861) came into being because J. M. Hutchings was put off by the *Pioneer*'s "ponderousness." It mainly promoted the state's natural wonders and prefigured recreational and literary interest in mountains. Hutchings scored an earlier literary success of sorts when his comic parody, "The Miner's Ten Commandments," sold a phenomenal ninety-seven-thousand copies as a letter sheet.

The *Hesperian* (1858–1863), founded by women (Mmes. F. H. Day and J. D. Strong) for women, promulgated culture—from the sublime thought of Milton to the art of muffin-making. Poems like Anna Fitch's "The Song of the Flume" and articles like W. Wadsworth's "A Digger Woman of Olden Times" added seriousness to the main attraction, colored fashion plates. Other publications disparaged western women for being too forthright and assertive; the *Hesperian* forthrightly countered that view.

"A Question of Title."

RATTLESNAKE JOURNALISTS IN ALKALI HELL. The gold rush didn't last long, and cycles of inflation, panic, and depression plagued the 1850s. Discovery of Nevada silver (1859) kindled feverish activity; once again the miners, promoters, and speculators were on the move. Virginia City, San Francisco's mining suburb, shot up overnight in the waterless, treeless "alkaline hell and high winds" of Mount Davidson in Washoe County. The Comstock Lode yielded over $400,000,000 in ores, but fortunes were made by only a handful of bonanza kings and bankers. Of interest to literature are the riotous years of the first bonanza.

J. Ross Browne depicted the frontier spirit in this illustration of Comstock in *Crusoe's Island*.

Joseph T. Goodman, typesetter at the *Golden Era*, headed over the Sierra Nevada; bought the *Virginia City Territorial Enterprise* for $40; and with a staff of boisterous young newsmen, set out "to keep the universe thoroughly posted concerning murders and street fights, and balls and theaters, and packtrains, and churches, and lectures, and highway robberies, and Bible societies . . . and the thousand other things which it is in the province of local reporters to keep track of and magnify into undue importance for the readers of a great daily newspaper."

Goodman was twenty-three then; his paper and its writers were to make history. There was Rollin Daggett, restless at the *Golden Era*, who joined the freewheeling *Enterprise* and wrote *Braxton's Bar*, an adventure novel of placer mining that included the true story of his rescue by a phantom bull in the Sierra Nevada. Daggett's political involvement ultimately led to his election to Congress and appointment as minister to Hawaii. There was city editor William Wright, better known by his pen name, Dan de Quille. Like Goodman a lifelong friend of Mark

Twain, he wrote *The Big Bonanza*, about the legendary Washoe era, for Clemens's publishing house. Sam Clemens himself joined the staff; so did "Unreliable" Rice and Steve Gillis, whose barroom brawl and arrest led to Twain's fast exit (1864–1865) to the Sierra foothills, where he stayed in Jim Gillis's cabin and heard a yarn about a jumping contest between two frogs. Many years later, Goodman's interest in Amerindian culture took him to Central America where he did scholarly work on Mayan inscriptions in Yucatan, writing a book on deciphering glyphs.

Mark Twain thought the early days in Nevada and Mother Lode country the happiest time of his life. He wrote in *Roughing It* (1872), the incomparable comic account of his greenhorn mining days, "It was an assemblage of two-hundred-thousand young men—not simpering, dainty, kid-gloved weaklings, but stalwart, muscular dauntless young braves, brimful of push and energy, and royally endowed with every attribute that goes to make up a peerless and magnificent manhood—the very pick and choice of the world's glorious ones. No women, no children, no grey and stooping veterans. . . . It was a wild, free, disorderly, grotesque society! Men— only swarming hosts of stalwart men— nothing juvenile, nothing feminine, visible anywhere!" If Twain immortalized Washoe and the Comstock Lode, his experiences and associations there inspired and formed him. Arthur McEwen reminisced, "It was there that Mark got his point of view—that shrewd, graceless, goodhumored, cynical way of looking at things as they in fact are—unbullied by authority and indifferent to traditions— which has made the world laugh."

MARK TWAIN (Samuel L. Clemens, 1835–1910) was, at age twenty, pro-Union, then pro-Confederacy as he steamed up and down the Mississippi as a riverboat pilot. He joined a Confederate militia in Hannibal, Missouri, but resigned after two weeks, "incapacitated by fatigue through persistent retreating." When Orion Clemens was appointed secretary to the territorial governor of Nevada, he took his younger brother Sam along as his secretary; thus, like many other migrants of the 1860s, Sam came west to escape the Civil War. His mining ventures failed; but after a couple of crude burlesques he signed "Josh" were printed by the *Territorial Enterprise*, he accepted Joe Goodman's offer of a regular job in 1862. For the next two years, he reported Comstock news and concocted hoaxes, burlesques, and fantastic comic tales. He tried out the free-association style of humorist Artemus Ward, who passed through Virginia City on a lecture tour, and for the first time used the name "Mark Twain."

On a visit to San Francisco (1863), he checked in at the Lick House and sold some articles to the *Golden Era*, run then by Colonel Joseph T. Lawrence, who was transforming it for a more sophisticated city. Twain was keen to make some money in silver stocks in San Francisco's "gambling carnival"; so when the opportunity arose, he moved permanently to the city the following year. He lodged at the Occidental Hotel ("Heaven on the half shell"); he'd met so many people already that a walk down Montgomery Street was "just like being on Main Street in Hannibal and meeting the old familiar faces." He began straight reporting for the *Daily Morning Call*, "fearful drudgery, soulless drudgery . . . awful drudgery for a lazy man."

Soon he entered a circle of young writers who met in the offices of the *Golden Era* at 732 Montgomery Street,

which, with the nearby saloons, was the locus of a rising literary constellation. Bret Harte, who worked at the Mint next door to the *Call*'s offices on Commercial Street, gave Twain instruction in the craft of writing: "He trimmed and trained and schooled me patiently," Twain wrote later, "until he changed me from an awkward utterer of coarse grotesqueness to a writer of paragraphs and chapters that have found a certain favor in the eyes of even some of the very decentest people in the land." For the *Era*, he wrote "The Washoe Wit—Mark Twain on the Rampage" and for the *Dramatic Chronicle* and *Californian*, articles on theater, society, earthquakes, and police. He cast aspersions on a trip to the Cliff House, a perennially foggy excursion San Franciscans inflict upon visitors. On the invitation of Artemus Ward, he sent "a villainous backwoods squib" for publication in the East, where it made its way into the *New York Saturday Press* under the title "Jim Smiley and His Jumping Frog." Twain played penny ante in the Montgomery Block Turkish baths with a man named Tom Sawyer, who years later hung a sign over his tavern on Third and Mission reading, "Ale and Spirits—The Original Tom Sawyer, Prop."

In 1866, he went to Hawaii to write travel sketches for the *Sacramento*

San Francisco journalists. Number two is thought to be Mark Twain.

Union and on the invitation of the *Alta California*, toured Europe and the Holy Land, writing hilarious, irreverent views of the Old World, collected as *Innocents Abroad.* During this period, he put

31

his talents to lecturing, at which he grew superb. The menu for a Lick House Banquet he invented on return to San Francisco in 1868 listed such items as Ku-Klux-Klan soup; Boiled Job (obscure, but Scriptural); Invited Guest, stuffed; Mexican Mustang Liniment; Terrapin, Seraphim, Cherubim, and sich. It was the audaciously humorous fare that made the most amusing of the West's journalists into one of America's great writers.

Not only was his comic gift unsurpassed, but when he damned the hypocrisy of the dominant culture, he spoke directly to a war-torn and disturbed nation. The dark side of that happy, wide-open frontier society didn't elude his eagle eye. When the *Call* refused to print his articles undermining political corruption, police brutality, and the mobs hounding the Chinese, he sent them to be printed in the *Enterprise*. As early as the mid-1860s, the shadows that filtered through his youthful humor had become apparent to the press, which joked about his having become the coast's foremost moralist. Twain's articles, "What Have the Police Been Doing" and "The Black Hole of San Francisco," prefigure the perspective of the man who was to write the bitter note on Puddin' Head Wilson's calendar: "October 12, the Discovery. It was wonderful to find America, but it would have been more wonderful to miss it."

$\mathscr{B}$LACK EMANCIPATION. Although the territory was preponderantly Democratic, fear that slave owners would have an unfair advantage working gold claims led to California's admission as a Northern free state in 1850. Because the new state was physically isolated and the draft impracticable, California sat out the war, contributing gold to the Union cause. Each side claimed supporters among the San Francisco authors. Charles Warren Stoddard, C. H. Webb, and Eliza Pittsinger championed the Northern cause with Bret Harte, who wrote over thirty pro-Union poems. Thomas Starr King and Edward Dickinson Baker employed oratorical arts to support President Lincoln. Southerners Adah Menken and John Rollin Ridge were for the Confederacy, as was Oregonian Joaquin Miller, for reasons unknown. Still others promoted California secession or dreamed of flying the Bear Flag again over the so-called California Republic that had lasted only a month in 1846.

Black poet James Madison Bell (1826–1902) of Gallipolis, Ohio, had been a friend and abettor of John Brown before coming to San Francisco in 1860. An excellent orator, he declaimed *The Day and the War* at Platt's Hall on January 1, 1864. The twenty-five-page poem on the heroism of the Black Brigade in Civil War combat was dedicated to "the hero, saint, and martyr of Harper's Ferry." In his introduction, Bell "laments the long years of enslavement of his race, but rejoices that the Emancipation Proclamation is the harbinger of the good time coming."

Times had grown worse for blacks since the pioneer days when William Leidesdorff was a respected city founder and Captain Ferguson of the Brannon Guards wrote poems like "Crispus Attucks" under the nom de plume "Jeams." The poetry of William J. Wilson,

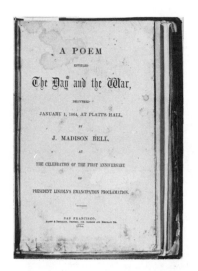

Cecilia Williams, and others envisioned future social justice in a period of degrading, discriminatory laws. Priscilla Stewart published "A Voice from the Oppressed to the Friends of Humanity" shortly after the passage of a bill demanding all free Negroes leave the state—many accepted a British invitation to emigrate to British Columbia in 1858. James M. Whitfield agitated for colonization of Latin America, an issue he had debated with Frederick Douglass.

The *Mirror of the Times* (1855), the first Negro newspaper, fought for blacks' right to give testimony in trials and for an end to slavery. Later, as the *Pacific Appeal* (1862), its motto was "He who would be free, himself must strike the first blow." The *Mirror* was founded in conjunction with the San Francisco Athenaeum, a library and debating society located in a building owned by Mifflin W. Gibbs, author of *Shadow and Light*, who was elected the first black justice in America. Editor Philip Bell, "the Napoleon of the Afro-American press," wrote for both black and white dailies and founded San Francisco's *Elevator* (1865) under the banner "Equality before the Law."

Fitz Hugh Ludlow New York

ITINERANT LITERATI. In the mid-1860s, the *Golden Era* was invigorated by some adventurous literati who before the war had gathered at Pfaff's beer cellar on lower Broadway in New York. Though Pfaffian Charles Henry Webb insisted in his *Golden Era* column that he considered "Bohemianism a misnomer for any literary growth which exists on this continent," the press identified the group with the characters in Henri Mürger's *Scenes de la Vie Bohéme* (1844), which sketched life in the Latin Quarter of Paris, where writers and artists had been defying the bourgeoisie and exalting socialist ideals and romantic love since the Revolution of 1830. It was true that Walt Whitman and other avant-garde easterners at Pfaff's were up against an entrenched puritanical bourgeoisie and the eastern establishment, which a generation before had failed to appreciate Edgar Allan Poe's genius and now supported restrained formalism.

Quite a different situation existed in the West. In San Francisco, a vulgar nouveau riche was trying to live down its rapacious ride to respectability. The decaying Victorian tradition was far away, and what passed for a literary establishment consisted of boisterous journalists and boosters. San Francisco's hazy idea of Bohemia emerged in Bret Harte's affected columns of whimsical vignettes, "The Bohemian Feuilleton" (1860–1861); but the only thing vaguely resembling Mürger's starving artists were roistering drifters down on their luck whose only ambition was to strike it rich quick. As Webb punned, "I had dreams, poetic dreams of name, fame . . . now, alas, my dreams are ore."

Literary rebelliousness took a distinctly western form: exaggeration, a taste for the fantastic and macabre, impossible coincidence, the illogical and heretical. The chaotic and remote metropolis had a tolerance for violence and excess of every kind and a liking for drunks and madmen, providing they were interesting.

One of the most intriguing New Yorkers was the arrant drug fiend, Fitz Hugh Ludlow (1836–1870), who came into town via Yosemite with landscape painter Albert Bierstadt. Ludlow was known as the American de Quincey after publication of his romantic classic, *The Hasheesh Eater; Being Passages from the Life of a Pythagorean*, described by Franklin Walker as "a most unusual, brilliant, and now inexplicably neglected work." Ludlow wrote theater and literary criticism for *Harper's* and the *Atlantic*. He was urbane, erudite, and recommended in particular the recently published *Origin of Species* by Charles Darwin. His intellectual interests ranged from law to Amerindian languages to esotericism. During his stay, he published several essays, a fantasy, and a lengthy weekly column for the *Golden Era*, "Reminiscences of an Overlander," one of which detailed the discomforts of his trip. "Webster's Unabridged closes its covers in despair before the task of giving expression to the misery suffered from Salt Lake to the Sierra," he wrote. He encouraged Twain, advised the stripling poet Charles Warren Stoddard, and impressed everybody, though not because he was an infamous exotic. In fact, it was Ludlow who said of San Francisco, "To a traveler paying his first visit, it has the interest of a new planet."

THE *CALIFORNIAN* (1864–1866), a literary weekly, was launched by another New Yorker, Charles Henry Webb (1834–1905), correspondent for the *New York Times* assigned to San Francisco. Shortly after his arrival in 1863, he became literary editor of the *Evening Bulletin* and wrote sketches, satire, and a scintillating column, "Things," for the *Golden Era*, using the names "Inigo" and "John Paul." Webb was a great wit and punster, once describing Sam Brannan, who had made millions in the gold rush by tithing his Mormons, as "a thing of booty and a bore forever." He challenged Fitz Hugh Ludlow and Mark Twain to a writing battle, proposing an elimination contest between the Inigo Boy, the Hasheesh Infant, and the Washoe Giant: "Inigo bent on giving Ludlow Fitz, and rending Apostolic Mark in Twain."

Webb's grand venture was the sophisticated *Californian*, printed elegantly and conceived as a counterpart of New York's *Round Table*. He advertised it as "The Best Journal on the Pacific Coast, and the Equal of Any on the Continent," and through it, he hoped to raise local literary standards. Bret Harte was a ready collaborator and so was Twain, who disclaimed the *Golden Era* for the new magazine. He wrote in a letter, "I quit the 'Era,' long ago. It wasn't hightoned enough. The 'Californian' circulates among the highest class of the community, and it is the best weekly literary paper in the United States."

The *Californian* combined provocative feature writing with international news, political editorials, Civil War dispatches, and straight stories on timely issues— financial panics, flogging as a punishment for rape, brutality at sea.

Covering the cultural scene were "Our Atlantic Gossip," theater and music criticism, notices of new books unloaded from the latest ship, and sharp

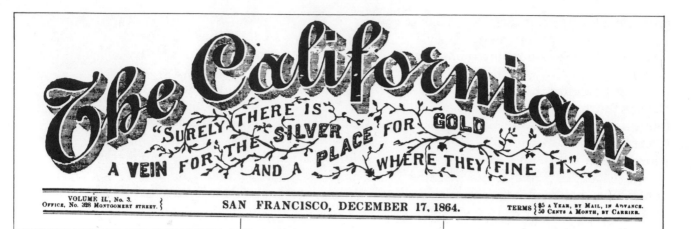

The Californian.

"SURELY THERE IS A VEIN FOR THE SILVER AND A PLACE FOR GOLD WHERE THEY FINE IT."

VOLUME II., No. 3.
OFFICE, No. 328 MONTGOMERY STREET.

SAN FRANCISCO, DECEMBER 17, 1864.

TERMS { $5 A YEAR, BY MAIL, IN ADVANCE. { 50 CENTS A MONTH, BY CARRIER.

observation of the city's social life. The *Californian* conjectured about strange and macabre phenomena: second sight, hauntings, vampires, Haitian voodoo, and other foreign mysteries. Articles on fashion, home furnishings, food and dieting ("every thin woman wants to be stouter") were directed to women. Serialized novels ranged from Mario Urchard's *The Countess Diana* to Miss M. E. Braddon's *Only a Clod.*

Among Bret Harte's contributions were "Neighborhoods I Have Moved From; by a Hypochondriac," "Fixing Up Old Houses," and a series, "San Francisco, By the Poets," burlesquing the city's various districts, such as "North Beach—After Spenser." He wrote delightful condensed parodies: one, for instance, of *Robinson Crusoe* with female protagonists because Harte, the father of daughters, noticed that children's stories gave all the heroic enterprises to boys.

Mark Twain ran a very funny correspondents' column that advertised: "Courting Etiquette, Distressed Lovers, of either sex, and Struggling Young Authors, as yet 'unbeknown' to Fame, will receive especial attention." He wrote effervescent absurdities, drifting from subject to subject with an admirable disregard for logic. In "Daniel in the

Lion's Den—and Out Again All Right," he began to describe the stock exchange but ended by making nonsense out of brokers' jargon. He claimed to have been asked to write art criticism; in an article on the paintings at the California Art Union, he launched at once into a rambling reminiscence of Calaveras County, where a dictionary sashayed around from one mining camp to another, the miners wrestling with the words. Then he reconstructed a scathing political rebuke to the Lillie Union and Constitution Fire Burglar-Proof Safe Party; that led him to safes and sewing machines, and soon to the museum exit and out for a drink. Twain's view of "art" was shared by many San Franciscans; in the 1870s the Chamber of Commerce sued and collected damages from the Wells Fargo express company for damaging a replica of the Venus de Milo, shipped from France to the Hopkins art school, the statue having arrived without arms.

Chief editor Webb satirized California chauvinism, the Forty-niners, conventional virtues, and the provincialism, illiteracy, and pretentions of the bourgeoisie. The city proved not to be high-toned enough for the *Californian.* Webb departed in 1866, with many enemies and nearly bankrupt from losses in mining stocks, describing his three years there as "a comparative eternity."

*A*LOVE POEM printed in New York's *Atlas* in 1855 was the beginning of Jane McElheny's uncommon literary career. As Ada Clare (1836–1874), she published candid poems and stories in various journals, then went to Paris to live among the bohemians, where she wrote sprightly letters for the New York papers about her unconventional life and gave birth to a son by Louis Moreau Gottschalk, a musician as well known for his philandering as his virtuosity. With her boy, she traveled unmarried and unashamed as "Miss Ada Clare and Son," shocking respectable society. In New York, she wrote uncompromising, often caustic, book and theater criticism for Henry Clapp's *Saturday Press* and the *Sunday Mercury*. She found friends at Pfaff's, where Walt Whitman thought her the New Woman born too soon.

At the *Golden Era*, a block away from the Barbary Coast's glittering saloons and gambling palaces, the Queen of Bohemia did not seem so wicked. The editorial announced, "As regards what is popularly and eccentrically known as the 'Bohemia' of newspaperdom, she is unquestionably a Queen in every essential of literary and social superiority that supports a legitimate claim to such eminence . . . the fairest and most accomplished lady ever associated with American journalism." During her stay in San Francisco, Clare was a principal contributor to the *Era*, writing a lengthy weekly column on a variety of topics—travel, theater and book reviews, fashion, parodies, essays on wit and humor, and impressions of local scenes. Of Californians, she wrote, "They seem to be people without any remembered Past save as it may sometimes come to them in a confused sense of having been born in some other place at some vaguely remote period." She did not stay long and wrote

irritably of San Francisco's rude customs, poisonous winds, and malarious atmosphere.

After her stage debut in *Camille* failed, she went with Stoddard to the Sandwich Islands. She was ever controversial and subject to criticism; her autobiographical novel, *Only a Woman's Heart*, was not well received. There is poignance in her statement that she got tired of exciting curiosity rather than interest.

$\mathcal{B}$EFORE Adah Isaacs Menken (1835–1868) came to San Francisco in 1863, she had danced with the New Orleans ballet and in Havana, learned Hebrew, French, Spanish, and German, taught, established a paper in Texas, and studied painting and sculpture. She had given Shakespearean readings and done Vaudeville, contributed to the *Israelite*, frequented Pfaff's, written avant-garde poetry, published in the *New York Sunday Mercury*, and begun an illustrious career as an actress.

"Miss Menken, stripped by her captors, will ride a fiery steed at furious gallop onto and across the stage and into the distance," read the advertisement for the August 24, 1863, performance of *Mazeppa* at Tom Maguire's Opera House in San Francisco. Customarily, a dummy was tied to a horse in the scene where Byron's hero undergoes his ordeal, but Menken was an expert rider and insisted on realism. Costumed in a body stocking, she thrilled Victorian audiences. This contemporary playbill features the daring equestrienne in action.

The *Golden Era* reviewed one of her 1864 performances in this role: "Poetess as well as actress, the Menken attains the finest ideal of Byron's Tartar prince, and her portraiture of 'Mazeppa' will be a classic of art in the records of future historians of the American stage." She played several other roles during her year on the coast, and wherever she appeared, "the enthusiasm of the audience was a mad frenzy."

She charmed Joe Lawrence's writers and strode into the saloons and gambled with the men; women sympathized with what they sensed was tragic about her. A brilliant, generous woman, Menken was among the first to recognize Whitman's importance; the admiration was mutual. Every week a new poem by Menken appeared in the *Golden Era*, poetry described by Dante Gabriel Rossetti as really remarkable, with a long, surging

free verse line. J. W. Davidson (*The Poetry of the Future*) called it "frantic soul cries of poetic aspiration, shrieked, as it were, out of the Darkness into the ear of Humanity and of God." Some found her unchecked emotion offensive and her poems undisciplined, but her passionate intensity and opulent imagery were unique in nineteenth century San Francisco. When others were writing, "Oh, may we never fail to bless and cheer/ The widow's path and wipe the orphan's tear/ To gather near the sick and lowly bed,/ and strew memorial flowers o'er the dead," Adah Isaacs Menken was writing, "Let us follow the heavy hearse that bore our old Dream out past the white-horned Daylight of Love/ Let thy pale Dead come up from their furrows of winding-sheets to mock thy prayers with what the days might have been/ Let the Living come back and point at the shadows they swept over the disk of the morning star."

Menken's third husband, Robert Henry Newell, accompanied her to San Francisco, writing for the *Era* under the name "Orpheus C. Kerr," referring to a political aspirant, a stock character in early sixties lampoonery. The marriage did not long survive the California tour.

After San Francisco, Menken made triumphant European appearances and her salons in London and Paris attracted Charles Dickens, Charles Reade, the Rossettis, George Sand, Theophile Gautier, Alexandre Dumas, and Algernon Swinburne whose "Dolores" she was. In the year of her death, John Thompson edited her poems, dedicated to Dickens and published as *Infelicia*. She died at thirty-three and was buried at Père Lachaise cemetery in Paris, her memorial stone inscribed "Thou Knowest" from Swinburne's *Ilicet*.

PRENTICE MULFORD (1834–1891) appeared in one of Charles Warren Stoddard's novels with the name Diogenes. Like his namesake, Mulford took a dim view of his era and searched in vain for an honest man in the daylight of California. On disembarking the ship *Wizard*, the twenty-two-year-old seaman wandered about Portsmouth Plaza, where criminals were tied up on display. He recalled in *Prentice Mulford's Story*, "In San Francisco, it was nothing but fog in the morning, dust and wind in the afternoon, and the Vigilance Committee the rest of the time." After quitting a job as a seagull-egg sorter, he spent several hard years prospecting in the Tuolumne River country. He ran for public office and so amused the populace by substituting nonsense for "eagle screaming" (pompous patriotic oratory) that he won the nomination, but his satire went too far and he lost the election.

On the basis of his droll sketches, Joe Lawrence invited him to write for the *Golden Era*, moving him into the Occidental Hotel, where Mark Twain and C. H. Webb were luxuriating. He lectured and wrote a sardonic column popular with the miners because it was based on firsthand experience. Mulford was skeptical of material "progress," extolled laziness, and defended women's rights. He wrote a series of "Compressed Novels," most of them burlesques and parodies. Among the best of them is *Barney McBriar the Shootist*, a gem of black humor, satirizing the stereotyped, tough gunman hero. McBriar boasted a private graveyard where he buried a multitude of annoying people whose heads he shot off on the spur of the moment.

Disliking city life, Mulford moved onto an old whaler and lived entirely on the bay, coming ashore only to deliver stories and pick up supplies. Mulford believed that one's personality traveled during sleep, and he dreamed of a more exalted existence. He spent his days cruising and his nights anchored in lonely coves; in reveries he heard voices, perhaps sensing the spirits of the bay the California Indians knew. He began a series called "The Invisible in Our Midst," for the *Era*, which evolved into a unique philosophy combining neo-Platonism, telepathy, and psychic power. Though interested in spiritualism, Mulford rejected what he called ghoulology, the "spiritualistic ghouls . . . deluding their hearers with the idea that they are the original Platos, Aristotles, St. Peters, or George Washingtons, and delighting in the wonder, credulity, and spiritualistic flunkeyism which their presence inspires. . . . An idiot is not precluded from having a mediumistic organization and serving as a door for invisible idiots to come and gibber through."

A hater of dogmas, Mulford sought a way to unite the material and the spiritual. "Don't imagine," he wrote in the *Golden Era*, "the visible things of the earth are worthless, because you have discovered the invisible. The earth, its wonders, its men and women, are here to be seen, to be studied, to be enjoyed. . . . It is the earthly eye that educates the spiritual."

In the early 1870s, he went to England, ostensibly to encourage immigration while sending back amusing travel letters to the *San Francisco Bulletin*. But to Diogenes, the squalid industrial towns, exhausted workers, and even the zoo were depressing. After he rewrote Joaquin Miller's *Life Among the Modocs* for him, he returned to the United States, where he lived in a New Jersey swamp, developing the White Cross Library. He was widely regarded as a major force in occultism; John Greenleaf Whittier, in his poem "Mulford," called him a sage and a seer. In 1891, Mulford's body was

discovered in a small boat floating off the coast of Long Island. On a writing tablet beside him were written his enigmatic last words, their meaning still a mystery.

IN HIS MEMOIRS, Twain wrote of Francis Bret[t] Harte (1836–1902), "He said to me once with a cynical chuckle that he thought he had mastered the art of pumping up the tear of sensibility. The idea was that the tear of sensibility was oil and by luck he had struck it." Harte's luck began with "The Luck of Roaring Camp," a short story set in the gold rush. The oil came in the form of an unprecedented contract with the *Atlantic Monthly*; for a single poem or story an issue, Harte was to receive annually $10,000, an enormous sum in 1870. It was more than enough to take him from California, which he'd never much liked anyway.

He had come at seventeen to Oakland, drifted through odd jobs, and worked for newspapers in Humboldt County until his article castigating the slaughter of Indian women and children in the despicable Gunther Island Massacre got him run out of the Eureka area in 1860. He began typesetting and writing for the *Golden Era*, signing himself "Bret" and "The Bohemian." The formidable Jessie Benton Frémont, herself a writer (*A Year of American Travel*), helped get him a sinecure so that he could devote himself to writing and the Republican cause. A prolific and versatile contributor to the *Californian*, he published his *Condensed Novels*, clever parodies of other authors, and *The Lost Galleon*, poems, in 1867. When bookseller Anton Roman founded the *Overland Monthly*, he persuaded Harte to edit it. Harte gave it its name and snarling grizzly logo, and his stylish editing brought it success. In the second issue, "The Luck of Roaring Camp" was to change Harte's destiny.

The story of a child, "Luck," born to the camp prostitute, and the revelation of sterling qualities in rough miners countered conventional Victorian hypocrisy (the religious press anathematized it). At the same time, its theme of self-sacrifice ensured acceptance. Harte's early masterpieces, "Luck," "The Outcasts of Poker Flat," "Tennessee's Partner," and ensuing tales applied a Dickensian combination of pathos, humor, and picturesque characters to the abnormalities of early California life. Each tale introduced "sinner" types who proved their superior virtue in heroic renunciations. It was the perfect moment for Harte's formula, which appealed to a generation ready to romanticize the gold rush. If western humorists had always used the contradiction between ideal and real to cast out terror and guilt, Harte redeemed an era of random violence, drunkenness, mob hysteria, and obsessive slaying of man and beast by displacing moral questions to safer ground. Always the superb craftsman, Harte was a dexterous storyteller too; in the wake of his achievement, "local color" fiction came to life in other regions of the United States.

Harte won a dubious triumph with "Plain Language from Truthful James" (popularly titled "The Heathen Chinee"), a poem he considered trivial. Because it referred to cheap Chinese labor, it was widely exploited in California and soon known to the world. Harte boarded the new transcontinental train for the East. However, his star fell as fast as it had risen. His was an urban sensibility, and he lacked experience at the mines, so he ran out of the substance his frontier tales required and never was apt at applying his formula to the city. His work for the *Atlantic* was disappointing; he spent more money than he made and by 1878 was ruined. He lived in Europe, mostly in England, where he ground out new versions of the same tales.

THE

Overland Monthly

DEVOTED TO

THE DEVELOPMENT OF THE COUNTRY.

JULY. 1868

SAN FRANCISCO:

A. ROMAN & COMPANY, PUBLISHERS,

417 and 419 MONTGOMERY STREET

LONDON: Trubner & Co.   NEW YORK: A. Roman & Co.
60 Paternoster Row.   27 Howard Street.

EXCELSIOR PRESS. BACON & COMPANY, PRINTERS.

*O*VERLAND MONTHLY. Anton Roman planned the *Overland Monthly* (1868) as a promotional organ for the city, but Bret Harte made it one of the fine magazines of its time with hard work and a high critical standard. The name "Overland" referred to the railroad "each day drawing West and East closer together" physically and intellectually. The bear is "crossing the track of the Pacific Railroad and has paused a moment to look at the coming engine of civilization and progress—which moves like a good many other engines of civilization and progress, with a prodigious shrieking and puffing—and apparently recognizes his rival and his doom."

Harte rejected the customary newspaper verse, using only a small number of understated, polished poems, with short stories by Emma F. Dawson, Prentice Mulford, Frances F. Victor, and local color fiction inspired by the success of Harte's new work. Ambrose Bierce published his first story, "The Haunted Valley," in the *Overland.*

Harte emphasized nonfiction for changing times. Segments of Henry George's *Progress and Poverty* predicted economic disaster; J. W. Watson blistered the city's failings; and Georgiana Kirby urged prison reform. There were essays by Reverend A. W. Loomis on the Chinese in California, by Stephen Powers on the coast Indians, and by Louis Agassiz on the animal kingdom. The indefatigable J. S. Hittell undertook the cultural history of mankind. Frances F. Victor disclosed the charm of the Northwest and Stoddard made a prose breakthrough with "Chumming with a Savage," a sensuous remembrance of his stay in the South Seas.

After Harte left (1871), new editors struggled on for three quarters of a century. An 1880s revival under the editorship of Millicent Washburn Shinn, though dubbed by Bierce "the warmed-Overland Monthly," included significant newcomers: California's idealist philosopher Josiah Royce, Edwin Markham, Kate Douglas Wiggin, Edward Rowland Sill, Frank Norris, Gertrude Atherton, and Jack London.

Abe Warner's Cobweb Palace Saloon

POPULAR POETRY—from The Cobweb Palace Saloon to Cupids to Kneecapping. William Cullen Bryant in 1872 discerned two kinds of poetry, both of value: first, great poetry by acknowledged masters and, second, poetry of "common apprehension," popularly understood and esteemed. Nineteenth-century California poetry fell entirely into the second category. Westerners, like other Americans, were great readers and writers of verse; that most of it was very bad did not deter them. Poetry had a decided use—to educate, amuse, comfort, and affirm common values. People might appreciate Shakespeare and Virgil, but at the same time they enjoyed comic or sentimental verses. The poet was never more honored; people read verse aloud at home, memorized it in school, and composed and recited it on every public occasion.

With the gold rush, rhymes, jingles, and ballads were printed in broadsides and newspapers. Mining and pioneer songs attained national fame: "Clementine," "The Gold Digger's Lament," "The Fools of Forty Nine," "Sweet Betsy from Pike," "The California Emigrant." The boy editor Edward Kemble inaugurated the ubiquitous front page "Poets Corner" in the *Star* (1847) with a long poem of his own. Bret Harte was astonished by the number of manuscripts he received. "It seemed as if all the able bodied inhabitants of the Pacific Coast had been in the habit of expressing themselves in verse." Bierce wryly congratulated Twain because "he suffused our country with a peculiar glory by never trying to write a line of poetry."

45

Edward Pollack

Joaquin Miller

Charles Warren Stoddard

Edward Rowland Sill

Edward Pollack was San Francisco's early hope for boasting a master poet, for Pollack had risen from child factory laborer to attorney-at-law and had written many lyrics for the dailies after the fashion of Poe and Coleridge. Moreover, he aspired to compose the national epic, to be the Homer or Milton of America. But Pollack died at thirty-five before he'd begun his *chef d'oeuvre*, living on only in revered memory, his "Evening" anthologized through the century. It began, "The air is chill, and the hour grows late/ And the clouds come in through the Golden Gate/ Phantom fleets they seem to me/ From a shoreless and unsounded sea."

The *Golden Era* said the ill-fated W. A. Kendall ("Comet Quirls") "existed as a kind of literary waif" from the time he left his Petaluma farm to be a San Francisco poet. In the 1850s, his verbosity and bathos were frequent targets of the *Era*'s barbs. For two decades, he was published in the newspapers, literary journals, and the anthologies; but Kendall's sensual obsessions, mildly erotic fancies about bare breasts and warm caresses, were considered inappropriate subjects. "But alas," wrote Ella Sterling Cummins in *The Story of the Files*, "he lacked mental balance, and when not writing these rich and lurid poems of love and imagination, he sat in the Cobweb Saloon, 'entranced,' and gazed at vacancy, until he became a burden to those who believed him to be a genius." He suicided in 1876 with an overdose of morphine.

California's scenic grandeurs overwhelmed its versifiers; nature was far and away their favorite theme. They ran the gamut—from Joaquin Miller's heroics to Charles Warren Stoddard's effusions to Edward Rowland Sill's moralizing in the Bryant manner. Flowers, rivers, tamer places left behind, Yosemite, the Golden Gate, and Mount Shasta had been written about too often, thought Harte, who remarked that "a beautiful bird known as the 'California canary' appeared to have been shot at and winged by every poet from Portland to San Diego."

Every holiday, dedication, fraternal party, or public ceremony called for an ode or two. Newsworthy events, covered now by television, required verses to express shared beliefs and feelings. Typical were William "Caxton" Rhodes's "Enobling of Liberty" and Anna Fitch's "Flag on Fire." Abolition of slavery, women's rights, and Civil War issues were common themes. The death of Lincoln inspired thousands of poems, ranging from Joe Goodman's soaring

Poetry alfresco in Carmel, 1912. Left to right: George Sterling, Clark Ashton Smith, James Redfern Mason, Peggy Wallace, Ethel Duffy Turner, John Hilliard Alma F. Duffy. Late nineteenth- and twentieth-century poets, notably Sterling and Smith, transmuted nature into mythic and cosmic dimensions.

Anna M. Fitch

Eliza Pittsinger

slaves." Calvin B. McDonald, known as "The Thunderer" for his pro-Union editorials, noted, "When her muse came down from the sacred mount it was at the invocation of serried battalions, not smiling Cupids beckoning from beds of roses."

Women did answer the cupids, however, in sentimental poems about hearth, babies, motherhood, and giving comfort in a harsh land. Among them were the coy Elizabeth Chamberlain, who wrote as "Topsy Turvey"; Clara Doliver, whose "No Baby in the House" was in such demand it was issued as a book; and Alice Kingsbury, who had twelve children and still found time to write verse, children's books, a novel, and an autobiography. Men's verse confirmed the worth of physical strength, hard work, and responsibility to family and country. Most of it was sentimental and didactic (for example, Lyman Goodman's "The Fair Tamborinist," which aimed to save a girl from prostitution, and James Bowman's tearjerker "Together," which was about a couple on a sinking ship— "We sink! we sink! One kiss, on earth the last!").

The high-spirited Comstock poets enjoyed nothing so much as a poetry competition to see who could write best and fastest. Then they blasted one another's poems in reviews: "a pale Wordsworthian imitation . . . diluted through a brain enfeebled with the fumes of contraband opium and moonshine whiskey." They liked to stir up a good battle, like the time C. W. Stoddard basked in the approbation of James Bowman's review of his *Collected Poems* (1867) until he discovered that the same Bowman had written a scathing critique for another paper. Sometimes the wars of words got a little rough. Arthur McEwen recollected that Joe Goodman once "called out the silver tongued Tom Fitch and shattered his knee with a pistol ball . . . in return for an unpleasant article that appeared in the course of a controversy."

elegy, "Abraham Lincoln," to the obituary lines penned by an unnamed rhymster: "Gone, gone, gone/ Gone to his endeavor/ Gone, gone, gone/ Forever and forever," to which Mark Twain replied in the *Territorial Enterprise*, "This is a very nice refrain . . . but if there *is* any criticism to make upon it, I should say there was a little too much gone and not enough forever."

"Thought is speeding, time is waning/ Let your banners be unfurled/ Tyranny has long been gaining/ hidden marches on the world" wrote the "Prophetess" Eliza Pittsinger, who raged at tyrants, male supremacists, and the pope. She had a sense of humor: "A wonderful toe doth the Pope possess! Kiss it ye vassals, and then confess!/ Unbosom your secrets to bigots and knaves/ 'Tis a custom they cherish of making you

OUTCROPPINGS. Most violence was confined to the printed page; and of all the mid-century feuds, the most exhilarating raged over California's first poetry anthology, *Outcroppings*, issued for the Christmas trade in 1865. With such an abundance of poetic activity, it seemed time for a collection; so when Mary Tingley left a sheaf of clippings on Anton Roman's desk, he gave it to Bret Harte, who selected forty-two poems by nineteen authors and provided a disparaging preface. But they had not accounted for the fury of the unrecognized versifiers. The *News Letter* reported, "Within two hours after it was known to be in town, a mob of poets, consisting of one thousand persons of various ages and colors, and of both sexes, besieged Roman's bookstore, all eager to ascertain if they had been immortalized by Harte. . . . By Thursday the news had been circulated throughout the state, and the 'country poets' were in a state of fearful excitement. Yesterday it was rumored that three to four hundred of these were coming down on the Sacramento boat in a 'fine phrensy' and swearing dire vengeance upon Harte."

Vitriolic reviews poured in from the foothills and in particular from the Washoe crowd, who devoted five columns in the *Virginia City Territorial Enterprise* to lambasting the "feeble collection of drivel," which, they suggested, ought to be washed down the sluices and out to sea—"effeminate," "purp-stuff," "trash," "a quantity of slumgullion that would average about 33½ cents a ton." An epidemic joke, it evoked some wicked satire from the city journalists and colossal laughter all around.

A few months later, H. H. Bancroft opportunely issued another anthology. *The Poetry of the Pacific*, edited by May Wentworth, included all the poets of local repute—all except Harte.

OUTCROPPINGS:

BEING

SELECTIONS OF CALIFORNIA VERSE.

Compiled by
F. Bret. Harte. 1839-1902

SAN FRANCISCO:
A. ROMAN AND COMPANY.
NEW YORK:
W. J. WIDDLETON.
1866.

INA DONNA COOLBRITH (1841–1928) was an imposing figure through three literary generations: from young pioneer lyric poet to distinguished editor and librarian to California's "loved laurel-wreathed poet," the first poet laureate (1915–1928) named in the United States.

Born Josephine D. Smith (niece of the Mormon prophet), she rode west on the saddle of James P. Beckwourth, famous mulatto scout, Crow chief, raconteur, and mountain man. He led her family across the Sierra Nevada and announced to the ten-year-old, "There is California; there is your kingdom!" In the small pueblo of Los Angeles, young Ina's poems were published in the *Los Angeles Star* and admired by San Francisco poet Joseph Duncan, who placed them in his *California Home Journal*. Ina married, then divorced, a flamboyant traveling actor, Robert Carsley, who proved insanely jealous and was shot in a duel. So Ina headed north to the metropolis of San Francisco to begin a new life.

With a literary reputation already established in 1861, she began writing for the *Golden Era* and *Californian*, using the name Ina Coolbrith. Her wistful, graceful, and polished lyric poems are collected in *A Perfect Day, The Singer*

of the Sea, and *Songs of the Golden Gate*.
She had renowned intimate friendships
with Bret Harte, Mark Twain, Charles W.
Stoddard, and Joaquin Miller; even
Bierce sang her praises: "If for every
10,000 Susan B. Anthony's there could
be one Ina Coolbrith, the world would
be a better place." Coolbrith was the
ideal, the muse, the unthreatening
bountiful lady.

Dubbed the "Golden Gate Trinity,"
she, Harte, and Stoddard had high times
editing the *Overland Monthly* together.
"There is a poetic divinity/ Number One
of the Overland Trinity/ Who uses the
Muses/ Pretty Much as She Chooses/
This dark-eyed young Sapphic divinity,"
ventured Harte once in a playful mood.
Coolbrith replied, "There once was a
young writer named Francis/ Who concocted such lurid romances/ That his
publishers said/ 'You will strike this firm
dead'/ If you don't put a curb on your
fancies."

The men went to New York or abroad,
but Coolbrith had her sister's children
and Miller's abandoned daughter, Cali-
Shasta, to support, so she took a job at
the Oakland Free Library. There she
guided the reading of the great dancer
Isadora Duncan, who remembered Ina
in *My Life*: "She had very beautiful eyes
that glowed with burning fire and passion.
Afterwards I learnt that at one time my
father had been very much in love with
her. She was evidently the great passion
of his life and it was probably by the
invisible thread of circumstance that I
was drawn to her."

She also introduced the schoolboy Jack
London to "the big books," and he took
several volumes from her personal collection with him on the *Sophie Sutherland* on his first trip to sea. He wrote
her in 1906, "No woman has affected me
to the extent you did. I was only a little
lad; I knew absolutely nothing about you,

yet in all the years that have passed, I
have met no woman so 'noble' as you."

Throughout her life, she gave generous encouragement to writers; and she
entertained the literati, especially at her
Russian Hill home near the historic park
that bears her name.

ONE DAY Charles Warren Stoddard (1843–1909) spoke to a thin, intriguing figure stopped momentarily in front of his house high on Telegraph Hill. The stranger introduced himself as Robert Louis Stevenson, and Stoddard invited him to come in to his "plover's nest." Stevenson recorded in *The Wrecker* that he found himself "in the midst of a museum of strange objects—paddles and battle clubs and baskets, rough-hewn stone images, ornaments of threaded shell, coconut bowls, snowy plumes—evidences and examples of another earth, another climate, another race, and another (if ruder) culture." Except for writing poetry, Stoddard most enjoyed collecting art and primitive artifacts, occupations that, combined with his sweet, sensitive temperament, made him an anachronistic figure in the Wild West among the macho mining poets and brawling literary rivalries.

The introspective Stoddard came to San Francisco as a child and began contributing effusive poems to the *Golden Era* in 1860 under the pen name "Pip Pepperpod," simultaneously lauded and exploited as the city's "boy prodigy." His *Collected Poems* (1867), edited by Bret Harte and printed in a luxurious volume by Edward Bosqui, created such an uproar that Stoddard decided to be an actor instead of a poet. His autobiography, *For the Pleasure of His Company; An Affair With the Misty City Thrice Told*, discloses his confusion, a struggle against torpor and the enticements of the city's literary milieu. All his life he sought equilibrium, his instability stemming in part from his grandparents' early infliction of terroristic Protestantism upon him. Attracted by the beauty and mystery of its ritual, Stoddard later became an aesthetic Catholic, teaching at Catholic universities while retaining a dislike of work, rules, and priests.

Stoddard was happiest while traveling and preferred "going about with my roots in my pocket." His best book, *South Sea Idylls*, celebrates, in muted homoerotic prose, the indolent life he led there while his money held out. He wrote Walt Whitman in 1870, "I must get in amongst people who are not afraid of their instincts and who scorn hypocrisy . . . barbarism has given me the fullest joy of my life and I long to return to it and be satisfied."

Stoddard's career spanned forty years, although today he is remembered not for his writing but as an enthusiastic litterateur, co-editor of the *Overland Monthly*, Twain's secretary in London, traveling companion of Prentice Mulford, Joaquin Miller, and Ada Clare, and friend to all. He stands here (on the right) with playwright Clay Green (center) and writer-musician Frank Unger (left) on the way to the Bohemian Jinks in 1877.

𝒞INCINNATUS HINER MILLER (1837–1913), named Cincinnatus after his father's hometown and Hiner after the doctor who delivered him, acquired the name Joaquin from verses he wrote about the bandit during the Murieta craze. Miller left his Oregon home for the Siskiyou mining camps, living briefly with Paquita, an Indian woman who bore their daughter. Under the spell of Mount Shasta, he began keeping journals and composing poems.

Through a newspaper correspondence column, he courted the rustic poet Minnie Myrtle Dyer, locally known as "the Sweet Singer of the Coquille." In 1862, the impetuous newlyweds dashed to San Francisco to make their mark in the literary world. The *Golden Era* offered neither pay nor encouragement, and Joaquin soon returned Minnie to her family, saying, according to Minnie, "a man never becomes famous until he leaves his wife, or does something atrocious to bring himself into notice."

Miller went to Canyon City, where he got favorable notice by leading a punitive expedition against the Indians. He reconciled with Minnie, edited a secessionist newspaper, self-published two books of poems, got admitted to the bar without legal training, and became a judge. He tried San Francisco again in 1870, but still his poems were unappreciated. Bret Harte would not publish him in the *Overland Monthly*, returning his manuscripts with a note suggesting he had "a certain theatrical tendency and feverish exultation, which will be better under restraint."

Ina Coolbrith urged Joaquin to seek fame abroad, where they liked the primitive Whitman, and suggested the fantastical costume he was to affect until he died. It happened that she was incensed over Harriet Beecher Stowe's "Lady Byron Vindicated," an insult, she thought, to the memory of Lord Byron. So she and

Joaquin Miller

Minnie Myrtle Miller

Miller gathered laurel leaves on Mount Tamalpais for him to place on the poet's grave.

After depositing the wreath, Miller tramped over England, paying his respects to the haunts of the English poets. In London, he showed his Byronic verses celebrating frontier life to everyone; and at last, with the help of the English poet

53

Joaquin Miller entertains admirers at the "Hights." This cottage and his handmade monuments to Moses, John C. Frémont, and Robert and Elizabeth Barrett Browning are now part of Oakland's Joaquin Miller Park.

Tom Hood, he got *Pacific Poems* and *Songs of the Sierras* in print. Like an outlandish dime-novel hero, dressed in sealskin cloak, sombrero, boots, and spurs, he fascinated English dinner parties with tall tales about his exploits. He reputedly smoked three cigars at once, galloped on all fours, and bit the ankle of a Victorian lady in a Mayfair drawing room. He met Browning, Tennyson, Arnold, and the pre-Raphaelites, who seemed attuned to his own deepest feelings. He tried to recall every word spoken at the home of Dante

Gabriel Rossetti, where "these giants of thought, champions of the beautiful earth, passed the secrets of all time and all lands before me like a mighty panorama." His charming, brief *Utopia* is based on these London associations.

At home he was not warmly received. Not only did people think his behavior set an example unworthy of American letters, but the abandoned Minnie Myrtle, her own poetic career stifled, took to the lecture circuit to denounce her husband. Her "Man, His Past, Present, and Future" suggested Joaquin's future ought to be the gallows.

Though he was a popular poet in his day, Miller was regarded by critics as banal, imitative, and prolix; and they sneered when he tried to rhyme Goethe with teeth. He seemed doomed to spend the rest of his life living up to his reputation as a wild bard. "On returning to my own country," he said, "I found that this unpleasant and entirely impossible figure ever attended and even overshadowed my most earnest work." He traveled then, exhibiting a genius for self-dramatization, continuing to write rhetorical, exuberant poems as well as some solid wilderness tales. In the late 1880s, he acquired land in the Oakland Hills and built "The Hights," where he became a kind of California monument, performing, prophesying, and entertaining literary friends: George Sterling, Ambrose Bierce, Jack London, Edwin Markham, Herman Whitaker, Edward Rowland Sill, Harr Wagner, Frank Norris, Yone Noguchi. From time to time, he came down and planted thousands of eucalyptus trees around the bay. He had, it was said, four great loves: women, whiskey, poetry, and trees, in that order; and it was to these he devoted his last years.

Frances Fuller Victor

*L*ITERARY INDUSTRIES. In 1851 the Fuller sisters published a book of their poems. Then they married the Victor brothers, and they both had successful, if very different, careers as writers.

Metta Fuller Victor stayed in the East, where she was active in the new mass-produced fiction industry. When Ann Sophia Stephens's *Malaeska* (1860) sold sixty-five thousand copies in the first few months, Beadle and Adams's dime novel publishing house was on its way. Escapist plots with plenty of action, suspense, romance, and a touch of sex—the "dimes" were snapped up by a million Civil War soldiers, selling four million copies between 1861 and 1865. Metta Victor's *Maum Guinea and her Children*, a best-selling novel of slave life, was admired by President Lincoln. She went on to write *Who Owned the Jewels, Born to Betray*, and many others in the sensational gothic line.

Frances Fuller Victor (1826–1902) went West in 1863, but she did not write dime novel westerns, though others did—with titles like *The King Pin Tramp; or Hustling Frisco Hoodlums*. Instead, she wrote city editorials for the *Evening Herald*, a colorful weekly column for the *Golden Era* (using the pen-name "Florence Fane"), poems and essays for the *Californian* and *Overland Monthly*.

Bancroft's "history factory"

Collected in *New Penelope* are her humorous observations of early California. A move to Oregon stimulated her interest in Pacific Coast history; and she published *Atlantis Arisen* and *The River of the West*, a biography of Joe Meek, the mountain man, which drew her into another kind of mass-produced book business, Bancroft's "Literary Industries."

Hubert Howe Bancroft (1832–1918), who opened his ambitious bookstore on Market Street in 1856, began amassing a personal collection of sixty-thousand items pertaining to western America from Alaska to Patagonia. In addition to bookselling, his huge shop printed and published law books, stationery, texts, and maps, sold musical instruments, and employed hundreds of researchers and a subscription book sales force.

At first Bancroft planned to compile an encyclopedia, but settled on a thirty-nine-volume history issued between 1882 and 1890 as *The Works of Hubert Howe Bancroft.* Twelve "assistants," headed by Henry Lebus Oak, wrote most of the works while the tireless Bancroft organized and controlled the project, imbuing his writing staff, as Ella Sterling Cummins said, "with his own morbid instinct for history." Initially, the *Works* aroused controversy, partly because Bancroft praised the City's founding fathers excessively, partly because people thought his business practices unethical, and above all because the writers were not credited with authorship.

Frances Fuller Victor, who moved back to San Francisco at Bancroft's invitation in 1878, wrote four volumes on the Northwest and much of the text on British Columbia and California, working steadily (and anonymously) until completion of the project. In 1893, she proved a rebellious worker in the "history factory" by exhibiting three of her volumes at the Chicago World's Fair with her name on the title page as author.

The University of California, Berkeley, acquired Bancroft's prodigious collection. As the Bancroft Library, it is now open to scholars, an invaluable repository of western history.

$\mathcal{W}$ILD WEST SEANCES. By 1850, every town in America had a spiritualist medium; the fortune seekers and gamblers who took their chances in nineteenth-century San Francisco accommodated hundreds. Not only did séances produce practical tips, but they allowed people to reveal their secret wishes in public and circumvent cultural restrictions. It was an era open to supernatural marvels, reveries of invisible worlds, apparitions of the wild, anticipations of scientific wonders. Dreams and desires, unincorporated in the conventional poetry of the period, flowered on lecture platforms, marking the transition from the Puritan vision of Michael Wigglesworth's "hellish fiends" of "a waste and howling wilderness" to the psychic daemons of the West's asocial wilderness.

Prentice Mulford communicated regularly with the spirit world, his messages laying the groundwork for a new method to change life through mental power. "When you are in a certain mental condition, your physical life and fortune will be an exact correspondence or material reflection of that condition," he claimed in his autobiography. Eliza Pittsinger was encouraged in her causes by a purple-robed being with a harp, who descended to her on Telegraph Hill.

Emma Hardinge gave frequent Lyceum lectures and imparted information on other worlds in *Leaves from Dark Volumes; or Sketches of Life from Underground Cities*, serialized in the *Golden Era*. Hardinge, an authority on the subject, wrote in *Modern American Spiritualism* that San Francisco was an ideal spot for this practice to thrive, because the transparency of the atmosphere encouraged phenomena, heavy charges of magnetism from gold deposits set up favorable currents, and the strong passions of the forty-niners tended to create "unusual magnetic emanations." Hardinge used her calling to campaign for Lincoln and the Union; other women spiritualists got supernatural support for feminism

C. H. FOSTER
WITH SPIRIT OF ADA ISAACS MENKEN
SPIRIT PHOTO BY MUMLER

and social reform, as well as an opportunity for erotic dalliance. Stoddard wrote that one of them tried, unsuccessfully, to seduce him. Mediums were accused by the press of driving men mad and/or being a cover for prostitution. Adah Isaacs Menken had "passed to the other side" long before this spirit photograph was taken, but she was perhaps still capable of driving C. H. Foster insane.

Even the skeptic Mark Twain went to séances and wrote a series of investigative articles on the "new wild-cat religion," concluding that it was no more fanatic than the Methodists and Campbellites, whose revival meetings back home "used to stock the asylums with religious lunatics."

S. S. Baldwin, a spectacular demystifier, produced the best shows at Platt's Hall—ectoplasm, flying guitars, bells, cracking bones, voices, weird whistles, and mists—then showed how they were produced by tricks of legerdemain. His performances were known to culminate in lively fistfights between believers and debunkers.

Janette Hagar Phelps

Victoria Claflin Woodhull

*C*ONTROVERSY CENTER STAGE. After the 1848 convention at Seneca Falls, New York, the struggle for the emancipation of women gained western adherents, San Francisco's women having had unusual opportunities for greater liberty. Among early feminist writers, "Hagar" (Janette H. Phelps) supported equality in the *Golden Era* but met with such spiteful replies from her male colleagues that she turned to lecturing, the better to debate her adversaries. Mark Twain spoke for the old guard: "This Iniquitous Crusade Against Man's Regal Birthright Must Be Crushed." Speaking at Platt's Hall in response were Susan B. Anthony, Julia Ward Howe, Elizabeth Cady Stanton, and Charlotte Perkins Gilman.

The public lecture vitalized nineteenth-century American education and letters, beginning with the Lyceum and continuing through the Chautauqua movement. San Franciscans flocked to the hotels, the Mercantile Library, and Platt's Hall, where speakers on public affairs, science, and the arts dispensed information and rendered opinions. Civil War orators debated rebellion and slavery. Reformers and revolutionaries argued reform and revolution. Contro-

versial speakers drew big audiences and plenty of hecklers. The "Great Agnostic," Colonel Robert Ingersoll, delivered "The Mistakes of Moses" at Platt's Hall, where he provoked Christians into denouncing him, then devastated them with logic and style. Reverend Henry Ward Beecher, America's most beloved churchman, pleaded for progressive social change.

Beecher was blasted into the century's hottest scandal by Victoria Woodhull, who printed astounding details of the pastor's amatory exploits with dozens of ladies in his flock. While Woodhull scorched Beecher's hypocrisy, she positively applauded his sexual prowess, spurring him on to further pleasures. Victoria and her sister Tennessee were the first American publishers of the *Communist Manifesto*, in their *Woodhull and Claflin's Weekly*. New York's boldest journal on issues of women's liberation, abortion, free love, human rights, and revolution. A brilliant orator, reputed to equal Lincoln himself, Woodhull went on tour after she (with running mate Frederick Douglass) lost her first madcap bid for the United States presidency. On tour in 1874, she spoke at Platt's Hall for 150 consecutive nights, while the presses hummed with texts of her speeches "Tried as by Fire" and "The Scarecrows of Sexuality."

THE MODERN MESSIAH.

Charles Crocker
(with white goatee)

Daniel O'Connell
(short man with mustache)

Thomas Maguire
(on face of padlock)

Ambrose Bierce
(with white hair)

Mayor Isaac S. Kalloch
(with glasses and broken daisy)

Governor Leland Stanford
(with top hat and dark beard)

Frank Pixley
(dark hair and sideburns)

*B*ARDS AT BAY. The most famous authors of the times spoke and read from their works at Platt's Hall: Matthew Arnold, Anthony Trollope, Bayard Taylor, Charles Dickens, John Greenleaf Whittier, F. Marion Crawford, James Russell Lowell, William Dean Howells, and Walt Whitman in his old age. When Ralph Waldo Emerson came in April 1871, the *Chronicle* noted, "The most original, profound, and incomprehensible American essayist, lecturer and philoso-

THREE OF A KIND.

The Wasp, Friday, April 14, 1882.

59

pher, is at present sojourning in San Francisco. . . . He has already lectured on *The Immortality of the Soul* and will probably soon deliver another of his characteristic imponderable dissertations." After Emerson's concluding lecture, a reviewer noted with relief that although his audiences "dropped off," he was met with "a minimum of derision." Emerson, undaunted, journeyed to Yosemite to drop in on John Muir. Muir's attempt to persuade him to sleep on the ground under the stars was unsuccessful, but Emerson did name a Sequoia after Chief Samoset.

"It is an odd thing, but anyone who disappears is said to be seen in San Francisco. It must be a delightful city and possess all the attractions of the next world," said Oscar Wilde, who arrived in town on an 1882 publicity tour. His lectures on aesthetics and home beautification were sponsored by the D'Oyle Carte Company, whose production of Gilbert and Sullivan's comic opera *Patience* was playing in theaters across the country. One of its characters, Bunthorne, was a caricature of Wilde, who posed on tour as an Aesthete in velvet breeches and coat and silk stockings, carrying an ivory cane. The significance of costume in making a statement about national and personal identity was as evident in Wilde's aesthete garb as it was in Joaquin Miller's dime-novel western attire. In spite of Wilde's undeveloped elocutionary style and the gigantic flower he carried, the six-foot-two-inch, two-hundred-pound Wilde won the respect of the male heavies when he drank them under the table at the Bohemian Club and won a poker game at the Cliff House, feats he seems to have had to duplicate at every stop in the country. His lectures on Irish poetry and independence excited much comment in the press, pro and con, the latter crowned by Ambrose Bierce's stings in the *Wasp* to a rival wit and epigram-

matist. The *Wasp* printed fifteen anti-Wilde items, a satiric parody, four burlesques, venomous verses, and many cartoons and called him an intellectual jellyfish, a gawky gowk, an ineffable dunce, and a bore with an opulence of twaddle and a penury of sense. And this was before Wilde's conviction for "abnormal sexual vice" or the publication of *The Soul of Man Under Socialism*. But Wilde had the last word. In an interview with an *Examiner* reporter, he said, "I have the most sympathy with the writers of the articles which strive to be what is called here in the United States 'funny.' Their hard work has been apparent."

Wilde's support came from the fervent Irish admirers of his mother, the insurgent patriot poet "Speranza" (Jane Francesca Elgee). Nearly a quarter of a century later, another Irishman echoed Wilde's Irish themes. The *Chronicle* reported (1904) that "when William Butler Yeats, the famous Irish poet and leader of the Celtic revival in Ireland, came out to the front of the stage in the Alhambra Theater last night unanimous applause stormed and restormed while a big Irish-American audience of more than 2000 persons gave the modern Gaelic patriot his first public welcome to San Francisco." Yeats spoke first about "reviving the mother tongue of the island by restoring its folk lore to the compelling dignity of masterly verse, and by developing throughout the land a genuine passion for real Irish drama." The reporter went on to note, "Yeats then read a powerful and anonymous poem that went all over Ireland, giving vent to a most remarkable curse . . . God's wrath was called down upon England that she might reap the harvest of her wrongs to the weak and oppressed all over the world. . . . Irish Ireland is Ireland of the centuries. English Ireland is Ireland of the decades. . . . Better an age-long battle than a civilization that brings death of the soul."

Denis Kearney and followers near City Hall

A MORAL PENAL COLONY. Of San Francisco, Ambrose Bierce wrote, "It is a moral penal colony. It is the worst of all the Sodom and Gomorrahs in our modern world. . . . It is the paradise of ignorance, anarchy, and general yellowness. . . . It needs more than all else a steady trade wind of grape-shot." Conditions in the 1870s and 1880s made good targets for grapeshot as the national postwar slump slid into the depression of 1873, followed by the failure of the Bank of California. The promise of Theodore Judah's transcontinental railroad was obliterated by four ruthless malefactors—Collis P. Huntington, Charles Crocker, Leland Stanford, and Mark Hopkins—whose control of the Central Pacific (later the Southern Pacific) made them absolute dictators in the state. The economic collapse gave these voracious Sacramento merchants the opportunity to monopolize capital, raw materials, transportation, and land; by the 1880s they owned the government. A hundred thousand Chinese laborers who had laid the Sierran tracks were now deemed expendable and thrown on the labor market by the "Big Four." Demagogue Denis Kearney rampaged through the city with his unemployed followers.

Speculation and stock swindles prevailed on Montgomery Street as the parvenu kings of Comstock joined the railroad magnates in ostentatious palaces on Nob Hill overlooking the misery below. The "reign of gilt" in San Fran-

Black Bart Bolton

Henry George turned his attention to economics. Robert Charles O'Hara Benjamin, a leading black attorney, looked to Africa (*Africa, Hope of the Negro*) and wrote a *Life of Toussaint L'Ouverture*. John Franklin Swift, a writer of Twainesque humor and travel letters, shook the city with an exposé of stock frauds and political corruption in a satirical novel, *Robert Greathouse*. The identities of villains were so thinly disguised that the publisher was forced to reissue an expurgated edition. Robert Collins wrote an early muckraking novel, *John Halsey, the Anti-Monopolist* (1884), a crusade against fraudulent silver stocks and stolen equities set in the turbulence of the financial district and the empty sandlots where Denis Kearney harangued the mobs, inciting them to attack the Nob Hill plutocrats and Chinese immigrants alike.

Black Bart (1830?–1888?), a most audacious and glamorous criminal, achieved twenty-eight successful stage robberies between 1877 and 1883, terrorizing the countryside, though he never fired a shot. He left poems behind him, signed "Black Bart PO8" (for poet), such as, "I've labored long and hard for bread/ For honor and for riches/ But on my corns too long you've trod,/ You fine-haired sons of bitches." A massive manhunt came to an end at last, when Wells Fargo agents traced him through a laundry mark to his modest house on Sansome Street—to the surprise of his friends, who knew him as Charles E. Bolton, a mild-mannered chap with a gift for conversation. The defiant antihero, pictured here, told his captors he called himself Black Bart after reading Caxton's story about a man who contended he had the secret by which he could destroy the world. Black Bart Bolton was sent up to San Quentin prison, where he served five years; and then disappeared.

cisco was more conspicuously exaggerated than anywhere else, where almost overnight, Irish saloon keepers had millions to invest in marble stables with hot and cold running water for the horses. With few exceptions, the first generation of writers boarded the new train for the East and Europe. Those who remained grappled with disaster.

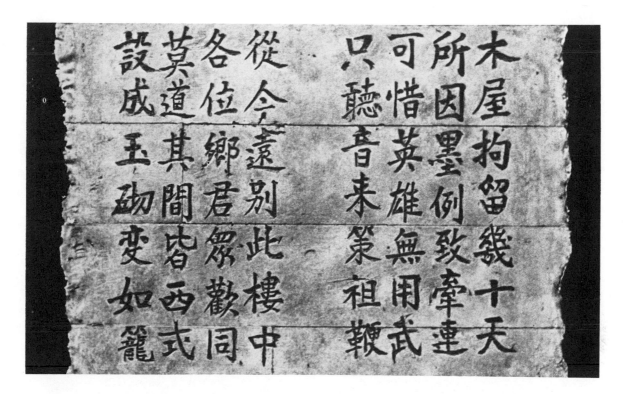

W RITING ON THE WALL. The first Chinese came to California with the gold rush and like other ethnic groups, founded newspapers: the *Golden Hills News* (1854), then the bilingual *Oriental* (1855). The maneuvers of European imperialism, war, and famine in Kwangtung Province motivated further Chinese immigration. A large, desperate Chinese population built the railroad under dangerous, inhumane conditions, an enterprise orchestrated by Charles Crocker. A great many of these workers did not survive. The Chinese called themselves *k'u-li*, bitter strength. Even in adversity, they maintained the Wên-hua-she, the Society of the Splendors of Literature.

After the railroad was completed, the depression hit, and the Chinese were squeezed in a classic double bind. If they were allowed unlimited entry, they competed "unfairly" with white workers; if they were excluded, they denied the economy cheap labor and consumers. Governor Leland Stanford and his cohorts exploited both sides. Vicious anti-Chinese legislation was passed throughout the 1870s. Men were not allowed to bring their wives and families; taxes were extortionate; lynch mobs attacked Chinatowns, burning and murdering. Hysterical campaigns by demagogues and newspapers led to the passage of exclusion laws in the 1880s.

Asian immigrants were held at the Angel Island station, where they were treated like prisoners while waiting permission to enter San Francisco. Many inmates in the holding barracks wrote poems on the walls, like the one pictured here—poems expressing despair and loneliness for home.

From this moment on, we say goodbye to this house,/ My fellow countrymen here are rejoicing like me./ Say not that everything is western styled./ Even if it were built with jade, it has turned into a cage.

Several scores of days detained in this wood house/ All because of some inked rules which involved me./ Pity it is that a hero has no way of exercising his power./ He can only wait for the word to whip his horse on a homeward journey.

——Translated by Kai-yu Hsu

63

*T*HE LITERARY FIGURE dominating a brutal era was the uncompromising Ambrose Bierce (1842–1914?), who blasted sham, pretentiousness, and assorted enemies in his newspaper columns for three decades. Additionally, he wrote ironic, macabre, and supernatural stories, collected in *Can Such Things Be?* and *In the Midst of Life*, and he created the immortal *Devil's Dictionary*.

Bierce was the second person to enlist in the Union Army after the firing on Fort Sumter. He entered the war as an eighteen-year-old drummer boy and was mustered out a brevet major. He was wounded at Shiloh, won many citations for distinguished service, and saw one-third of his brigade killed in action.

In San Francisco in 1868, he took over the *News Letter*'s "Town Crier" column, the tradition of which was to exercise unlimited abuse in the style of frontier humorists. From the outset, Bierce continued Twain's ridicule of the police, adding the mayor, the Caucasian Society, the forty-niner pioneers, and fraternal organizations. He specialized in the art of vituperative jesting, in which he surpassed his predecessors in audacious blasphemy and epigram. His "Telegraphic Jottings," terse satire based on humorously shocking juxtapositions of news and comment, initiated a free-flow invective he continued through his "Prattle" columns.

In the early 1870s, he delighted England, where he spent time with expatriots Twain, Mulford, and Miller; refined his satire on Tom Hood's *Fun* and *Figaro*; and issued (as "Dod Grile") three books of sketches: *The Fiend's Delight, Nuggets and Dust out of California,* and *Cobwebs from an Empty Skull*. Reluctantly, he returned to a turbulent and corrupt San Francisco. He never overcame his feeling of alienation and estrangement there.

"It is my intention," he said, "to purify journalism in this town by instructing such writers as it is worth while to instruct, and assassinating those that it is not." He did the former as associate editor of the *Argonaut* (1876–1879), the *Wasp* (1881–1887), and on Hearst's *Examiner*. Writers were not his only targets.

As he railed against the railroad barons, "bloated bondholders," political grafters, Denis Kearney, and his unruly Workingmen's Party of California, Bierce's prejudices against the possibility of improvement crystallized, his contempt for contemporary civilization scaling Nietzschean heights. After he moved to the *Wasp*, his wit grew ever more sardonic, as he threw the cold light of negation over everything. He was indiscriminate and unsystematic. He raged against dog lovers and teetotalers, scorched W. C. Bartlett's Wordsworthian nature poetry, and hoped to howl over the grave of his employer, Hearst. He was intransigent about Jack London's socialism, and, according to Charlotte Perkins Gilman, at his best in scurrilous abuse of hard-working women writers. Quite often, as Franklin Walker pointed out, he attacked with more heat than profundity, under a "misapprehension that he was a social philosopher rather than a wit." But with outrageous black humor, he was capable of ferreting out hypocrisy, fraudulence, and the tyranny that sleeps in the heart of ideologies. At times he was flawless: "No sane man of intelligence will plead for religion on the ground that it is better than nothing. It is not better than nothing if it is not true. Truth is better than anything or all things; the next best thing to truth is absence of error."

His campaign in Washington against Huntington's Funding Bill was effective realpolitik. The measure would have canceled the railroad's obligation to repay government loans. Bierce described

the Senate testimony: "Mr. Huntington appeared before the committee and took his hands out of all pockets long enough to be sworn." "Huntington Lying in his Last Ditch," read a Bierce headline. In the end, Huntington tried to bribe his adversary: "Well, name your price; every man has his price." Bierce replied that his price was the amount owed the government and that Huntington might pay it to the Treasury.

Bierce's masterpiece, *The Devil's Dictionary*, a compilation of mordantly brilliant definitions developed from an early "devil's wordbook," was serialized in the *Wasp*. Some examples of his distilled wit:

Politics, *n*. A strife of interests masquerading as a contest of principles.

Pray, *v*. To ask that the laws of the universe be annulled in behalf of a single petitioner confessedly unworthy.

Radicalism, *n*. The conservatism of tomorrow injected into the affairs of today.

Realism, *n*. The art of depicting nature as it is seen by toads.

Religion, *n*. A Daughter of Hope and Fear explaining to Ignorance the nature of the Unknown.

Saint, *n*. A dead sinner, revised and edited.

Bierce defined a cynic as "a blackguard whose faulty vision sees things as they are, not as they ought to be," and so he regarded himself. His many enemies saw him as a pure blackguard, a Svengali, and a scourge. Upton Sinclair called him "a great writer, a bitter black sinner, and a cruel, domineering old bigot." Bierce once told Jerome Hart, "When I was in my twenties, I concluded one day that I was not a poet. It was the bitterest moment of my life." Mary Austin thought his savage irony stemmed from a sense of failure to fulfill his titanic creative power. His friends considered him an archaic romantic with an almost morbid sensitivity, a moralist whose unrealistically lofty expectations led to quarrels and disillusionment; his daughter Helen spoke of his electric personality and the strange power he had to attract wild birds and animals to him when he called.

At the age of seventy-one, after surveying the old Civil War battlefields where he had seen a truth of human behavior and set many spectral stories, the old enemy of disorder decided to go to South America. "Dressed for death," he crossed the Mexican border with a vague idea of joining Pancho Villa, and disappeared forever. He wrote to Lora Bierce, "Goodbye—If you hear of my being stood up against a Mexican stone wall and shot to rags, please know that I think it a pretty good way to depart this life. It beats old age, disease, or falling down the cellar stairs. To be a Gringo in Mexico—ah, that is Euthanasia!"

THE ARGONAUT.

FRANK M. PIXLEY, } - - - - - *Editors.*
FRED. M. SOMERS. }

*N*IGHTMARES AND GHOULS. Named after a Bret Harte story, the *Argonaut* was founded by Frank Pixley (1877) as a weekly with a dual purpose: "rampant Americanism on one side" (that is, a pro-railroad, anti-labor, anti-immigration slant) and literature and art on the other. Early writers included Ambrose Bierce, a regular columnist for two years; C. W. Stoddard, with a department called "Fancy Free"; and Gertrude Atherton, whose "The Randolphs of Redwood," a sizzling exposé of a prominent dipso-maniac heiress, shocked the elite.

Jerome Hart joined the *Argonaut* in 1880 and encouraged the short story; an admirer of the supernatural and fantastic, he ran translations of Maupassant, Gautier, and Mérimée as well as tales of terror by American authors. The combination of rampant Americanism and fictional horror struck a perfect harmony.

The supernatural hoax, science fiction, and horror story flourished on the frontier, where uncertainty and the terrors of an unprincipled society, thrust into sharp relief, could be eclipsed momentarily by gruesome invention. As the mythic Garden of the West was cultivated over the corpses of an indigenous people, western literature excelled in "horror," as if fictional cannibals and macabre effects might outshadow the savagery of American life.

William "Caxton" Rhodes

Ralph Keeler

William C. Morrow

The contemporary fascination with UFOs, intergalactic denizens, apocalyptic science, and vampires echoes back through the nineteenth century. Mark Twain's account of a three-hundred-year-old petrified man excited amazement in a credulous public. William H. Rhodes ("Caxton"), an urbane lawyer with a talent for prose, created a panic similar in impact to the one following Orson Welles's 1938 broadcast of a Martian invasion, a radio drama based on H. G. Wells's *The War of the Worlds*. Caxton's hoax, "The Case of Summerfield," printed in a daily paper in 1871, alarmed the community with a supposedly true story of a fiend who had devised a means to destroy the planet by setting the oceans on fire through the use of potassium. Other fictional ventures into mad science by Rhodes were "The Telescopic Eye" and "John Pollenfaxen," the latter about a photographer who used living animal and human eyes for experiments.

Ralph Keeler, the author of *Gloverson and His Silent Partners*, the first novel of California life (which "failed instantly and decisively," according to William Dean Howells), was far better at weird tales, nightmarish and metamorphic. Keeler ran away from home at eleven and worked as a cabin boy on Great Lakes steamers. He was a prodigy—dancer, singer, poet, and vagabond. He worked as an actor in Mississippi riverboat minstrel shows, then worked his way through college. He wandered to Germany, where he attended Prince Rupert University in Heidelberg (and learned seven languages), then showed up in San Francisco in 1864 to spread German romanticism and write fantastic stories. His end was as strange as his tales. Sailing somewhere between Santiago and Havana, he either fell or was pushed overboard and was never seen again.

Among the masters of the ghastly and uncanny in the *Argonaut* were William

Emma Frances Dawson

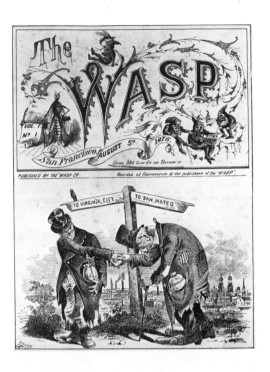

C. Morrow ("Awful Shadows," "The Rajah's Nemesis," "A Remarkable Case in Surgery," "Mated Rubies," and "The Ape and the Idiot"), Robert Duncan Milne ("Ten Thousand Years in Ice"), Annie Lake Townsend ("Metempsychosis" and "The Withered Hand"), Emma Frances Dawson ("A Warning Ghost" and "Singed Moths"), E. H. Clough ("The Kiss of Death"), and Nathan "the Essenian" Kouns, who, like Ambrose Bierce, set horrific stories in the Civil War.

Ambrose Bierce was the consummate genius of the genre; everything he wrote—psychological, realistic, or supernatural—illustrates Paradise Defeated. Out in the poisoned western Eden, Bierce, with sardonic humor and cruel accuracy, denied the heroism of the Civil War, the omnipotence of the individual, and the inevitable satisfaction of rampant American dreamers.

THE WASP. A weekly journal of social commentary featuring vitriolic colored cartoons, the *Wasp* achieved distinction under the editorship (1881–1886) of Ambrose Bierce, who wrote most of the text. Although he focused on political issues—corruption, the machinations of the Big Four, and Chinese immigration—intriguing literary items surfaced from time to time:

An enterprising maniac is making himself felt in the journalistic line. *The Asylum Appeal*, published at Napa and edited by lunatics entirely, has improved steadily in lunacy ever since its start, and is now a most queer and interesting piece of bric-a-brac. All through it, in poem, prose, and short item there is a *sauce piquant* of dementia that is charming and unlike anything in literature.

This mansion of ours—o'er its turrets and towers/ Let us wave the broad banner of light/ Was built by *the beast*, who'll be first at the feast/ When Confucius comes with his kite.

The precise relevancy of the mythical beast and the advent of Confucius with an aerial toy is not apparent, but the imaginative wealth of the lines is indubitable.

$\mathcal{P}$OETES MAUDITS. After Bierce read
Herman Scheffauer's poem "The
Sea of Serenity," he agreed an amusing
controversy might be started. In the
tradition of Poe's own balloon hoax in
the *Baltimore Sun*, they would publish
Scheffauer's poem in the *Examiner*,
claiming it a historic discovery of a lost
Poe poem.

Bierce was always fond of stirring
things up. Some of his hoaxes were celebrated: for instance, his damning review
of a book on the waltz, *The Dance of
Death* (which he had had a hand in

writing), incited a sale of eighteen
thousand copies. Unfortunately for the
Poe Hoax, Hearst's bold 1899 Spanish
American War headlines overwhelmed
this small literary mischief.

Scheffauer, pictured with Bierce, was
one of the latter's protégés for a while.
He wrote poems, collected in *Of Both
Worlds* and *Looms of Life*, and Grove
Plays for the Bohemian Club's summer
entertainments. He returned to his
native Germany, where he became a
propagandist for the Kaiser. In 1926,
crushed by the aftermath of World War I,
he killed his woman companion, slashed
his wrists and throat, and jumped from a

high building in Berlin. It was said he took life too seriously.

Scheffauer's lurid death contributed to the macabre legend surrounding Bierce and his poet associates. First, there was the matter of Bierce's own mysterious disappearance in Mexico.

Josephine C. McCrackin, writer and preserver of forests, lost everything in a forest fire. Then, Bierce's friend and favorite student, the poet George Sterling, took a fatal dose of cyanide. Another protégé, fantasy writer Emma Frances Dawson, starved to death in Palo Alto. The brooding poet David Lesser Lezinsky, an admirer of Whitman, was supposedly suicided by Bierce's unkind reviews. And Richard Realf, poet, suicide, and fellow Civil War veteran, was hounded to death by what he called a "nemesis"—a woman he married "in a fit of aberration after a period of prolonged debauch."

Realf had been raised by Lord Byron's widow. In this country, he worked with John Brown and was appointed Secretary of State in the provisional government of his liberated territory. Realf, sent to bring help from England, was waylaid several months converting to Catholicism, and by the time he returned John Brown had been hanged at Charles Town. He fought in the war, became a Perfectionist at the Oneida Community, went on the road as a temperance lecturer, and married a number of women without bothering about divorces. One of his wives, Catherine Cassidy, refused to be deserted and pursued Realf around the country until he poisoned himself.

Before he died, he wrote three widely admired sonnets inspired by his domestic difficulties. Bierce, in his eulogy, quoted from one of them: "Born unto singing, and a burden lay/ Mighty on him and he moaned because/ He could not rightly utter in the day/ What God taught in the night."

David Lesser Lezinsky

Richard Realf

Josephine Clifford McCrackin

Helena Modjeska

UTOPIANS. If the Civil War had derailed the radical programs of the Abolitionists, the victory of the industrial North unloosed the dynamos, stratified classes, and bloated the trusts. A restless, exploited urban proletariat and discontented farmers saw their control over society and old dreams of a new world disappearing. Programs for social reconstruction and spiritual regeneration went hand in hand; amorphous reform movements amalgamated curious combinations of ideas—socialism, phrenology,

the Grange, feminism, syndicalism, theosophy, trade unions, spiritualism. Behind Jacob Coxey's army of the unemployed, a rudimentary labor organization, was a theory of "soul absorption." Upton Sinclair, a practicing telepathist, put equally sincere energies into *King Coal* and *The Fasting Cure*. Utopias sprang from premises humanitarian, millenarian, mechano-scientific, and dietary. Late nineteenth-century communitarian societies were based on Henry George's *Progress and Poverty* and Edward Bellamy's *Looking Backward*, which envisioned a total realization of human potential. Before rationalist and imaginative thinking were separated into mutually exclusive spheres, utopian novelists dared dream of transforming the world, of making a radically better society. Undeveloped California, which attracted people escaping constraints of established society, missed the prewar Owenite and Fourieran movements; but from 1875 to 1900, it initiated more utopian colonies than the other states combined, some with curious literary connections. North of San Francisco, the Icaria Speranza community based itself on French socialist Etienne Cabet's utopian book, *Voyage en Icarie* (1840); and the Altruria colony was inspired by readers of William Dean Howells's *A Traveller from Altruria*. Other utopian communities ranged from aristocratic to theosophic to revolutionary.

Chafing under Russian domination in Warsaw, Count Charles Bozenta Chlapowski and his wife, Helena Modjeska (1840–1909), conceived a scheme for setting up a Polish Brook Farm in California with a few friends. They saw themselves cooking under the sapphire sky, playing guitars, and listening to mockingbirds while Indian maidens

Henryk Sienkiewicz

adorned them with wreaths of wild-flowers. Acting on this improbable fantasy, they found land near Anaheim and struggled for almost a year at making a utopia there, but inexperience and the rigors of agriculture defeated them. Henryk Sienkiewicz (1846–1916), best known for his novel *Quo Vadis?*, was discouraged almost immediately and sat under a tree, writing. Before long, he returned to Poland, his impressions of San Francisco recorded in *Portrait of America*. Modjeska, former hostess of a Warsaw salon of intellectuals, perfected her English and in San Francisco resumed the theatrical career for which she was celebrated in Poland. She became a famous actress on the American stage, settled permanently in Anaheim, and left a charming memoir, *Memories and Impressions*.

*T*HOMAS LAKE HARRIS (1823–1906), poet and sage, aimed to found the New Harmonic Civilization north of San Francisco after he split with his community at Brockton, New York, having gained some two thousand followers from both sides of the Atlantic. Influenced by Pythagoras, Charles Fourier, and Robert Owen, Harris had been a spiritualist and a Swedenborgian minister in New York City. He was acquainted with Horace Greeley, Edgar Allan Poe, H. W. Longfellow, and Nathaniel Hawthorne, who didn't think much of his poetry. Lady Byron had heard Harris read poems dictated to him by Spirit-Byron and had been gracious to him.

In 1875, with his favorite disciples, he established Fountain Grove to develop a theocratic social order based upon his theory of esoteric sexual sublimation and a metaphysic of a bisexual deity—the Masculine Love and the Feminine Truth. Harris received a poem a day in trance states, and issued them and other writings at Fountain Grove Press: *Wisdom of the Adepts, The Republic of the Sun*, and *Luminous Life*, among them. His verses were collected in *The Golden Child* and *Battle Bells, Verse Studies in Social Humanity*. Many of the verses expounded his ideas of pleasurable living: "If you would slay the Social Snake/ That brings the Bosom grief and ache/ Dance while you may, dance while you may/ For heaven comes forth in Social Play"; others reflected his preoccupations with sex mysticism and apotheosis.

Calling himself Primate and King, Harris struggled to break through the forces of evil by rallying "vortical atoms" by means of capturing *vril* through the Principle of Internal Respiration, a yoga-like breathing technique. He aspired to divine union with Lily Queen, his heavenly female counterpart, but was rumored to have used earthly stand-ins. Scandal

Thomas Lake Harris

Burnette G. Haskell

beset Fountain Grove, but fortunately, by 1894, Harris had succeeded in becoming immortal, proceeding to New York under the name Theos. There he reconnected with a disciple and fellow poet, Edwin Markham. When Harris died, Markham and Harris's wife tried to keep the news from the press, because they thought what had occurred could not possibly have been death. After three days of expecting him to rise, they had to admit the Trance Poet would have to be buried. After the disappointed disciples had given up hope of his resurrection, Harris's adopted heir, Kanaye Hagasawa, guided the utopia in a more prosaic direction, namely viticulture, developing the excellent Fountain Grove wines of Sonoma.

𝓑URNETTE G. HASKELL (1857–1907), a brilliant graduate of the University of California, Berkeley, recruited San Franciscans into secret organizations, first the Invisible Republic and then the Illuminati, which were to infiltrate society for the purpose of sowing the seeds of radical enlightenment among the citizenry. Haskell took over the editorship of his uncle's labor journal, *Truth*, converting it into an organ of the revived International Workingmen's Association. This late branch of Marx's First International had, in San Francisco, more in common with the anarchist "Black International" (also claiming a small, active membership in the city). The motto of *Truth*, with Haskell at the helm, was "Truth is five cents a copy and dynamite is forty cents a pound." The visionary Haskell was exceedingly impatient:

Kaweah colonists before the fall

"Arm to the teeth! The Revolution is upon you!" he urged in 1883.

When the revolution failed to occur, Haskell turned his attention to Edward Bellamy's ideas, publishing *What Nationalism Is, the American Cure for Monopoly and Anarchy*. While he was living on Clay Street in 1886, he founded the Kaweah Colony, conceived as "the purest and most radical democracy." Organized in San Francisco, its members located their utopian community where Sequoia National Park now stands. The experiment was short-lived, mainly because the lumber interests fought it tooth and nail. The Karl Marx Tree was renamed for General Sherman; and Burnette Haskell died in obscurity, buried by the Sailors' Union of the Pacific he had helped found.

HENRY GEORGE (1839–1897) wrote in *Progress and Poverty* (1879), "What change may come, no mortal man can tell, but that some great change must come, thoughtful men begin to feel. The civilized world is trembling on the verge of a great movement. Either it must be a leap upward, which will open the way to advances yet undreamed of, or it must be a plunge downward, which will carry us toward barbarism." Henry George's answer to this call for a leap upward was the single tax, a theory resembling that of Victor de Mirabeau and the eighteenth-century Physiocrats.

George's career followed a pattern typical of other emigrants. He ran away to sea at thirteen, prospected for gold in California and British Columbia, and filibustered on behalf of Mexican President Benito Juarez, who was fighting Maximilian's installation on the throne by Napoleon III. George worked mainly as a newspaperman and wrote for the literary journals—essays on the pseudoscience of phrenology and ghost stories. He even contemplated a novel. But at the same time, he became absorbed with the paradox that progress (like the coming railroad) meant wealth for a few and poverty for the many. George paid particular attention to the awesome misuse of land in California. No yeoman farmer class had usurped the privileges of the semifeudal estates that virtually enslaved Chinese coolies and were sites of sporadic squatter violence. With the huge land grants to the railroad's Big Four, around twenty million acres of arable land were concentrated in the hands of a few hundred people. Land that became available fell to speculators, who drove prices up and forced farmers to pay excessive and unfair rents.

A single tax on land, George argued, would end speculation, redistribute wealth, and provide all the revenue

Henry George with baby Henry George Jr.

required for society's needs. Because "neither labor nor capital would be taxed on their just earnings," many small property owners as well as laborers found this simple solution persuasive. George's integrity, eloquence, and impassioned prose made *Progress and Poverty* an international best-seller, admired by Leo Tolstoy, George Bernard Shaw, and, briefly, Daniel de Leon. Sidney and Beatrice Webb thought it did more than anything to stimulate the revival of interest in socialism in England, where it influenced the formation of the British Labour Party. In that it responded to the bitterness and rebellious tradition of dissent in agrarian America, it was a significant force in the Populist and Greenback movements. Socialists and utopians considered the tax a partial and superficial remedy but saw that George clearly recognized the limitations of "equality of political rights" and demanded nothing less than "the Golden Age of which poets have sung and high-raised seers have told in metaphor."

"The Prophet of San Francisco" ran for mayor of New York, polling more votes than Teddy Roosevelt, but was defeated by the Tammany Machine. When he died, multitudes lined the streets for his funeral cortege, but already his specific proposal was an anachronism in the swift tides of developing industrial capitalism.

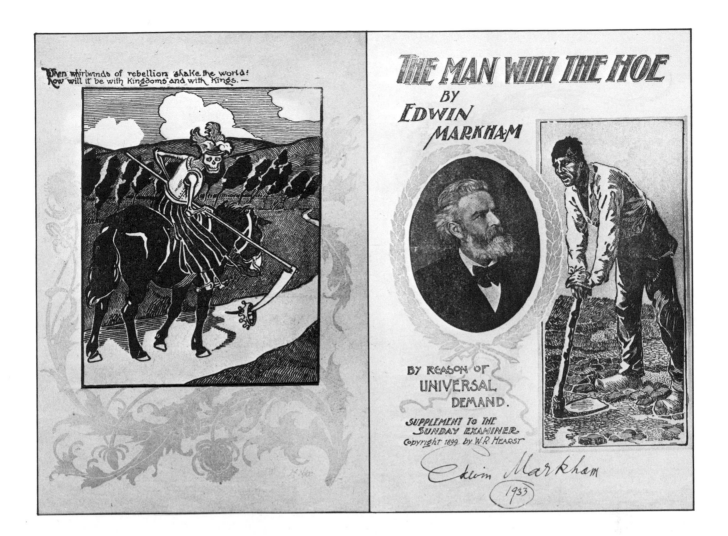

SO SOMBER and terrible was Edwin Markham's (1852–1940) youth that he identified with the hero of Victor Hugo's *The Man Who Laughs,* Gwynplaine, who was disfigured in childhood by cuts made from mouth to ears, leaving him a monster with a hideous grin. Markham endured his own psychic scars, working as a sheepherder, got what education he could manage, and taught in small country schools. He read and collected books, admiring especially Ruskin, Fourier, Marx, Kropotkin, Ignatius Donnelly, Keats, and Shakespeare.

The literary center of gravity shifted in the 1870s and 1880s to Oakland, where Ina Coolbrith reigned at the library and Joaquin Miller tippled with the poets at "The Hights." Because of his asthma, Bierce could never stay long in San Francisco and so was often in the drier climate of the East Bay. Edward Rowland Sill, a Berkeley teacher, wrote poems on themes of religious doubt and won laurels with "The Fool's Prayer," a poem thought to be impressive in public recitations. (The West proudly claimed him as its intellectual.) David Starr Jordan and Charles Warren Stoddard also met with this literary circle, and as Markham contributed to the revived *Overland Monthly* and the new *Californian*, he became regarded as a promising newcomer. Through his involvement with Thomas Lake Harris, he developed his own brand of mystical insurgency, keeping a "book of darkness" and writing notes on social protest and poems dealing with the oppressed and rebellious.

A single poem exploded in the *San Francisco Examiner* on January 15, 1899, and changed the destiny of this ordinary man and poet. "The Man with the Hoe," a protest against the brutal exploitation of farm labor, was inspired by Jean François Millet's painting of the same name. By a peculiar irony, the painting was owned by the family of labor exploiter Charles Crocker, and Markham saw it on display at the Hopkins Art Gallery on Nob Hill. The poem thrust Markham into international furor and fame; translated into forty languages, it earned him $250,000 in royalties over the next thirty years. He was much in demand as a speaker by labor and radical groups; his poetry was popularly and critically acclaimed. In 1922, over a hundred thousand persons came to hear him read "Lincoln" at the dedication of the Lincoln Memorial, broadcast on radio nationwide.

There were exceptions to this universal admiration. Collis Huntington offered a $750 prize for a poem to oppose Markham's dangerous viewpoint (won by John Vance Cheney). And "The Man with the Hoe" inspired Bierce's most terrible blast: "If ever, (which Heaven forbid!) I stumble upon the mortal part of the late Edwin Markham, Poet of the People, I shall turn it upon its back in the sure and certain expectation that the throat has been cut by a hoe." Markham survived both prophecy and prophesier; his stamina was legendary as he spun through the country on perpetual tour, even traveling the length of Mexico at the age of eighty-three, a peripatetic embodiment of the populist impulse.

*M*OUNTAIN ECSTASY. Among the prose writers covering the California landscape, the most remarkable were two eccentric geologist naturalists. Clarence King (1842–1901), mad mountain climber and fabled raconteur, collected his scattered writings in *Mountaineering in the Sierra Nevada* (1872), which Wallace Stegner called "the most delightful book of its decade—along with *Roughing It*, the highwater mark of frontier literature." The first real literature of the wilderness, it includes climbing thrills, character sketches, and three narrative stories: "The Newtys of Pike," "Kaweah's Run," and "Cut-Off Copple's."

Scottish-born John Muir (1838–1914), escaping a severe Protestant background, headed across the country on foot from his log cabin in Wisconsin. In California, he hiked to the most austerely beautiful places he could find and rarely left the wilderness, walking thousands of miles, daring the elements, and pushing himself to the extremes of possible experience. His rapturous essays were published first in the *Overland Monthly* and collected in *The Mountains of California, My First Summer in the Sierra*, and *The Yosemite*. Some found his enthusiasm unnerving, but Mary Austin, a sensitive writer captivated by the spirits of the desert, understood his mystical intensity. In *Earth Horizon*, she describes meeting Muir in Carmel, "a tall, lean man with the habit of soliloquizing. He told stories of his life in the wild and of angels; angels that lifted him and carried him. I know something of what went on in Muir . . . for him, quite simply, the angels were spirits of the wild, who bore him on their wings through perilous places."

Muir explored the Arctic and Alaska, visited forests all over the world, and advocated the preservation of wilder-

ness. For his efforts on behalf of con-
servation and national parks, Muir
Woods National Monument was named
for him. Muir is seated here (right) with
John Swett, pioneer and educator.

WHEN ROBERT LOUIS STEVENSON (1850–1894) first came to San Francisco in 1879, he was a penniless, twenty-eight-year-old vagabond in mad pursuit of the woman he loved. Nine years later he returned to charter Oakland millionaire Dr. Samuel Merritt's yacht for a voyage to the South Seas. Between these two trips, he published most of his well-known books, including *Treasure Island, Dr. Jekyll and Mr. Hyde, Kidnapped*, and *The Master of Ballantrae*.

Stevenson fell in love with the unhappily married Fanny Van de Grift Osbourne at Grez, an art colony outside the Forest of Fontainebleau. Their two-year idyll ended when Fanny's husband called her and the children home; but the lovers found it impossible to be apart, and a letter from Fanny precipitated the ill and unpublished Scottish writer six-thousand miles to California. To preserve proprieties during divorce proceedings, Stevenson rented a room at 608 Bush Street in a private home. His San Francisco experience is preserved in *The Wrecker* (1892): good $.50 meals at Donadieu's French Restaurant at Grant and Bush, hours spent writing on a bench in Portsmouth Square, and long walks through the strange foreign city. One day the amateur emigrant encountered Charley Stoddard, who became his friend and talked to him of the South Seas: "It was in such talks," wrote Stevenson, "that I first heard the names—first fell under the spell—of the islands;

and it was from the first of them that I returned (a happy man) with *Omoo* under one arm and my friend's own adventures under the other." Stoddard gives a curiously animated picture of Stevenson in *Exits and Entrances*, "that inspiring man . . . talking volubly, flicking the eternal cigarette, flinging his arms in eloquent Gallic gestures . . . soliloquizing with the fine frenzy of an Italian improvisatore."

As Stevenson's funds ran out, he ate at cheaper restaurants, finally limiting himself to four ounces of food a day. In his shabby velvet coat, thin and tubercular, he sat in the Bohemian Club, reading, and tried to land a regular job with a city newspaper, an effort that ended in failure. He came down with influenza-pneumonia and was writing his epitaph when the strong-willed Fanny Osbourne threw convention to the winds and moved him into her Oakland home until he recovered. They were married in April 1880; and at the suggestion of friends Dora and Virgil Williams, they set off for the drier climate of Mount Saint Helena, where they lived rent-free in an abandoned mining dormitory, the setting of Stevenson's *The Silverado Squatters* (1883). Just as in a plot of a romantic novel, Stevenson's disapproving father reconciled himself to the marriage, enabling the couple to return to Europe, forgiven and financed.

Only Kipling (whose *Light That Failed* was rejected by the *Chronicle* during the author's visit in the 1880s) aroused comparable admiration during the 1890s rage for boyish adventure romance.

Pictured here is Stevenson (on the right) on his return trip (1888) on board the *Casco* in the Oakland estuary. Fanny Osbourne Stevenson is seated (center front); immediately behind her is Lloyd Osbourne, her son; and above him, bearded, is Sam Merritt. Though Merritt at first refused to lease his boat to "one of those cranks who write books," Fanny was able to prove to him that Stevenson was now a respected, wealthy man of letters. They eventually settled in Samoa, where Stevenson spent his last years on the estate "Vailima," where he was known as *Tusitala*, the teller of tales.

IN THIS OUR WORLD

AND OTHER POEMS

By CHARLOTTE PERKINS STETSON

Would ye but understand!
Joy is on every hand!
Ye shut your eyes and call it night,
Ye grope and fall in seas of light—
Would ye but understand!

SAN FRANCISCO
JAMES H. BARRY AND JOHN H. MARBLE, PUBLISHERS
1895

*R*EFORM. Charlotte Perkins Stetson Gilman (1860–1935), grandniece of Harriet Beecher Stowe, came to San Francisco to recover from the nervous breakdown she later converted into a brilliant short story, "The Yellow Wallpaper." Her first writings were poems, reflecting her dedication to Fabian socialism, Edward Bellamy's Nationalism, and feminism, collected in *This Our World* (1893) and *Suffrage Songs* (1911).

In her autobiography, *The Living of Charlotte Perkins Gilman*, she describes the highpoints of her life in Oakland and San Francisco—the California Woman's Congresses she organized in 1894 and 1895 and the vivid events of the Pullman strike. She recalls meetings with Ina Coolbrith and Joaquin Miller, who was entertaining Hamlin Garlin and James Whitcomb Riley at "The Hights," and Bruce Porter, who designed one of her books. Active in the Pacific Coast Women's Press Association, she edited its magazine, *Impress*, and worked with visitors Jane Addams and Susan B. Anthony as well as local journalists and writers.

Hounded by the press and plagued by debt and difficulty during her San Francisco years, Gilman left without regret.

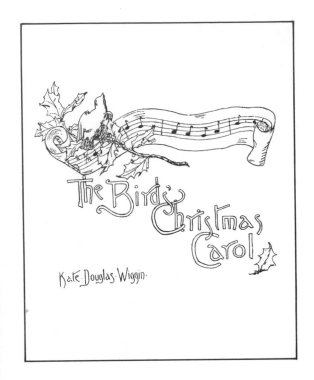

Among her many books are *Man-Made World, His Religion and Hers*, and the feminist milestone *Women and Economics* (1898), a cogent argument for economic, rather than merely political, change. Her utopian novel, *Herland*, recently reprinted, was originally serialized in *The Forerunner*, a journal of fiction, editorials, and poetry—written, edited, and published entirely by Gilman herself.

$\mathcal{A}$MONG HER COLLEAGUES were feminist and heretic Sarah B. Cooper and Kate Douglas Wiggin (1856–1923), who established in the "wretched slums" of Silver Street the first free kindergarten west of the Rockies. Wiggin turned to writing as a means of supporting schools for the poor; the substantial proceeds from her first stories, *The Story of Patsy* and *The Birds' Christmas Carol*, encouraged her to become a professional author. Her optimistic juveniles, especially *Rebecca of Sunnybrook Farm* (1903), were read by generations of youngsters. Wiggin returned to San Francisco nearly every spring to lecture on educational topics at the teacher training center she had founded there.

IN HER AUTOBIOGRAPHY, *Adventures of a Novelist*, Gertrude Atherton (1857–1948) related that when her husband died at sea (his body returned to her preserved in a keg of rum), she was freed to pursue the literary career she wanted. Her elopement with her mother's fiancé, George Atherton, the wealthy son of a San Francisco Peninsula merchant and a Chilean aristocrat, resulted in a disappointing marriage. She confessed in her autobiography that though she had two children, "the maternal instinct had been left out of me with all the other domestic virtues." She found life on the huge Spanish land grant estate demanding, oppressive, and boring. She had been a headstrong, rebellious child; over the objections of her husband and conservative Castillian mother-in-law, she contributed articles and fiction to the *News Letter* and *Argonaut* in the 1870s and 1880s. But still she longed to escape her restricted circumstances. "A novelist should know the world. . . . What opportunity have I to study it in a hole like California?"

With George gone (1887), she traveled over the next fifty years between San Francisco, New York, and various European cities, writing dozens of novels (many of them selling hundreds of thousands of copies), short stories, essays, histories, memoirs, magazine articles, and biographies. Sensations when they were issued were *A Daughter of the Vine* (1899), based on the sordid lives of prominent citizens; *Patience Sparhawk and Her Times* (1897), with a Lamiel-like heroine; and the best-seller, *Black Oxen* (1823), one of several fictional treatments of sexual rejuvenation, a glandular therapy with which Gertrude was involved in the 1920s and 1930s. Like Helen Hunt Jackson, whose popular *Ramona* (1884) appealed to nostalgia

for Amerindian-Spanish California, Atherton wrote fiction set in the early days, then carried her sixteen-novel saga into contemporary times. The rebellious spirit of her first works degenerated into slapdash romanticism, later books transcribing Gertrude's aristocratic fancies.

Neither San Francisco's struggling working people nor its literary Bohemia had anything in common with Atherton's social world. To the wealthy Atherton, the city seemed dull and eventless. "I doubted if anywhere on earth could one feel so isolated, so blue, so stranded, as in San Francisco. Well it had been called the Jumping-Off-Place. In the 1890s, despite the sentimentalists, it was gray and ugly and depressing." She preferred a less provincial milieu.

Atherton's heroines, unlike their sentimental sisters in the usual woman's novel, combine beauty, wealth, sexual freedom, independence, brilliant careers, and sometimes marriage. Her own ideals were the emancipated intellectual beauties whose salons in late eighteenth-century France attracted the literary and political greats. Gertrude was famous for her own salons, but they never quite satisfied her: "The salon was all very well for Madame de Staël who could sit in the middle of the room and pontificate, or for Madame Récamier who listened 'avec seduction,' but in these days the hostess does nothing but move about and stand about listening to scrappy conversation, wondering if she has forgotten to introduce anyone to the celebrities he came to see, and wishing they would all go home. I like the small group, and as for men, I have always preferred one at a time."

In her old age, she settled in San Francisco's Pacific Heights, where she was active in the P.E.N. Club and in literary and civic affairs. She continued writing until her death at age ninety-one.

FRANK NORRIS (1870–1902) was born in Chicago but in 1884 moved with his family to San Francisco, where he grew up in a large Victorian house on Sacramento Street near Van Ness. As a youth, he watched the cowboys driving herds down Van Ness Avenue and explored the shabby world of small shopkeepers on Polk Street, the scene of *McTeague*.

He studied art in Paris at the Atelier Julian, then at San Francisco's Art Association, but preferred writing romances (à la Kipling via Froissart), which he continued to do at the University of California. In Zola's naturalistic fiction, Norris saw ordinary lives sucked into a cold dynamic beyond their control but also given dramatic significance, a view that began to influence his writing.

After a year at Harvard, where he wrote parts of *Vandover and the Brute*, he wrote for the *Chronicle*, which sent him to South Africa (1895) to write travel articles. After capture by the Boers and a severe tropical illness, he returned to the West Coast, joining the youthful staff of the *Wave*. Impressed by his work there, *McClure's* hired him to cover the Spanish-American War in Cuba; but a renewed bout of fever cut his assignment short.

"Tell your story," said Norris, "and let your style go to the devil—we don't want literature, we want life!" Life in *Blix* is young love in scenic San Francisco's bohemian environment and looks to a hopeful future. In *McTeague*, it is the misery of the underside of America's acquisitive society as the inexorable destinies of an avaricious Polk Street dentist and his wife are spun out in Norris's greatest book (made into the unforgettable film masterpiece, *Greed*, by Erich von Stroheim). The joyous *Blix* and the gritty, realistic *McTeague*, both published in 1899,

exemplify a curious bridge between frontier romanticism and a new muscular realism. Norris heralded the coming generation of activist writers, goaded by the inequity and alienation produced by the implacable machines, inanimate and political. Norris treated this reality with more detachment than others; his sympathy tended to lie with the oppressed, but he admired brute power. This, as Alfred Kazin thought, made him a romantic naturalist, at once insurgent and reactionary.

When Norris and his lovely bride, Jeanette Black, moved back to San Francisco, he worked further on his trilogy-in-progress, *The Epic of Wheat*. The first volume, *The Octopus* (1901), written with exuberant vitality, is set in an agricultural California already in the grip of monopolies geared to industry. It is the dramatic story of San Joaquin Valley ranchers fighting the Southern Pacific Railroad, symbolized by a monster octopus strangling the land that feeds it. The book was based on real events. Huntington had managed to procure, in addition to $700,000,000 for the Big Four, land grants of 12,800 acres for every mile of track laid. The railroad invited poor settlers to lease this property with the promise that they could buy it later at a fixed price without charge for improvements. When, through mammoth labor, they transformed the arid desert into productive land, the railroad offered it at exorbitant prices to anyone who could pay. Norris's novel culminates in the Mussel Slough tragedy (1880), in which protesting ranchers, provoked to armed resistance, were shot down by Southern Pacific officials and their marshals.

Critic Oscar Cargill suggests that before publication of *The Octopus*, Norris was persuaded to see Huntington and that this visit to the impressive "ogre" of the Southern Pacific altered his perspective. Not only did Norris change the emphasis of the novel, developing the so-called equal culpability of the ranchers, but he also deflected his focus onto the broader, impersonal theme of wheat. *The Pit* (1903), the posthumously published uncorrected second volume of the trilogy, takes place on the Chicago commodities exchange. The unfinished third volume, *Wolf*, was to follow the wheat to a famine-stricken European village; but Norris died at the age of thirty-two of complications following surgery for appendicitis.

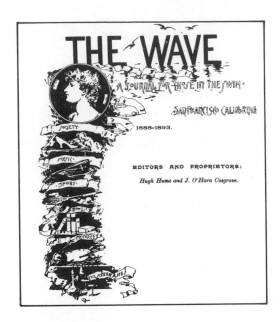

THE WAVE was a weekly journal founded and first edited in Monterey to promote the Southern Pacific's luxurious Del Monte Hotel. In 1895, it moved to San Francisco, where under the lively direction of John O'Hara Cosgrave and Hugh Hume it attracted "those in the swim," featuring drama and book reviews, social and political news, fiction, and poetry.

It is ironic that Frank Norris served his literary apprenticeship on the magazine set up to counter the anti-railroad campaigns of the *Examiner* and *Wasp*. Norris wrote some one hundred and twenty pieces for the *Wave* between 1891 and 1898, many under the pen name "Justin Sturgis." As associate editor and principal writer in the last two years, he covered the city scene—restaurants, colorful neighborhoods and characters, shows, and happenings—gathering background for his San Francisco novels, *Blix*, *McTeague*, and *Vandover*.

Other *Wave* contributors were Ambrose Bierce, Gelett Burgess, Will Irwin and novelist Inez Irwin (his wife), Jimmy Hopper, Emma Frances Dawson, Juliet Wilbor Tomkins, Frank Bailey Millard, W. C. Morrow, Jack London, and Wallace Irwin.

*I*N ELEGANT *FIN DE SIECLE* attire, Gelett Burgess (1866–1951) stands outside his home on Russian Hill, a neighborhood—not far from the Montgomery Block and other Barbary Coast bohemian haunts—favored by writers and artists of the period. Boston-born Burgess had studied engineering at MIT and taught topographical drawing at the University of California, Berkeley, but he was not the usual sort of engineering professor. On his first day in San Francisco, an odd telepathic communication with friends back in Boston moved him to write a story, "The Twenty-Third Séance." His interest in extraordinary occurrences appears again in his novel, *The Heart Line*, a detailed picture of "San Francisco improbabilities" and the bohemian milieu of séances and wild studio parties. He was dismissed from his teaching post in the aftermath of an inspired caper. He had pulled down a cast-iron statue of the eccentric teetotaling dentist, Dr. Henry Cogswell, who had given the city a number of similar monuments featuring himself proferring a glass of water kept full by means of a hidden pipe.

After this gesture against abstemiousness, Burgess set out to counter the genteel ladies' writing tradition then fashionable and, additionally, the specious bohemianism of the Bohemian Club. With other members of *Les Jeunes*, he hatched the *Lark*, a little magazine that specialized in undermining rationalism with euphoric anarchy. Burgess contributed a great many items of "sheer, premeditated absurdity."

The first issue of the magazine introduced Burgess's infectious quatrain: "I never saw a Purple Cow/ I never hope to see one/ But I can tell you anyhow/ I'd rather see than be one." After it had swept the nation, he wrote another: "Ah, yes, I wrote the 'Purple Cow'—/ I'm Sorry, now, I wrote it/ But I can tell you Anyhow/ I'll Kill you if you Quote It."

A staid reviewer for the *New York Tribune* called it "one more hysterical magazine . . . from the realm remote from the moorings of intelligence," a view that delighted *Les Jeunes*. The *Lark* followed in the wake of the *Yellow Book*, but *fin de siècle* San Francisco shared none of the melancholic aestheticism of England or the anguish of the French decadence Burgess lightly mocked: "A is for Art of the age-end variety/ We Decadents simply can't get a satiety."

Burgess later joined the staff of the *Wave*, taking Frank Norris's place writing and editing. After he left the city, he exhibited "Experiences in Symbolic Psychology," thirty watercolors, in New York, and he continued writing in an ebullient vein as a professional author.

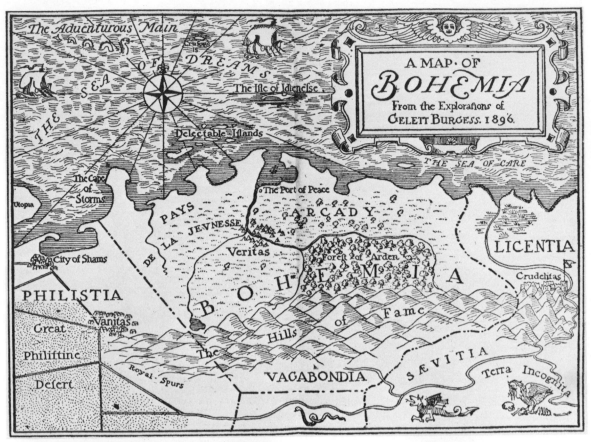

A MAP OF BOHEMIA From the Explorations of Gelett Burgess. 1896.

THE LARK

THE·ROSE·ON·ROSES·FEEDS·THE·LARK···ON·LARKS·=·THE·SEDENTARY·CLARK
ALL·MORNING·WITH·A·DILIGENT·PEN;·······MURDERS·THE·BABES·OF·OTHER·MEN
R.L.·STEVENSON.

 N receipt of Fifty Cents, a cover for the Lark, bearing a reduction of the Lark's first Poster (the Piping Faun), in two colors, printed on hinged boards, six by eight inches, will be sent by addressing WILLIAM DOXEY, 631 Market Street, San Francisco, California

"IT IS THE LUXURIES that are necessary," claimed Gelett Burgess. So the journal the *Lark* (1895–1896) was elegantly designed and printed on imported bamboo paper with hand-set type; and it confirmed the luxuries of nonsense and surprise. Bruce Porter's original announcement for the *Lark*, "The Piping Faun," accurately symbolized it as the blithe spirit of the redwoods as well as the city. Published by William Doxey's bookstore, a frequent gathering place of *Les Jeunes*, it attained a circulation of three thousand copies.

Burgess's map of Bohemia appeared in the March 1896 issue, and its various territories display the world view of *Les Jeunes*, who were inclined to stay in the Pays de la Jeunesse with an eye on The Hills of Fame and tended to steer clear of Philistia and Licentia.

LES JEUNES was the name given by the newspapers to the originators of the *Lark* for their youthful, robust, and joyous style. Besides Gelett Burgess, the group included Bruce Porter, landscape designer, muralist, and maker of stained-glass windows; Porter Garnett, calligrapher and fine printer; and architect Willis Polk. Other artists, wits, and poets associated with the group as contributors were book illustrator and author Ernest Peixotto, artist Florence Lundborg, and writers Juliet Wilbor Tomkins, Yone Noguchi, and Carolyn Wells. *Les Jeunes* are pictured here in the editorial offices of the *Lark* in its last days.

91

*P*ORTER GARNETT (1871–1951) poses as Pan in the Bohemian Grove. A native of San Francisco, Garnett, one of *Les Jeunes*, flew with the *Lark* and graced the city with his own soaring verve. His literary criticism for the *Pacific Monthly* was fresh and intelligent; for instance, in "The Importance of the Unimportant," he proposed a new way of looking at literature, hoping to free it from the endless warfare among pedants who try by conventional means to determine the "best" writers. Without these strictures of analysis, wrote Garnett, "We can then measure Ella Wheeler Wilcox with the Marquis de Sade, Rabelais with Cardinal Newman, Nietzsche with James Whitcomb Riley, Havelock Ellis with Gelett Burgess, and Alfred Austin with Mary McLane." He went on to note that McLane, the self-proclaimed genius monomaniac of Montana, was without question a far more interesting phenomenon than the poet laureate Alfred Austin. Time has confirmed this judgment.

Porter Garnett was variously a calligrapher, woodcarver, designer, teacher, critic, theater producer, and fine printer. His play *The Green Knight* was performed in the Bohemian Grove, and he ventured into the science of the absurd with *The Oop Unit; or the Science of Conometrics, an Extraneous Opuscule*. His experience in fine printing and type design in San Francisco eventually took him to the Carnegie Institute of Technology in Pittsburgh, where he founded the Laboratory Press, famed for its excellence in typography.

*W*ITH THE END of the *Lark* after only two years, *Les Jeunes* scattered. Burgess explained in *Bayside Bohemia*, "Our mood was too spontaneous or rather too enthusiastic, for we had dwelt overlong with gayety; there was the world's sober work to do." But Burgess never took the world's work too seriously. With Porter Garnett, he edited *Le Petit Journal de Refusées*, each copy printed on hideous patterned wallpaper cut in unique trapezoidal forms, with a content more extravagant than ever. This magazine had one number only; San Franciscans, observed Burgess, were too accustomed to the unusual to pay it much attention.

contempt, so he did not remain long in various menial jobs. At the O'Farrell Street headquarters of the Aikoku Domei, a political league whose object was to reform the bureaucracy in Japan, Noguchi met young firebrands involved in local immigrant issues. In *The Story of Yone Noguchi* he described the sometimes violent disputes between the group represented by the newspaper he edited, *Soko Shimbun*, and a rival faction. Poetry, however, was his passion, and he soon abandoned political activity, hoping to meet American poets.

Because Joaquin Miller, who had visited Tokyo, had a reputation as a crazy-wisdom hermit poet, Noguchi trekked to "The Hights," where Miller greeted him courteously and offered him work with room and board as payment. Though he was disappointed that the hard-drinking old bard wasn't a reader of books, Noguchi did admire Miller's genuine feeling for nature. He stayed four years and did odd jobs, including turning on a hidden sprinkler during Joaquin's rain-making ceremonies for visiting ladies. More precious to him was his intimate friendship with Charles Warren Stoddard; in his autobiography, he memorializes "dear Charley," with whom he stayed in San Francisco and in Stoddard's bungalow in Washington, D.C.

Gelett Burgess printed many of Noguchi's poems in the *Lark* and assisted in the publication of his first book, *Seen and Unseen* (1896), "nocturnes set to the music of an unfamiliar tongue." During his years in America, especially in his association with *Les Jeunes*, he stimulated Western interest in Japanese artists.

Noguchi became a distinguished professor, critic, and poet after he returned to Japan. He is the father of the sculptor Isamu Noguchi.

*W*ITH A BOOK of Poe's poems under his arm, eighteen-year-old Yone Noguchi (1875–1947) disembarked at the port of San Francisco, intending to learn all he could about American culture. Racism was his first lesson. As a kitchen boy and dishwasher he was treated with

$\mathcal{T}$HE MONTGOMERY BLOCK. When construction began in 1852 on the bay shore with a redwood log raft foundation, they called it "Halleck's Folly"; but the Montgomery Block endured earthquake and fire for over a century and was San Francisco's most illustrious literary landmark. Money made on Mexican land grant settlements after the U.S. takeover financed construction of the tallest, most luxuriant building west of the Mississippi. Occupying the block between Montgomery and Sansome, Washington and Clay, this "wonder of masonry" was built by Henry Wager Halleck, engineer, lawyer, military strategist for Lincoln, Civil War general, archivist, secretary of state, gold surveyor, quicksilver entrepreneur, and, according to rumor, alchemist.

The ground floor was resplendent with marble-floored, chandeliered saloons and restaurants. The entire basement was used for making and storing Kohler and Froeling wine. Newspapermen liked the Montgomery Block establishments because they were central to the ruthless city's wheelings and dealings. In 1855, editor James King of William lashed his enemies one stroke too many on the pages of the *Bulletin* and was shot down the following year in front of the block's Bank Exchange Saloon; thus the Vigilance Committee was reborn. During the Comstock bonanzas, the neighborhood was jammed with mining investors speculating along Montgomery Street, the West's wildest casino. The *Golden Era* crowd exchanged outrageous stories with the characters down from the foothills in the street's saloons—the Bank Exchange, the Occidental, Lick House, and Barry and Patten's.

In the 1870s, Duncan Nichols began his long reign at the Bank Exchange Bar, serving Pisco Punch, a drink likened by block manager Otto Stidger to "the scimitar of a Harroun whose edge is so fine that after a slash a man walked on unaware that his head had been severed from his body until his knees gave way and he fell to the ground dead."

As business interests crept south, the neighborhood changed character; some oldtimers remained in the building, but new, smaller enterprises moved in. Among the tailors, Chinese herb dealers, and geomancers, Sun Yat-sen drafted the constitution of the Republic of China in a third-floor lawyer's office and A. P. Giannini opened an office of the little Bank of Italy, now the Bank of America. In the 1880s, artists living in the Latin districts of North Beach and Telegraph and Russian hills rented studios around Washington, Clay, and Pacific streets, where Montgomery met Montgomery Avenue (now Columbus). It was here that Robert Louis Stevenson met with Fanny's son-in-law, Joe Strong, Virgil Williams, and Jules Tavernier—chief instigators of San Francisco's bohemia. When some of the young artists noticed the "Monkey" Block's attractive skylights and low rents, they took over.

More than two thousand writers and artists are reputed to have lived in the building. Among the writers, Stoddard and Joaquin Miller had rooms. Ambrose Bierce wrote his blistering "Prattler" column there from time to time. Sadakichi Hartmann entranced audiences with readings from the works of Paul Verlaine and J. K. Huysmans. Frank Norris painted in Charles Dickman's studio and plotted *McTeague*; and the other Norrises, Kathleen and Charles, wrote there. Gelett Burgess and his friends worked on the *Lark* and plotted their high-spirited pranks. Yone Noguchi sowed his wild oats with American writers. Jack London stayed in his friend Xavier Martinez's studio after nights on the town; and George Sterling, resembling Pan or Peter Pan, kept a room for his many secret amours.

Giuseppi Coppa, Turinese chef and bon vivant, served his specialty, chicken Portola, in his Monkey Block restaurant, extending credit to impecunious writers and artists. Frequented by virtually all the Bay Area avant-garde, Coppa's was the most important turn-of-the-century bohemian rendezvous. One day *Les Jeunes* asked permission to improve upon Papa Coppa's new red wallpaper. Porter Garnett drew a five-foot lobster standing on the island "Bohemia"; sculptor Robert Aitken added a couple of monumental nudes; Xavier Martinez made an elegant frieze of black cats; and the Coppa murals were underway. Using only charcoal, crayon, and chalk, they covered the top half of the restaurant by the time they were finished.

Names from the illustrious past interspersed with those of local habitués were inscribed around the top of the Temple of Fame: ARISTOTLE, NEWBERRY (Perry, editor of the Carmel *Pine Cone*), VELAZQUEZ, ISABEL I (Fraser, journalist and local Queen of Bohemia), DANTE, MARTINEZ (flamboyant Mexican-born painter, VILLON, BUTTSKY (Perry Newberry's wife, who was ever desperate for a cigarette), RABELAIS, GARNETT, GOETHE, MASIE (writer Mary Griswold Emerson), NIETSCHE (the omitted Z was caught above in a cat's mouth), BURGESS, WHISTLER (under whom Martinez had studied abroad), LAFLER ("Fra" Henry, writer-editor), STERLING, VERLAINE, AITKEN, and KANT.

Inspired graffiti were added to the caricatures, goops, and sketches. George Sterling's much-quoted lines, "The blue-eyed vampire sated at her feast smiles bloodily against the leprous moon," were placed in one scroll, and in another was Lewis Carroll's " 'Curiouser and Curiouser,' cried Alice." Porter Garnett painted a line from Oscar Wilde's *Salome*: "Something Terrible is Going to Happen." It did.

The murals were destroyed in the great earthquake and fire of 1906, but the Montgomery Block stood intact, one of the few buildings to survive. Rents shot sky high until the city was rebuilt, and it was never to regain its former grandeur; but writers and artists found cheap living-studio space again and continued to haunt the valiant old structure through the next decades. In 1959, this unofficial historic monument was razed to make way for a parking lot. Today, standing in its place on "Little Wall Street" is the metronomic Transamerica pyramid.

$\int$ ON OF AN ITINERANT astrologer and a spiritualist medium, Jack London (1876–1916) was born in San Francisco on Third Street, south of Market. He was raised in Oakland by a mother who didn't want him and a kind but financially troubled stepfather, John London.

In his teens, London read voraciously, worked in a cannery and jute mill (sometimes sixteen hours a day), and lived recklessly on the tough Oakland waterfront. He drank with roustabouts in Heinold's First and Last Chance Saloon, raided oyster beds in the bay, then went sealing aboard the *Sophie Sutherland* off the Japanese and Siberian coasts. In 1894, London marched with Kelly's division of Coxey's army of the unemployed and went on the road, riding the rods and blind baggages across America. He did time in the Erie County penitentiary, where he saw what happens to those at the "bottom of the Social Pit." Inspired by the *Communist Manifesto*, he became a dedicated but "unscientific" socialist. Back in Oakland, he managed a year of high school and passed entrance exams to the University of California, where he spent six months.

At twenty-one, he joined the gold rush to the Klondike, and his experiences there provided background for his most popular stories. After the publication in the *Overland Monthly* of "To the Man on the Trail" in 1898, London averaged more than two books a year and another two dozen contributions to periodicals. His translation of an adventurous life into fiction made him, as his friend Upton Sinclair wrote in *Mammonart*, "the true king of our storytellers, the brightest star that flashed upon our skies. His classic arctic story, *The Call of the Wild* (1903), a cleanly written lyric exaltation of the younger world, is still a razzle dazzle favorite around the globe.

He spent a seminal summer in the London slums, covered the Russo-Japanese War as a Hearst correspondent in 1904, and went on a nationwide lecture tour as president of the Intercollegiate Socialist Society. London stepped up his activities in the nascent western socialist movement. Marrying Bess Maddern and having a home provided him the opportunity to entertain new friends—the brilliant tramp philosopher Frank Strawn-Hamilton, activist George Speed, and English writers Austin Lewis and Herman "Jim" Whitaker. He ate at Coppa's with other young radicals and met the spellbinding socialist lecturer, Anna Strunsky, with whom he collaborated on *The Kempton-Wace Letters* (1903), a curious book dealing with the relations between men and women. London joined the Socialist Labor Party, lectured and met with Frederick Irons Bamford's Ruskin Club, Nathan Greist's

forum, Ben Reitman, Emma Goldman, and the *Mother Earth* anarchists. His elemental tales, set in the wilderness and at sea with red-blooded heroes and Nietzschean superdogs were best-sellers, but London's favorite was *People of the Abyss* (1903), which he "put more heart into than any other," a true account of the destitute, struggling "work beasts" in industrial London.

In the last decade of his life, he wrote more than thirty full-length books, hundreds of stories and articles, and thousands of letters to fans and aspiring writers. After 1910, London applied himself to scientific agriculture and animal breeding on a model estate, "Wolf House" at Glen Ellen in the Valley of the Moon. Attempting too much, he worked at a frenetic pace and suffered chronic illness, disappointments, and depression. He died at forty, probably by his own hand.

Jack London's life spanned the nation's perplexing, violent transformation from laissez-faire to corporate capitalism, from continental frontier society to international empire. Progressive Era America, exemplified in Theodore Roosevelt's strenuous life, stood for reform, nationalist pride, individualism, confidence in agrarian values, and belief in the superiority of the Anglo-Saxon race—an ideology that affected London's viewpoint just as it did that of Frank Norris and other authors at the turn of the century. A self-educated working man, London read everything and tried to incorporate it all into his writings, mixing swashbuckling and science with Nietzsche, Spencer, Darwin, Ernst Haeckel, and Marx. His undirected eclecticism had idiosyncratic results. "London seems to have thought of the Superman as a Western work giant like Paul Bunyan, a brawny proletarian eligible for membership in the I.W.W.," observed Alfred Kazin in *On Native Grounds*.

Talking with Frank Strawn-Hamilton

Jack London was America's first working-class writer, one of the highest paid and best known over the world. He wrote for money; he wanted to show the capitalists he could beat them at their own game. He wrote adventure, autobiographical novels (*The Cruise of the Dazzler, The Road, John Barleycorn*, and the fine *Martin Eden* among them), oneiric science fiction (*The Star Rover*), and essays on revolution. *The Iron Heel*, a crystallized metaphor of revolution and reaction, as clearly anticipated the repressive intent of today's multinational oligarchs as it did 1930s fascists.

London wanted to infuse the working class with his own driving intensity, to persuade everybody to bring to the fight a commitment equal to his own.

That they could not brought him to despair in the Valley of the Moon. Underlying the violence in his work is a passion for transformation, a dream of explosive departure. He worked for "the fate of man" with a furious imagination, if not with sweet consistency. H. L. Mencken wrote in *Prejudices: First Series*, "The man, in truth, was an instinctive artist of high order, and if ignorance corrupted his art, it only made the fact of his inborn mastery the more remarkable. . . . There was in him a vast delicacy of perception, a high feeling, a sensitiveness to beauty. And there was in him too, under all his blatancies, a poignant sense of the infinite romance and mystery of life."

$\mathcal{G}$OD'S OWN MAD LOVERS. London and his second wife, Charmian Kittridge, whom he married on his socialist lecture tour, are pictured here during their *Snark* trip. In Charmian, Jack found his "Mate-Woman"—the kind of androgynous ideal portrayed in Maud Brewster of *The Sea Wolf*—a woman who combined femininity with athletic prowess, childlike enthusiasm with intellectual interests. However closely Charmian approximated the New Woman in some respects, she nonetheless subordinated her life to her husband's, allowing him to manage everything and otherwise devoting herself to his work, needs, and interests. Still, they invented their own romantic destiny. Together they worked and played, swam, rode, boxed, farmed, sailed, and wrote. The marriage was not without tension and difficulties, but their love and loyalty endured.

Jack and Charmian London stayed with the Sterlings in Carmel after London's lecture tour, which was marred by a vituperative press and public hostility to his divorce and remarriage. He decided that they would take a seven-year trip around the world. The *Snark* was a dangerous vessel by all accounts, the crew was inexperienced, and the ship's mate, Charmian's Uncle Roscoe Eames, was an adherent of the hollow earth theory, which held that the earth's surface is concave and that we live on the inside of a sphere. "Thus," said Jack, "though we shall sail on the one boat, the *Snark*, Roscoe will journey around the world on the inside, while I shall journey around on the outside." But London looked forward to learning navigation while pitting himself against the elements and writing a thousand words a day.

The Piedmont "crowd" came to see them off in Oakland. Pictured here on

deck are (left to right): Carrie Sterling, Lora Bierce, Charmian London, James (Jimmy) Hopper, George Sterling, and Jack London.

London's friend Jimmy Hopper, a former University of California star athlete and an adventure writer (*Caybigan*), lent his football jersey for luck and they hoisted it up the mast. The *Snark* set sail April 23, 1907. Unfortunately, everything went "wild and chaotic"—engine troubles, and then sickness: malaria, yaws, skin diseases. They returned to the states in 1909, the trip cut short, much to the intrepid Charmian's disappointment. London nonetheless managed to write five books, including *Martin Eden*, and Charmian wrote two.

*W*OLF AND GREEK. London stands on the dock with George Sterling, "the great Man-Comrade" he had always hoped to find. They called each other by their nicknames. George was "Greek," after his classic profile ("a Greek coin run over by a Roman chariot," someone had said). Jack was "Wolf," his elected lycanthropic identity. Their friendship was intense; Charmian called it an eloquent spiritual comprehension. In the early days, they hiked in the Piedmont Hills above Oakland and on the Carmel beaches, hunted, fished, and went to the fights, talked socialism and literature, stayed out drinking, and haunted the burlesque houses and bordellos of the Barbary Coast. George volunteered the arduous editing and proofreading of all Jack's books, even after the Londons moved to Glen Ellen in 1911. Jack wrote George into *Martin Eden* as the poet Russ Brissenden and into *The Valley of the Moon* as Mark Hall.

*J*INKS. Little did Jack London suspect when he wrote this check that the Bohemian Club Grove where he caroused with George Sterling and got roaring drunk once with Ambrose Bierce would be the future locale of annual secret meetings of the top echelons of America's ruling class.

The Bohemian Club originated in the 1872 breakfasts *Chronicle* newswriter James Bowan organized for colleagues in rooms at the Jolly Corks. As a drinking club, it was to promote good fellowship among WASP male journalists. Before long, membership was extended to writers, artists, and others interested in the arts. The club moved to Pine Street over the California Market, then to progressively finer quarters; after acquiring forest property on the Russian River, its members reveled there during the summer. The Bohemians entertained themselves in fraternal fashion with a Low Jinks (recitations and comedy) and a High Jinks (elaborate outdoor pageants) staged in the redwoods, written and produced by members.

Sterling's verse drama, *The Triumph of Bohemia* (1907), a celebrated Grove Play, concluded with a combat between the Spirit of Bohemia and Mammon to decide if the Bohemians "Shall hold this spot, or whether I, supreme/ Shall smite thee down, and dedicate this vale/ To desolation and unchanging dearth." Mammon is slain and placed on a bier, and a procession is formed for the annual Cremation of Care ceremony. Its symbolic purpose is to put away Care, or worldly concerns, freeing men to find

George Sterling prepares for *The Triumph of Bohemia*

in the Grove a "refuge for the weary heart" and a "balm for breasts that have been bruised." At the turn of the century, the Piedmont crowd, the Coppans, and the Carmelites were active Bohemians; even Grace Greenwood and Ina Coolbrith had honorary status, the latter serving as club librarian. Jack London tried to write a Grove Play, but sprites and wood nymphs in verse were too much for him.

Gradually, the Bohemian Club evolved from a group of men with talent and no money to a group of men with money and talent for ruling the world. Recent faces seen in the Grove have been those of David Rockefeller, Henry Ford, Henry Kissinger, Richard Nixon, Werner von Braun, and Edgar Kaiser. As G. William Domhoff has documented in *The Bohemian Grove and Other Retreats*, modern July encampments are unique exercises in ruling-class cohesiveness, a meeting place for the most powerful men in the country—the owners and managers of major banks and corporations, Pentagon brass, top-level elected officials, and policymakers. Artist members today are Bob Hope, Art Linkletter, and wealthy local amateurs; and the Cremation of Care rite offers a refuge for the weary hearts of the super-rich. Mammon triumphed after all.

George Sterling

*Y*OU SHALL BE THE POET of the skies, the prophet of the suns," proclaimed Ambrose Bierce to George Sterling (1869–1926) on publication of *Testimony of the Suns* (1903). From the time they met in 1892 at Lake Temescal, Bierce directed Sterling's reading, published his poetry in "Prattle," and advised him to look to the classics. Sterling submitted all his work to Bierce for assessment, although after 1896, when the latter moved to Washington, D.C., he was only a long-distance mentor.

Sterling was born in Sag Harbor, Long Island, and was chosen for the priesthood by his neurotic father; but George renounced the Church and was steadfastly irreverent. In Oakland, he worked (as little as possible) in his uncle's real estate office, a post that supported him as San Francisco's foremost bohemian poet. Between 1902 and 1926, he published eleven volumes of poetry, four verse dramas, and a critical work on Robinson Jeffers.

Bierce launched his protégé nationally, placing Sterling's "The Wine of Wizardry" in *Cosmopolitan*, accompanied by an introduction in an extravagant vein: "I hardly know how to speak of it. No poem in English of equal length has so bewildering a wealth of imagination. . . . If it had been written in French and published in Paris it would have stirred the very stones in the street." Such fulsome praise from a man with many enemies was more injurious than helpful.

Influenced by Baudelaire and the symbolists, Sterling was, in his work, a kind of leashed Swinburne. There was genuine vision in Sterling and some of his poems attain an exotic beauty, but many suffer from self-conscious grandiloquence. In the rising imagist movement, his strictly rhymed, highly ornamented poetry with an archaic diction belonged to the previous century. Sterling once admitted that Bierce "laid an icy hand on my youthful enthusiasm"; his prodigal nature was not suited to Bierce's formal models.

George and his statuesque wife, Carolyn Rand, settled in Piedmont, where they met Jack and Bess London at their rented Villa Capricciosa on Lake Merritt. In 1902, they found the Londons a home closer to their own. The two residences became meeting places for "the crowd" — Jimmy Hopper, Jim Whitaker, Blanche Partington, Xavier Martinez, Austin Lewis, the Emersons, and San Francisco friends who enjoyed lively parties in the country air.

To escape the distractions of the city and write undisturbed, George went with Carrie to build a bungalow in Carmel, which in 1905 was just a few farms and a dream of land developers. Photographer Arnold Genthe arrived later that year and described his life there in his memoir, *As I Remember*. Genthe, a dashing Prussian who took his doctor's degree at the University of Jena with a dissertation on Lucan in Latin, had developed an interest in photography on a vacation in San Francisco and financed his experimental work with high society portraits. Mary Austin joined them in early 1906; she described walks, climbs, swims, tea beside driftwood fires, abalone chowder, and "talk, ambrosial, unquotable talk." After the devastating San Francisco earthquake, many others made their way south, either as full-time residents or for stays of weeks or months. Sterling, who inspired affection in everyone, presided as a friendly "High Panjandrum" over the seaside colony, having attracted to him the environment he had intended to escape.

After 1910, Carmel began to lose its primitive appeal and the original crowd drifted back to the city as more bourgeois residents moved in. Van Wyck Brooks records in *Scenes and Portraits* that on his visit in 1911, "George Sterling, the poet . . . had precisely the aspect of Dante in hell," and the writers found themselves "becalmed and supine" in an existence "half operatic where curious dramas were taking place in the bungalows and cabins." After Jack and Charmian London's final visit after the *Snark* returned, Jack and George didn't see so much of each other. Ambrose Bierce broke with George in a series of violent epistolary denunciations of Sterling's socialism, which had escalated along with his friendship with Jack London, his tawdry bohemianism, and compulsive love affairs. These became abhorrent to Carrie, too, and she left him.

After Carrie's suicide in 1918, Sterling grew despondent, drank ever more heavily, and engaged in frolicsome, empty ventures. In 1926, on the night of a Bohemian Club dinner for H. L. Mencken, he took a lethal dose of cyanide in his room at the club where he lived. Fragments of poems were found by his body, "I walked with phantoms that ye know not of" and "Deeper into the darkness can I peer/ Than most, yet find the darkness still beyond."

Profligate, charming, a lyric personality, Sterling was a catalyst for renewal of literary activity in the Bay Area. Carey McWilliams assessed correctly that "the range and intimate quality of his acquaintance gave cultural significance to his career." San Francisco added his name to the roster of its legendary romantic eccentrics, unofficial laureate of "the cool grey city of love."

MARY HUNTER AUSTIN (1868–1934) had made a literary reputation with *Land of Little Rain* (1903), a collection of sensitive essays on southeast California and its people, just before arriving in Carmel. Austin had come to love the beauty of the region east of the Sierra Nevada range, "beyond Death Valley and on illimitably into the Mojave Desert," after she moved from Illinois with her family to an arid homestead in the Tejon, and then to the Owens Valley.

Austin visited San Francisco on several occasions, making early literary contacts. In 1892 at the Oakland Library, she met Ina Coolbrith, under whose friendly direction she prepared her manuscript and saw her first sketches published in the *Overland Monthly.* After a decade of solid writing, Mary came again to the city, and George Sterling took her to the festivities at Coppa's Restaurant and to Portsmouth Square to fill the Stevenson galleon with violets.

Austin researched *Isidro*, her early California romance, in Carmel in 1902; when she returned to live there early in 1906, she proved an independent and unconventional resident. Her studio was a treehouse modeled on a wickiup, and her long comfortable garments and unpinned hair defied convention. Respectable folk from nearby Monterey crossed to the other side of the street to avoid being seen with her. Furthermore, unlike many of the bohemians, she didn't drink, was not sexually promiscuous, and worked hard, producing books about the Paiute Indians (*The Basket Woman*), Mexicans (*Isidro*), and Basque sheepherders (*The Flock*).

Austin's autobiography, *Earth Horizon*, illuminates the San Francisco and Carmel literary scene with a wry, critical perspective. "We were not, in Carmel, inclined to the intellectual outlook, except that there was a tendency to take Jack seriously in respect to the Social Revolution," she observed. From the fundamental Protestant Midwest, Mary was unaccustomed to hearing men talk freely in front of women, as did Jack, George, and the rest. She found curious "the liability of men of genius to find their subjective activities on their way to fruition so largely at the mercy of the effect on them of women. I never needed a love affair to release the subconscious in me, nor did Nora May French, the only woman of the group with an equivalent talent to London and Sterling."

This snapshot catches Mary on the beach talking with (left to right) George Sterling, Jack London, and Jimmy Hopper.

Some of the Carmelites derided Mary Austin's dramatic sense of herself and her grave spiritual quest. On several occasions, as a child and later on the desert, she experienced intense moments of mystical ecstasy. In *Earth Horizon*, she described how "everything came alive together with a pulsing light of consciousness," how she saw clearly the inclusive relation of parts to the whole—"the sweetness of ultimate reality." She was ever aware of "that singular sense of presence lurking unseen in the wild." After researching world religions, she concluded the Paiute shamans expressed most closely her own intuition and showed her how to stay in touch with the creative principle of the universe. Through *Wakando* one might connect body, mind, work, and earth in perfect harmony. Mary once went up to San Francisco to interview William James, who confirmed what the Paiute taught— "a continuing experience of wholeness, a power to expand the least premonitory shiver along the edge of primitive apprehension to the full diapason of spiritual sophistication."

Austin believed she had, like an Indian *chisera*, the gift of prophecy. In the spring of 1906, she went to San Francisco to see her agent about publication of *Isidro*. When she arrived at the Palace Hotel, she felt oppressed by an impending sense of disaster. She called her brother and told him the hotel was threatening to fall on her, warned her friends, then went to stay with the Hittells. The city awoke the next morning to the confusion of the great earthquake.

In 1907, Mary suffered a keen disappointment when residents of her beloved Owens Valley were manipulated into signing away their water to supply Los Angeles. Even worse, she had elected Lincoln Steffens to be her "grand passion" when he visited the community; and her desperate infatuation was unrequited. She began to believe that she was dying of cancer. She said goodbye to Carmel and in Italy fortuitously recovered, her attention drawn to the great Catholic mystics.

A trip to London gave her access to a literary circle that included George Bernard Shaw, William Butler Yeats, Joseph Conrad, and H. G. Wells, who let it be known he regarded her as the most intelligent woman in America. Back in the United States in 1910, Austin worked on the New York stage production of her pioneering folk verse drama, *The Arrow Maker*, and she joined the group around Mabel Dodge (Luhan). She returned to Carmel in 1913, where she was active in the Forest Theater, but came rarely afterwards.

Active in the suffrage and birth control movements, she wrote on feminist themes: *A Woman of Genius* and *No. 26 Jayne Street*. Her interests were catholic: *The Ford*, a novel about farmers versus real estate developers; *Experiences Facing Death*, insights into *The Tibetan Book of the Dead*; *Outland*, a psychological fantasy based on the Sterlings; and *The American Rhythm*, a plea for freedom of form and a sense of place as bases for an indigenous American lyric poetry, using as example her moving translations of Amerindian songs and ritual chants.

"Casa Querida," the home she built in Santa Fe, was always open to artist and writer friends, among them Willa Cather, who wrote *Death Comes for the Archbishop* there. Of California writers, only Helen Hunt Jackson shared her profound appreciation of Indian values; Austin's last years in the Southwest were devoted to preserving the arts of that vanishing culture.

MIDNIGHT LURE OF DEATH LEADS POETESS TO GRAVE
Nora May French Drinks Acid in Poet's Home
Dies in a Few Minutes as Mrs. George
  Sterling Chafes Cold Hands
Had Beauty, Suitors, Fame, Many Friends
—*S.F. Examiner,* Nov. 15, 1907

*B*ORN IN AURORA, New York, Nora
May French (1881–1907) emigrated
with her family to southern California
during the big land boom. After attending Los Angeles schools and studying
art in New York, she took an oppressive
job in a leathercraft factory. Her first
poems were published in Charles Lummis's
Out West. Harry "Fra" Lafler, editor of
the short story magazine the *Blue Mule,*
placed some in the *Argonaut.* She and
Lafler corresponded often; and when
Lafler, estranged from his wife, visited
Nora May in Los Angeles, they fell in
love. A line from one of her letters was
added to the Coppa murals: "I fancy
that all sensible people will ultimately
be damned."

"Phyllis," as she called herself, moved
in November 1906 to deserted San Francisco, where Lafler had a makeshift
Telegraph Hill cottage made out of
earthquake debris. She was soon a mythic
figure in the anarchic bohemian life of
the devastated city, courted in time by
Alan Hiley, Bruce Porter, and Jimmy
Hopper as well as Lafler.

The following year she went to Carmel.
Carrie Sterling wrote a friend, "She is a
freak that has a dozen wheels going at
once." Life was frenetic in Carmel, too:
reading poetry and drinking until dawn,
the complexities of too many already
married suitors, worries about jobs and
money, and manic-depressive cycles.
French was the first of them to take
cyanide.

Her friends scattered her ashes over
Point Lobos and in 1910 brought out a
beautiful edition of her *Poems,* edited by
Lafler, printed by Porter Garnett, with a
portrait by Arnold Genthe.

A REUNION OF POETS. In 1905, Joaquin Miller (left) went to Monterey to deliver a lecture and sent a message to George Sterling (center) to meet him and Charley Stoddard (right). They met at the "dude saloon," where the older poets were drinking whiskey; and, feeling mellow, they all had their picture taken before going off to visit the old Spanish mission at Carmel. Stoddard passed out before he could savor the Catholic atmosphere, and Joaquin made passes at the Portuguese sexton's pretty daughter. George reported the lecture was a great success. Stoddard spent his last years in Monterey, where Charles Rollo Peters and other artists lived, not far from Carmel colony friends.

*P*ERENNIALLY HOPEFUL, maniacally dedicated, Upton Sinclair (1878–1968) was an extremist in the cause for social justice and greater human happiness. With the substantial royalties earned by *The Jungle* (1906), an exposé of the horrors of Chicago's stockyards, he established a communitarian society in New Jersey. Helicon Hall numbered among its participants a variety of socialists, anarchists, single taxers, spiritual experimenters, and authors. After five months, it burned down and with it the manuscripts of resident writers. Exhausted from a grueling writing pace (the twenty-nine-year-old crusader had just completed his tenth book), ill, and on the verge of a nervous breakdown, Sinclair accepted George Sterling's invitation to stay in Carmel. There in 1908, the romantic rebel relaxed, writing three radical plays, forming new plans for the advancement of socialism, and practicing a rigorous health regimen. He and Sterling went to a dull Ruskin Cub meeting in Oakland and to the Bohemian Club, which Sinclair considered a den of satyrs. Before long, Sinclair, an ardent prohibitionist, was as irritated by the heavy drinking and time wasting at Carmel as the bohemians were by his zealousness. He departed after three months.

In 1917, he moved permanently to Pasadena, where he wrote prolifically (over a hundred novels and tracts) and ran on the Socialist party ticket for Congress, the U.S. Senate, and governor in the 1920s. He ran again in 1934 on the Democratic ticket with a program to end poverty in California (EPIC). He lost, but the establishment took over many of his ideas in modified form.

Mississippi poet Mary Kimbrough Craig Sinclair, subject of Sterling's *Sonnets to Craig* (1927), and husband Upton Sinclair are pictured here in Bermuda in 1913.

INCLAIR LEWIS & OPAL PEET — CARMEL DUTCH FAI

$\mathscr{T}$HE ANNUAL DUTCH FAIR to promote crafts in Carmel was the occasion for this conversation between Sinclair Lewis (1885–1951) and Opal Heron Peet, who, with her husband, Herbert Heron Peet, and Perry Newberry, founded the Forest Theater, one of the first Little Theaters in the country.

Lewis (called "Hal" or "Red") was just out of Yale the year before and had been doing odd jobs and stoking the furnace at Helicon Hall until it burned.

Others from Helicon Hall who made their way to Carmel were Michael Williams, a green vegetarian and journalist, and sisters and novelists Alice MacGowan and Grace MacGowan Cooke, who brought young Sinclair Lewis along as secretary.

In Carmel, he interested himself in amateur theatricals and young girls, added to his file of story outlines, and despaired of getting published. An admirer of Jack London, he was delighted when the legendary older author bought the first of twenty-seven plots from him (for a total sum of $137.50), five of which London eventually used, though none was particularly successful.

William Rose Benét, a Yale classmate of Hal's, met him in Carmel and took him home to Benicia to stay with the family (younger brother Steven was ten at the time). George Sterling got Lewis a job on the *San Francisco Evening Bulletin*, but he was soon fired for incompetence. He visited the Londons whenever possible and prowled about town, hearing the fiery Tom Mooney speak in 1909. Mark Schorer suggests that Lewis's brief stay in San Francisco stimulated his interest in social problems and labor organization.

Mooney's frame-up trial was seven years in the future. Even farther in the future were Sinclair Lewis's provocative snapshots of middle America: *Main Street*, *Babbitt*, *Arrowsmith*, and *Elmer Gantry*, published in the 1920s.

$\mathscr{L}$INCOLN STEFFENS (1866–1936) stands (at the right of the horse) with his son Pete (astride) in Carmel, where he retired to write his influential *Autobiography* (1931) after a notable career as a muckraker and social reformer. Born in San Francisco, he spent his youth in Sacramento, where the family lived in the monumental Victorian house that became the governor's mansion (until Ronald Reagan found it too drafty). Before entering the University of California, Steffens was privately tutored for a year in San Francisco by English intellectuals who leaned toward philosophical anarchism. He studied in Europe, then held editorial positions on *McClure's*, *The American*, and *Everybody's* magazines, writing attacks on the trusts and government collusion with big business. After publication of *The Shame of the Cities* (1904), a national tour exposing graft in additional cities took him to San Francisco in 1907, where he muckraked the notoriously corrupt regime of Mayor E. E. Schmitz and Boss Abe Ruef, a Labor administration that had sold out to powerful corporate capitalists. Steffens had no hope that the prosecution would result in conviction of real culprits like Huntington's successor, William F. Herrin. "I labored humorously, and I think pleasantly, for the exposure in San Francisco of the universal state of business corruption of politics to show what was hurting us, and not who," Steffens wrote, and he confessed he was astounded by the enormous wealth and energy devoted to keeping things wrong.

By the time he moved permanently to Carmel in 1927, it had gone the way of the Bohemian Club, becoming the smug bourgeois resort town John Steinbeck encountered on his *Travels with Charley in Search of America* (1962): "And Carmel, begun by starveling writers and unwanted painters, is now a com-

munity of the well-to-do and retired. If Carmel's founders should return, they could not afford to live there, but it wouldn't go that far. They would instantly be picked up as suspicious characters and deported over the city line."

Steffens and his wife, Ella Winter, author of *Red Virtue*, wrote for the *Carmelite* and tried to be a part of the community, but they met crushing hostility because of their radical views, support of the longshoremen's and general strikes in San Francisco, and optimistic opinion of the Russian Revolution.

A stubborn supporter of the Soviet Union, even after the purges, Steffens was anathematized by many on the left as a Stalinist, while Communist Party stalwarts dubbed him "Mr. Liberal." In spite of his precarious stance, many old guard writers along with some new ones went to see him in Carmel: Max Eastman, Gertrude Stein and Alice B. Toklas, Robinson Jeffers, Carl Sandburg, Langston Hughes, Sinclair Lewis, and John Steinbeck. With Watergate, the neglected art of muckraking, "the letting in of light and air," revived Steffens's style of grass roots radicalism and sophisticated investigative journalism.

$\mathcal{R}$EADERS KNOW CLARK ASHTON SMITH (1893–1961) as a master of fantasy fiction, "in sheer daemonic strangeness and fertility of conception . . . perhaps unexcelled by any other writer, living or dead," according to H. P. Lovecraft in *Supernatural Horror in Literature*. Few, however, know that San Francisco once hailed Smith as a poetical genius and that there are poets today who sympathize with George Sterling's assessment: "Clark Ashton Smith is undoubtedly our finest living poet . . . in the great tradition of Shakespeare, Keats, and Shelley, and yet, to our everlasting shame, he is entirely neglected and almost completely unknown."

The self-educated Smith grew up near the gold town of Auburn, where he read Poe's poems and tales of terror, Thomas Lovell Beddoes's play, *Death's Jest Book, The Arabian Nights*, and gothic novels such as William Beckford's *Vathek*. He also went through *Webster's Unabridged Dictionary*, cover to cover, with particular attention to etymologies. He began writing stories at the age of eleven and a few years later sold *contes crueles* with Oriental themes to the *Black Cat*. After some of his poems were published in Auburn newspapers and he was discovered by San Franciscans, A. M. Robertson published his *The Star-Treader and Other Poems*, followed by other books of lyric poetry.

Smith preferred to live and work in the Sierra Nevada foothills, where his imagination inhabited spectral regions out of space and time, although he sometimes came to the city and visited the Sterlings in Carmel. In an article for the *Overland Monthly,* he recalled one happy summer there, during which he picked mint in the meadows for Sterling's bottomless pineapple punches.

In 1925, Smith wrote his first weird story; ill and in need of money, he began writing regularly for *Wonder Stories* and *Weird Tales*—the lush, visionary, intensely poetic fiction that stimulated later writers—Ray Bradbury, August Derleth, and Fritz Leiber. After 1939, he devoted much of his time to painting and carving exotic sculpture from unusual minerals.

In San Francisco, Smith stayed in Madelynne and Eric Barker's little apartment just below Telegraph Hill and liked to look across the bay toward San Rafael at a peculiar, haunted peak he called the hill of Dionysus.

THE SEACOAST OF BOHEMIA. Franklin Walker's delightful, affectionate account of *The Seacoast of Bohemia* tells the literary story of Carmel, from Robert Louis Stevenson's lonely stay in Monterey (1879) and Gertrude Atherton's early search for local color, to the 1930s, with Lincoln Steffens's persecution and Robinson Jeffers's solitary vigil in Tor House. The colony's literary glory was between 1906 and 1912, when San Francisco was rebuilding from the ruins of the great quake. In those days, residents, visitors, and part-time residents dashed in and out: there were Ray Stannard Baker, muckraking associate of Steffens; journalists Will Irwin and Blanche Partington; light-versifier Wallace Irwin; and novelists Inez Irwin and Geraldine Bonner. Ernest Peixotto and Florence Lundborg, artists from the *Lark*, visited their friends, and so did the beautiful Anna Strunsky and the Coppa bohemians. Fred Bechdolt, a bohemian drifter, collaborated with Jimmy Hopper on a prison novel, *9009*, and later wrote books on the old West. Harry Leon Wilson, editor of *Puck* and co-playwright with Booth Tarkington of *The Man from Home*, was an eccentric mainstay of the community after 1911. He created Ruggles of Red Gap and other characters familiar to *Saturday Evening Post* readers. Though his young wife Helen (Cooke) was an active participant in the Forest Theater, Wilson regarded it with scorn. Mary Austin, however, back from her travels, was keen to produce her folk-verse dramas. Pictured above is the cast of her play *Fire*. Below: Opal Heron as the Beast. Behind her to the left: poet & editor of the *Wanderer*, Ethel Duffy Turner as the Indian maid Laela. Top right: George Sterling with club; below him in the bearskin, Raine Bennett, editor of *Bohemia*.

117

HOTBED OF SOULFUL CULTURE, VORTEX OF EROTIC ERUDITION.

Carmel in California, Where Author and Artist Folk Are Establishing the Most Amazing Colony on Earth.

BY WILLARD HUNTINGTON WRIGHT.

Picnic at Point Lobos: (Left to right) Jack London, Alice MacGowan, Grace MacGowan Cooke, Upton Sinclair, Xavier Martinez, Mary Austin, George Sterling, Lucia Chamberlain, Fred Bechdolt, James Hopper, and "Fra" Harry Lafler.

Hotbed of Soulful Culture . . .

Carmel-by-the-Sea is a very temperamental town. Situated five miles from Monterey in a huge pine grove which slopes to the sea, Carmel has been blessed with much natural beauty. Its abundant foliage, lush ravines, picturesque hills and its austere, implacable coast have caught the imaginations of the artist-folk. The result is that Carmel has a great deal of temperament that originally was not indigenous. At present it is a hotbed of soulful culture, a vortex of animated erudition.

Of late it has become the magnetizing center for writers, near writers, notso-near writers, distant writers, poets, poetines, artists, daubers, sloydists, and those aspiring ladies who spend their days smearing up with paint what would otherwise be very serviceable pieces of canvas. In addition, there are at least twenty college professors, a club of well-meaning neophytes of the arts and crafts, esoteric Yogi, New Thoughters, Emmanuel Movers and last (but not the least, O Lord,) the dramatists.

In fact, if you have any hobby, caparisoned or saddleless, Carmel is the place where you may ride unmolested. The community is strictly highbrow. Thither gather the yearners for culture, the spirits with prominent auras, the favorites of the Muses, the children of the intellect, the over-souls, the chosen, the blest.

O You Sunset!

In a shady pine shadow sat a masculine tuft of hair in front of an easel. He was doing the sunset. But the sunset was divinely indifferent—it didn't know what was happening to it. From a bosky glade near by, an athletic figure snarked forth. It was Jack London, the progenitor of the red corpuscle in literature. He was joined by two languorous females, and they in turn gathered about them other personages of various dimensions and temperaments. And toward the beach they plodded merrily, calling to the houses as they passed: "Come, the sunset."

When the beach was reached, they seated themselves along a lupined hummock of posies: and what they did to that sunset was a-plenty. It was an adjectival orgy. One fair young thing, gazing rapturously, intoned the following:

" 'Tis like a wassailous Bacchante, reeling her westering route."

" 'Tis as a Cyclopean blacksmith," corrected Mary Austin, remembering her Browning, "striking frenzied sparks from the anvil of the horizon."

"Isn't it sweet?" (Was it Lucia Chamberlain's voice?)

Here London entered the commentative ring. "Sweet? Hell! That sunset has guts!"

Two Social Factions

Here are two factions in the artistic population of Carmel. One is the respectable element, and the other the eminently respectable element. At the head of the one is George Sterling. The favorite beverages of this faction are mint punch, Scotch highballs and Riesling. Its favorite pastimes, when it is not engaged in artistic pursuits, are singing and imbibing the aforementioned beverages. Jack London, James Hopper, Fred Bechdolt, Fra Lafler, Herbert Heron, Lucia Chamberlain and [Xavier] Martinez are on the Receiving Committee of this faction.

The Eminently Respectables are led by the two charming sisters, Alice Mac-Gowan and Grace MacGowan-Cooke. Arnold Genthe holds forth here and also Mary Austin. The habits of this faction are impeccable. Bedtime at 10 o'clock, and nothing more inhibitional than milk in the way of liquid febrifuges. The sunset and the old homely virtues for them.

The Professors

As I have stated, there are many college professors in Carmel. These classic pundits come down from Berkeley and Stanford to recuperate. David Starr Jordan has a bungalow there. For the most part these gentlemen have coagulated in one street. This honored highway is called "Professorial Row." Their principal pastime is engaging in catch-as-catch-can on the dialectic mat. The professors very studiously and religiously avoid the artistic element in Carmel for fear of contamination. These learned gentlemen represent law and order. And the habits of the artists from the beginning of the world have always been chaotic.

Very Temperamental

The temperament of Carmel manifests itself in many strange ways. Besides in the creation of the plastic and graphic arts, it breaks out sartorially, dietetically and hirsutically. Men and women alike are addicted to flowing cravats. These long, trailing Windsors are a sign of genius. It is impossible to be a genius without a necktie that looks like a fat woman's sash. I venture the assertion that Carmel has more hair per capita than any town in America. . . . All the hair one meets in Carmel is long: "Art is long; why not hair?" There is a barber in Carmel, but I hear he has an independent income.

[Temperament] has affected but a few victims dietetically. Chief among these are Upton Sinclair and Michael Williams, although Sinclair is really the more guilty. Williams is only used by Sinclair as a demonstrator, a kind of Exhibit A. to prove the practicability of his gastronomic theories. No one would dare attempt to unseat Sinclair form his digestive divan. He has left no gastronomic stone unturned. He is the Sherlock Holmes of the pork sausage, the ultimate germ eradicator, the bacilli Pinkerton, the microbe's dilemma, the milk-can poet, the final living authority on the dangerous and deadly pastime of eating. Sinclair and Williams wrote a book on their unearthly theories. It was called "Good Health and How We Won It." It proved conclusively that

Upton Sinclair

two human beings could live on nuts, zwiebach and fruit for a year and survive it.

The Carmelites

The Carmelites include a great many well-known writers and artists, as well as a great many writers and artists who hope to be well known.

It is here that Jack London creates his red-blooded yarns. Between chapters he skirts the fiords in search of abalone. His menu consists solely of underdone duck and Martini cocktails. I was told that last time he was at Carmel he came near exterminating the duck from that part of the coast.

Alice MacGowan and Grace Mac-Gowan-Cooke, consanguinary and literary sisters, hold forth at Carmel and write best sellers. They are the most indefatigable workers in the place. Once in a while they will stop long enough to give a tea to the Eminently Respectables . . . but most of the time they are making their pens hum.

In Carmel lives the wassail bard, George Sterling. But Sterling is not a real poet; his sense of humor is too keen, and he is too interested in life. In the early morning he may be heard at his wood-pile heaving valiantly away at pitch-pine logs. And a little later, one may behold him hoeing in his garden. Like Yates at Innisfree, Sterling has nine bean rows. He raises potatoes, and catches his own fish. He lives the life of the outdoor Indian. He is happily married, unlike many of the Carmelites,

George Sterling

Mary Austin

and when he writes, it is for his own amusement.

At Carmel also lives James Hopper, a favorite with the magazine readers. He is built like a young ox, and has a face as impervious as a stone wall. A beautiful wreath of yellow down hovers around his head, but like Sterling, he is only temperamental occasionally.

Mary Austin, however, is a radiating center of temperament. It seethes and bubbles from her like vortiginous heat waves. Her principal occupation is wandering among the pines with her hair flowing, and discussing the microcosmic aspect of neoplatonic theurgy. There have been many aspirants for Mary Austin's place as the temperamental mad molloh, but she does not ride side-saddle on her hobby, and any unhorsing process would be extremely difficult. She has dramatized her temperament so that it is almost a perfect piece of art.

Henry Anderson Lafler, the shagpated troglodyte, is a Carmelite. So is Lucia Chamberlain, the Blessed Damosel of the mystery tale. She wanders by the sea plucking posies and blowing Egyptian deity rings into the empyrean. Herbert Heron is the esthete of Carmel. He is an unappreciated poet who writes long iambic pentameter affairs concerning Actaeon and kindred personages. Mr. Heron's house is a massive vault of reinforced concrete with triple-plate doors of iron, and combination springs and padlocks. In this is kept his poetry.

From San Francisco comes Xavier Martinez the painter, whose features can only be seen at close range. There is evidently some bitter feud between Martinez and the tonsorial profession. His head resembles a huge black chrysanthemum. Only by parting the hirsute curtain in front can he look out upon the world.

It is at Carmel that Upton Sinclair holds forth and shakes the foundations of our social universe with his feverish novels.

To Carmel came Arnold Genthe, San Francisco's society photographer, the esthete of the off-focus portrait. Genthe can photograph you so that you will have no idea that it is you.

When the twenty-three-year-old Willard Huntington Wright journeyed up to Carmel in hope of getting a sensational story, the residents carefully guided him through the scene, anticipating a scandal. But he wrote instead this gentle spoof (abbreviated here). It appeared, with cartoons by Gale, in the *Los Angeles Times* on May 22, 1910. He missed Mary Austin and Upton Sinclair, who had already gone, but included them anyway. Their strong personalities, as they survived in local gossip, appeared to be of greater interest than anything else in Carmel. Three years later, Wright went to New York to edit the *Smart Set*, true to his reputation as boy iconoclast. He is best known today as the mystery writer S. S. Van Dine, creator of Philo Vance.

Part Two: The Twentieth Century

ALICE B. TOKLAS (next page, left) with Annette Rosenshine in a tintype depicting the Cliff House in San Francisco about the turn of the century. Alice Babette Toklas was born in the City on April 30, 1877, in her grandfather's house at 922 O'Farrell Street. Later she lived with her family at 2300 California Street. In her memoirs (*What Is Remembered*, 1963) she wrote about those early days in San Francisco:

> "Life went on calmly until one morning we and our home were violently shaken by an earthquake. Gas was escaping. I hurried to my father's bedroom, pulled up the shades, pulled back the curtains and opened the windows. My father was apparently asleep. Do get up, I said to him. The city is on fire. That, he said with his usual calm, will give us a black eye in the East."

Toklas lived through the earthquake and fire of 1906 but it did not shake down the Victorian conventions by which she had to live. Her life under the family roof was not the free life she envisioned in reading the novels of Henry James. His women (as Linda Simon says in her biography of Toklas), "though sometimes undone by circumstance, were nevertheless mistresses of their fate."

Annette Rosenshine later wrote, "Sex was an uncharted sea in the lives of the Victorian woman. . . . The difficulties of adjustment either psychologically or sexually were unknown in the tragic confusion of both men and women." Toklas was a feisty woman forced to be an onlooker in the San Francisco art world, although she was allowed to visit the Hopkins Art Institute and the Bohemian Club (where Henry James was supposed to appear but didn't). She met Maynard Dixon, Ralph Stackpole, Arthur Putnam, Arnold Genthe (who photographed her) and Jack London (whom she didn't like). She knew Gelett Burgess, whose *Lark* cried out euphorically for "emancipation from the narrow literary dicta of the nineteenth century." But for the emancipation of women, she looked in vain in the San Francisco of that green time. In August 1907, she left for Europe and (as Linda Simon puts it) "fled to freedom." And to Gertrude Stein.

Toklas returned to San Francisco with Gertrude in the mid 1930s. On the way, they stopped in Los Angeles and had dinner with Chaplin, Paulette Goddard, Lillian Hellman, Dashiell Hammett, and

Anita Loos. And they stopped in Monterey (California), as Toklas later remembered:

"We got to the Del Monte Hotel quite late that night and at once there was a telephone call from Mabel Dodge. I answered. She said, Hello, when am I going to see Gertrude? and I answered, I don't think you are going to. What? she said. No, I said, she's going to rest. Robinson Jeffers wants to meet her, she said. Well, I said, he will have to do without."

In San Francisco, Gertrude met the press and Alice stayed in the background, a grey presence. Gertrude was entertained by Gertrude Atherton, but whatever entertaining was said wasn't recorded. (Their aberrant thoughts on the situation of women in society would have made fascinating reading.)

Stein (who wrote like some superbright child might speak) was born in Pennsylvania in 1874; she moved with her family to Oakland in 1880. In 1891 they moved to San Francisco and lived a year or so in an ornate house on Turk Street. When she met the press in San Francisco in the 1930s, she didn't tell them that there's too much There there. She didn't really like the "Paris of the West." (Today there is an Alice B. Toklas Democratic Club in a gay district of the City.)

𝒦ATHLEEN NORRIS, born in San Francisco in 1880, went East when she
married novelist Charles Norris, brother
of Frank Norris. Her first big success in
sentimental fiction was *Mother* in 1911;
and she became the image of just that—
a Gibson Girl matron who could also
write—to generations of readers of
*Woman's Home Companion, Ladies'
Home Journal*, and other domestic bibles
of that ilk. (Her father was twice president of the Bohemian Club, and her
sister married poet William Rose Benét.)
Kathleen once stated that half her working time was spent playing solitaire while
characters and conversations unrolled in
her mind's eye. Most of her characters
were from the upper-class end of the
deck, with few deuces, wild cards, or
spades but lots of hearts and diamonds.

𝓡ABINDRANATH TAGORE visited the
United States five times between
1912 and 1930. On his second tour in
1916 there was a veritable "Tagore craze"
sweeping the country. He had been recently awarded the Nobel Prize for Literature, and Macmillan had undertaken
the publication of all his works in English. He was hailed as the fulfillment of
Whitman's prophecy (in "Passage to
India") that "Finally shall come the poet
worthy the name."

Tagore's physical presence overcame
the often derisive criticism of those who
viewed him from afar as "a clever Oriental
journalist" who came "to spread anti-
nationalism and heathenism in a
Christian country." His biographer,
Sujit Mukherjee, later wrote, "It is
possible to split the whole body of writing on Tagore, in India, or abroad, between writers who had some personal
association with him and those who had
none. That the former invariably incline
towards idolatry while the latter lean the
opposite way only perpetuates the gulf
that even now divides critical opinion
about Tagore."

Tagore's San Francisco visit, as with
many a famous wandering literary per-
sonage, did not turn out at all as expected.
He arrived on September 30, 1916; and
the most publicized aspect of his tour
was his lecture, "The Cult of Nationalism."

"According to Tagore's thesis," Mukherjee wrote, "nationalism was the unwhole-
some spirit which in one form had urged
England to enslave the Indian people, in
another had plunged the European nations
into war, and in general endangered the
peace and prosperity of the whole world.
The biggest sensation of the trip happened
in San Francisco when a scuffle in front
of Tagore's hotel between two groups of
[Far East] Indians was magnified by the
local press into an incipient plot to
assassinate Tagore. While headlines
screamed across the country, Tagore had
to undergo police protection much against

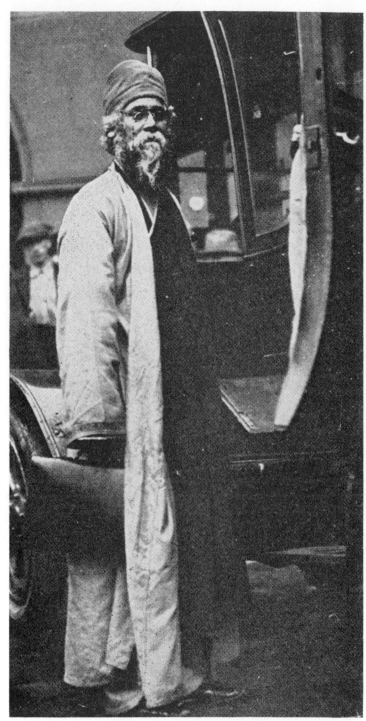

Tagore landing in San Francisco

his will and gave a statement saying "I do not believe there was a plot to assassinate me, though I had to submit to the farce of being guarded by the police, from which I hope to be relieved for the rest of my visit to this country."

"Tagore, Famous Poet, Dooms Occident" was the headline in the *San Francisco Call* the day after his lecture, October 3. The story reported,

Tagore, in an impassioned spiritual appeal, foretold the ultimate material downfall of material power and the triumph of the nations of India and China who now "sit sobbing in the darkness." The lecture was at the Saint Francis Hotel. There were society women and men in full evening regalia, there were university presidents, the city's biggest financial powers, there were artists, students, and clad in the careless costume of their calling, several of the well-known anarchists, advocates of direct action, all listening to Tagore's indictment against personal and material power, violence and greed.

Tagore said Western civilization "has erected gigantic idols of greed in its temples, feeding them with human souls and bodies. It cannot go on. There is a moral law, always at work. . . . You cannot drive engines through the heart of the people and escape judgement." He quoted for examples the fate of ancient Rome and Greece. In speaking of Japan, he said that her nationalism, "copied from the West, was destroying the beauty of her soul." (In an October 10 editorial after his departure, the *Call* rejected his condemnation as the words of an impractical mystic. If Christ came back today, with his beat sandals and hippy hair, he'd probably be rejected too.)

Tagore was to make three more tours of the United States. He abruptly ended his fourth visit, partly because of unpleasant cross-examination by U.S. immigration officials in Vancouver. Tagore addressed America for the last time in 1940, when he sent a cable to President Roosevelt reminding this country of her responsibility in stemming "the tide of evil that has menaced the permanence of our civilization." He died a month before Pearl Harbor, having received no reply.

126

ISHI (second from left) at the Orpheum Theater in the City sometime during the last years of his life (about 1914) while he was housed in the Museum of Anthropology, then located in San Francisco. Behind him (in black beard) anthropologist A. L. Kroeber, who cared for Ishi. His second wife, Theodora Kroeber, later wrote Ishi's story from his spoken words, the biography of the last wild Indian in North America (*Ishi, Last of His Tribe*, 1964).

This Stone Age man stumbled into Western civilization in August 1911. Exhausted and starving, he was found lying in a corral of a slaughterhouse near Oroville, California. Through Professor Kroeber of the University of California's department of anthropology, Ishi was brought to the Museum of Anthropology on Parnassus Heights, where he lived long enough to leave his record of the Yahi way of life.

SADAKICHI HARTMANN (1867?– 1944) is pictured here laying a wreath on the Robert Louis Stevenson Memorial, Portsmouth Square, in about 1916. That year Hartmann published two books in San Francisco: *Tanka and Hakai, Japanese Rhythms* and *My Rubaiyat*. It was the same year he was called "The Most Mysterious Personality in American Letters." Born on an island in Nagasaki harbor, of a German father and a Japanese mother, he was brought up in Germany but migrated to America, to San Francisco and eventually to southern California. His myriad talents—painter and poet, playwright and actor, art critic and literary essayist—fascinated generations of artists and intellectuals. J. G. Huneker described him as "the man with the Hokusai profile and broad Teutonic culture." Ezra Pound wrote, "If one hadn't been oneself, it wd. have been worthwhile being Sadakichi." In 1956, *Fortnight* called him the last bohemian. In 1969, *Swank International* mindlessly labeled him the first hippie. In 1970, the University of California at Riverside staged a retrospective of his life and art. A *Sadakichi Hartmann Newsletter* was published by the English department.

Samuel Dickson (in *San Francisco Is Your Home*) says Hartmann was arrested in San Francisco in 1918 and accused of being pro-German. He told the judge: "I hate Germany. I was arrested in Berlin for calling the Kaiser names." Dickson also reports that in 1917 at the Scottish Rite Auditorium he "horrified his audience by announcing 'California will eventually secede from the Union.'" Dickson says he saw Hartmann thrown out of Begin's Italian restaurant in 1917 because the owner was angry at what Hartmann had written about certain local artists. Dickson, however, was the kind of romanticizer whose dates and facts could not always be trusted.

Hartmann was a mad genius to some but to others he was the dean of American art critics, having established his reputation with *A History of American Art*. He was also associated with the anarchist movement, joining Emma Goldman and Edwin Bjorkman in founding the magazine *Mother Earth*. As for the possibility that anarchism might really work, he wrote, "A cook is needed even for the most frugal brew."

Margaret Anderson

*M*ARGARET ANDERSON (ABOVE) AND EMMA GOLDMAN (next page) were associated briefly in San Francisco when Anderson was editing the September 1916 issue of the *Little Review* from a studio in the old Montgomery Block. Anderson later wrote that she had discovered anarchism by reading Goldman just in time to become an anarchist for that issue. With Back East snobbism, she ran the main part of the issue with blank pages and a note on the title page that "The September issue is offered as a Want Ad." Following the blank pages was a cute little satirical cartoon showing "Light occupations of the editor when there is nothing to edit." Among the activities were swimming, suburban gardening, and puttering about the house.

She didn't mention she was actually living in rural Mill Valley at the time and thus certainly made small contact with the life that swirled around the Monkey Block in those days. Perhaps it is truer today than it was back then that editors

Emma Goldman

BOHEMIA, another review published in the City in 1916, really marked the end of the old turn-of-the-century literary world, although a few of the great old figures (George Sterling, Clark Ashton Smith, James Hopper) still graced its masthead. Its chief editor was Raine Bennett, and its patrons were the big money names of the City: the Crockers, the Gianninis, the Jay Goulds, etcetera (in contrast to government support of the arts today). The First World War was ushering in the modern world, and a new bohemia would arise around the old Montgomery Block, but here is what the editors saw at the time:

A deserving criticism has been passed to the effect that the recent issues of *Bohemia* have been about as funny as a crutch. To some the magazine ridicules its own name and decorates its covers with gay colors, while inside its articles have been mournful enough to print upon oxidized crape. To all this we bow in humble acknowledgment. We have tried to depict the true Bohemian spirit of San Francisco, and in seeking the truth we have found only grief. We have found a mournful procession of those who in days gone by have made fellowship respond with merriment. We have found places deserted and silent where once rare humor rang. We have had so-called "Bohemians" pointed out to us, and observed them to be anaemic wretches, sunk in the nausea of poverty.

In the old, inspirational days of San Francisco, the arts abounded in their manifold and colorful interpretations. But the thunder of mercenary pursuits has shattered that galaxy to atoms, and sent the angelic trumpeters of Memory shrieking to platonic shelter. Its lightning has struck the altar of the Muses, and the ambitious carol of worshipers has been choked to a death rattle. The barges of joyous throngs have forsaken shores once musical with revelry; the sirens of our nights have gone, and the pipes of Pan lie trodden under the hoofs of fleeing satyrs.

who do not live in the City can hardly have much contact with what's going on in its literary and artistic life, so much of it happening at night when they are safe at home in the slurbs. (The book editors of the San Francisco daily papers haven't been seen at nighttime literary events in the City for over twenty years.)

The back pages of Anderson's San Francisco issue contained a strong plea for Tom Mooney in "The San Francisco Bomb Case." (Mooney and Warren Billings were in jail, charged with planting a bomb in a Preparedness Day demonstration on Market Street. Anarchists Alexander Berkman and Emma Goldman went to bat for them. Mooney and Billings were convicted on perjured testimony and prowar hysteria.) Emma Goldman lectured at least five times in the City in behalf of various reform movements, including feminism and birth control.

The restaurants where once we sang and danced, have in numerous cases barred their doors because of a lack of public interest. Our bay, which early mariners imagined would be bristling with the masts of ships from the Orient in flourishing courtesies of travel, is calm with the serenity of idle waters. Throughout all the forest aisles of California no naiads of former imagery abide, no dryads dance; the laughing nymphs who once played about our fountain-heads of Genius have departed in tears, and in the metropolis of San Francisco every hall of yore is empty—the cherubs of our dreams have sought elsewhere to gambol, and Music sobs on her shrine, in desolation.

This is why *Bohemia* has found it difficult to frolic among its pages.

*　　*　　*

"Weaving Spiders Come Not Here" is a motto of the Bohemian Club. And yet, in the presence of that high principle which the evolutions of time and temperament have not effaced, a spider of hideous mien has been weaving silently. Its claws have clutched at the very heart of this illustrious body, and the shadow of its horrible form is hovering above the pinions of the Owl. Ten revered members have succumbed within the Winter's pall, and the Spider still is weaving, still is weaving. . . .

ISADORA DUNCAN is shown here with her husband, the great Russian poet Sergei Essenin, in 1922. They had just been married. Essenin committed suicide in Russia in December 1925, after he and Isadora had parted.

Born in San Francisco in 1878 in a small house on the northwest corner of Geary and Taylor streets, Isadora Duncan was brought up by her divorced mother "in an extremely permissive, agnostic, antipuritan, and poetic style," according to James D. Hart in his *Companion to California*. Francis Steegmuller in *Your Isadora* notes that the city of San Francisco placed a commemorative plaque on her birthplace in May 1973. Irma Duncan, who delivered the address at the ceremony, wrote, "It was a real 'Isadora Happening,' with some young girls in tunics and bare feet dancing on the sidewalk to music by Shubert, in the roaring traffic, to and in her honor. Speeches, cheers, tears.

"Isadora would have loved it! It was literally right down her alley! Amazing how her name can still arouse people." In *My Life*, Isadora wrote, "I am indeed the spiritual daughter of Whitman."

(How our perceptions of Walt Whitman have changed. Today his dominant image—at least in San Francisco—would seem to be the Good Gay Gray Poet. Isadora typified the nineteenth-century heterosexual view of the bard. Her life and her dance were her own "Song of Myself." She did not dance his "Calamus.")

LAUGHING HORSE, "Wherein the First Laughs are Awarded the University of California," was first edited at the university in Berkeley by "four more or less like-minded young persons who find education as it is perpetrated in America, and especially at California, to be a gaudy farce with lachrymous overtones. . . . Our aim is frankly destructive. . . . We are the wrecking gang, hurlers of brickbats, shooters of barbs, tossers of custard pie."

In April 1922, the magazine moved to Santa Fe and Taos, New Mexico. Its principal editor became "Spud" Johnson and its principle influence the D. H. Lawrence cult in Taos. The original tone was inspired somewhat by Gelett Burgess's *Lark*, Margaret Anderson's *Little Review*, H. L. Mencken's literary castigations, and Upton Sinclair's attack on the university as the training ground for Babbittry.

George Sterling, D. H. Lawrence, Jaime de Angulo, Witter Bynner, Upton Sinclair, Genevieve Taggard, Walt Whitman (with a letter), Clarkson Crane, and many others made up the "Laughing Stock." It laughed on 'til 1939, the horse laugh getting weaker all the time, until it finally dozed off into a permanent siesta against an adobe wall in the hot sun under a sombrero. It was 1939 and no more time for laughing.

The shift to New Mexico had proved a literary link between the Bohemias of the Bay Area, Carmel, and Taos, there having been much intercourse between them, beginning with Mary Austin and others of the Carmel group in the preceding decade. (Another way of putting it is that what eventually happened to Carmel—increasingly fashionable artsy-craftsy putterers, weavers, and ladies in serapes who "sculpt"—happened to Taos and Santa Fe.)

*C*ONTINENT'S END: *An Anthology of Contemporary California Poets* was published by the Book Club of California in San Francisco in 1925. Edited by George Sterling, Genevieve Taggard, and James Rorty, it was a real nexus of what had gone before and what was to come, the past and the future bound together, rather like the driving of the golden spike where Back East met Far West. In his introduction, Sterling said, "The age of Steel begins to sing in a voice of steel, calling us back from far musings, & demanding the actual instead of the imaginary." The iron horse of prose had arrived, snorting and puffing with its load of rhymed antiquities. Approaching the absolute staccato of machines (as well as the absolute "flat-out" sound of western speech) poetry was losing its winged rhyme, not to mention its inverted syntax and other affectations of the Old World. Poetry, while retaining the typography of poetry, began to sound more and more like prose. At best it took on the sound of impassioned speech.

Today, most big anthologies of contemporary poetry are at least two-thirds prose, albeit in the typography of poetry—finely written lyric prose, witty prose, beautiful, poetic prose, but rhymeless nevertheless, and incapable of being sung. (Try singing Ezra Pound's "Cantos." Try even reading them aloud, and you will hear what fine rugged prose it is. Read T. S. Eliot's "Four Quartets" and hear the most beautiful poetic prose written this century.)

In *Continent's End*, many of the older voices—George Sterling, Ina Coolbrith, Edwin Markham—still spoke in rhyme or with inverted poetic diction. The new young voices were not always rhymeless, but the syntax was more direct. Robinson Jeffers's fulsome title poem (the frontispiece to the book) was stuck on the

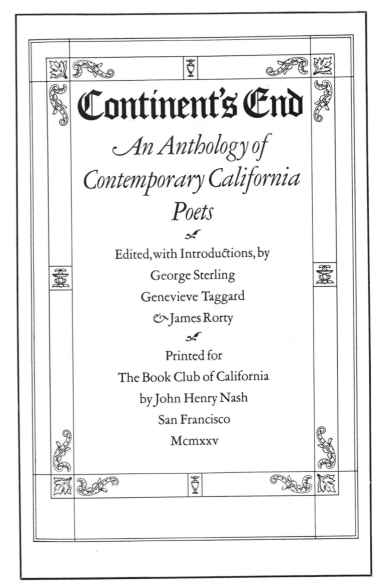

crags somewhere in between—rhymeless yet full of an antique rhetoric. (One of the newcomers in the volume was Stanton Coblentz, writing in the old-fashioned style. He was to become a holdout for it, editing *Wings*, a magazine of conventional rhymed verse, in Mill Valley as late as the 1950s.)

Some women in *Continent's End* did make breakthroughs to territory never touched by women writers—Mary Austin, for one, with the "Song of the Maverick":

I am too arid for tears, and for laughter,
Too sore with unslaked desires . . .

My body is bitter with baffled lusts. . . .

My feet run wide of rutted trails
Toward the undared destinies.

And Genevieve Taggard pointed to the future when "some swarthy Keats or electric Shelley will come." (But would she have recognized them in Gregory Corso or Bob Dylan at the Fillmore Auditorium?)

Surveying *Continent's End*, James Rorty in his Introduction concluded,

It has all been so huge and so sudden. Look from Twin Peaks over San Francisco and the bay region, and you will see the story of the youth of the West, its aspiration, its confusion, written large over the landscape: a splatter of buildings—homes, factories, apartment houses, office sky scrapers, quite without architectural unity, or even visible focus in church or market place—is flung against the sides and over the tops of sand-hills where seventy years ago the wind blew over barren sage; across the bay, which the crowded ferries churn so diligently, the white spire of the second-largest university in the world rises at the base of a hill-slope which a few miles back is still largely cattle-range. One would scarcely expect, in seventy years, to transform the chaos of a camp into a civilization. Yet it is being done. The West is beginning, as indeed all America is beginning. It is examining its traditions, sifting its attitudes, experimenting.

$\mathcal{D}$ASHIELL HAMMETT (1894–1961) worked in San Francisco as a Pinkerton detective in the 1920s, and he drew upon the city and its atmosphere for the books he began to write in the late 1920s. Plotted in San Francisco, *The Maltese Falcon* was made famous by Humphrey Bogart as the unconventional detective, Sam Spade, in the classic John Huston film. James D. Hart, in his *Companion to California*, wrote of Hammett: "Cool, tough, and hardboiled in attitude, his works allied Hemingway's mood with the subject of detective fiction, giving that genre a new tone and style which affected Raymond Chandler and other writers." Moving to Hollywood in the 1930s to write films, Hammett refused to testify before the Un-American Activities Committee and went to jail for it. His friend Lillian Hellman wrote about him in this era in *Scoundrel Time* (1976).

This is the cover of Francis Ford Coppola's weekly *City of San Francisco*, for November 4, 1975. The magazine began publication in July 1973 and lasted until late 1975. Seemingly inspired by a real affection for the City, but not above muckraking in the style of early San Francisco journalism, the magazine stimulated and published many of the liveliest writers in town, including poets able to bridge the yawning gap between the esoteric and the popular.

During its too short, extravagant life, *City*'s chief editor was the debonair and flamboyant Warren Hinckle, one of the founders of *Ramparts* (the New Left radical journal whose editors included the late great-hearted Paul Jacobs and Robert Scheer, now a hotshot feature writer and interviewer for the *Los Angeles Times*. Scheer's first book, written while a clerk at City Lights Bookstore, was *Cuba: An American Tragedy*, one

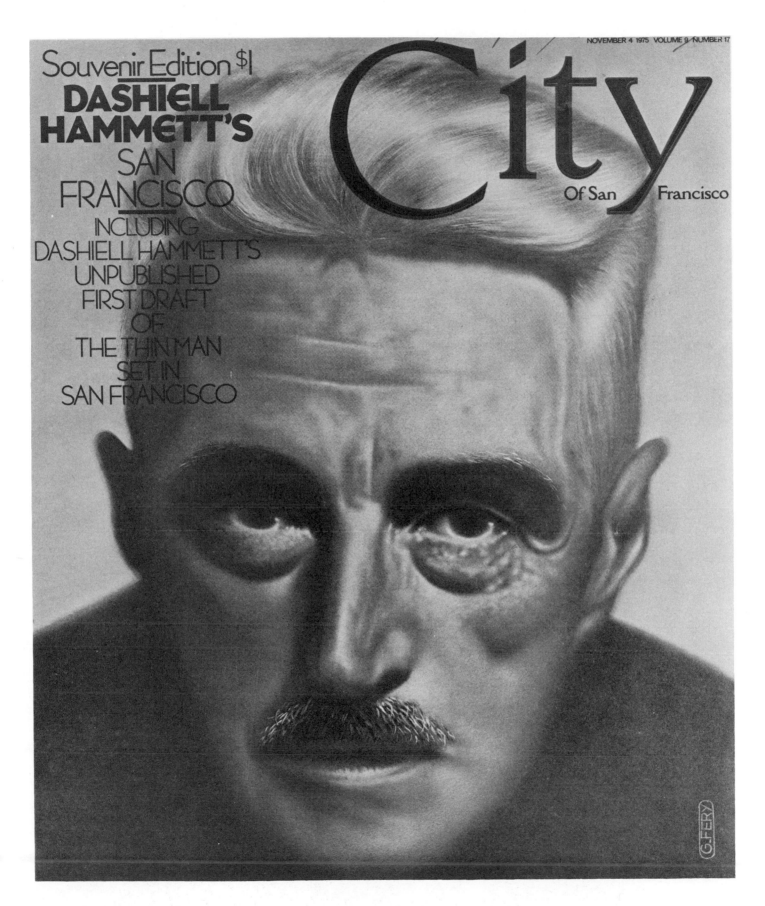

NOVEMBER 4 1975 VOLUME 9 NUMBER 17

Souvenir Edition $1
DASHIELL HAMMETT'S
SAN
FRANCISCO
INCLUDING
DASHIELL HAMMETT'S
UNPUBLISHED
FIRST DRAFT
OF
THE THIN MAN
SET IN
SAN FRANCISCO

City
Of San Francisco

G.FERY

Sam Spade's FRISCO

These photographs, made by Edmund Shea, show the places where Hammett's detective heroes — and Hammett himself — conducted much of their business and their lives. The descriptions are all from Hammett.

A

Geary Theatre, 450 Sutter Street:
"Spade went to the Geary Theatre . . . and posted himself on the curb in front, facing the theatre . . . At ten minutes past eight Joel Cairo appeared, walking up Geary Street . . . "

The Maltese Falcon

B

Golden West Hotel (now the Golden State), 114 Powell Street — where Josephine Dolan spent the night before she and Hammett were married.

Fact taken from the Hammett's marriage license

C

Flood Building, 870 Market — where the Continental Detective Agency office was (actually, Pinkerton's office):
"The Continental Detective Agency's San Francisco office is located in a Market Street office building."

The Op in "The Big Knockover"

D

Ferry Building:
"'She said she wanted to get a newspaper. . .' 'Which paper?' 'The Call. Then . . . just after we'd crossed Van Ness she knocked on the glass again and said take her to the Ferry Building.'"

Cab driver and Sam Spade speaking of Brigid in The Maltese Falcon

E

111 Sutter Street (Hunter-Dulin Building) — Spade's Office Building:
"In the doorway of Spade's office-building he came face to face with the boy he had left at Gutman's. The boy put himself in Spade's path, blocking the entrance, and said: 'Come on. He wants to see you.'"

The Maltese Falcon

F

Samuel's Clock, 856 Market Street:
Albert Samuel's Jewelry Store where Hammett worked on occasion.

G

Southern Pacific Passenger Station, Third and Townsend:
"We . . . went down Brannan to Third again, and over to Townsend — and we didn't see Babe McCloor. . . We stopped across the street from the Southern Pacific passenger station."

The Op in "Fly Paper"

H

Waverly Place in Chinatown — where the back entrance of Chang Li Ching's house was located:
"I couldn't guess which was the important house. Four doors from Jair Quon's gambling house, Cipriano had said, but I didn't know where Jair Quon's was. . Up the street [was] the Temple of the Queen of Heaven — a joss house. . ."

The Op in "Dead Yellow Women"

I

Spofford Alley in Chinatown — where Chang Li Ching's house was:
"I went up to Spofford Alley and found my house with no difficulty at all. It was a shabby building with steps and door the color of dried blood. . ."

The Op in "Dead Yellow Women"

ILLUSTRATED BY EDMUND SHEA

Sam Spade's

FriscO

J

St. Mark Hotel (The St. Francis) — where Miles Archer picked up the tail on Brigid and Floyd Thursby:

"Spade went through the St. Mark's long purplish lobby to the desk and asked a red-haired dandy whether Miss Wonderly was in."

The Maltese Falcon

K

Julius's Castle, Telegraph Hill:

"Spade and Effie Perine sat at a small table in Julius's Castle on Telegraph Hill."

"A Man Called Spade"

L

1805 Divisadero — where the Oakwood Hall was in Hammett's day:

"Rhino said: 'Ain't nobody's business where I got my money. I got it.' Minnie said: 'He won it in a crap game, mister, up the Happy Day Social Club. Hope to die if he didn't.'"

Speaking to the Op in
The Dain Curse

M

Redwood Street and rear of 580 McAllister — where the Whosis Kid went when he left his room:

"I ... reached the corner of Franklin and Redwood just in time to see my man ducking into the back door of an apartment building that fronted on McAllister Street... The building in which the Kid had spent the night and this building... had their rears on the same back street, on opposite sides, a little more than half a block apart..."

The Op in
"The Whosis Kid"

N

228 FILBERT Street, Telegraph Hill:

"I climbed Telegraph Hill to give the house the up-and-down. It was a large house — a big frame house painted egg-yellow. It hung dizzily on a shoulder of the hill..."

The Op in
"The Scorched Face"

O

Blanco's Restaurant, 859 O'Farrell Street — today the Great American Music Hall:

"It was then after five o'clock. Not having had any luncheon, I went up to Blanco's for food..."

The Op in
The Dain Curse

of the best pro-Fidel studies of the Cuban revolution.) Hinckle later carried his socko journalism to the *San Francisco Chronicle* where he carries on a kind of Mutiny on the *Bounty*, although one is never sure if he is Captain Bly or Mister Christian.

Another major contributor to *City* was Kevin Starr, who under Mayor Joseph Alioto became chief librarian. A cultural historian and Harvard Ph.D., he published *Americans and the California Dream, 1850–1915* (1973) and retired from the public library shortly thereafter to write a second volume (covering 1915 to the present) and to write a column for the *San Francisco Examiner*. In 1979, he published a San Francisco novel, *Land's End*.

Together with Hinckle, Starr may be seen to represent in some manner the Jesuit Catholic intellectual elite of the City, with roots in the University of San Francisco. (Another Catholic columnist, Charles McCabe of the *Chronicle*, is more shanty than lace-curtain Irish in his writing, describing himself as an old bohemian. He is a literate Falstaff among journalists.) On the preceding pages is reproduced the feature that ran in *City*.

CHARLES ERSKINE SCOTT WOOD (at left) is shown here with Albert "Mickey" Bender in the 1930s. (Although Wood once lived at Broadway and Taylor Street in San Francisco, this photo was probably taken in Los Gatos, California.) Wood was a West Pointer who fought against Chief Joseph of the Nez Percé (as well as in other campaigns to exterminate native Americans) before turning to law, literature, and liberal causes. During World War I he wrote for *The Masses* and produced *Heavenly Discourse*, satirizing economic and social injustice and the inhumanity of war. (It was probably his young wife, Sara Bard Field, a poet and feminist leader in San Francisco, who prompted his later liberal leanings.)

*R*OBINSON JEFFERS (at left) with Albert M. Bender outside Jeffers's Tor House in Carmel in the early 1930s. Bibliophile and patron of the arts in San Francisco, Bender was recently described by Kevin Starr in the *San Francisco Examiner* as "an 1890's bohemian in the grand manner, the last envoy of *fin-de-siècle* San Francisco." The crowded parties in his Russian Hill flat between the two wars were the liveliest literary and artistic soirées in town. "Bender," says Starr, "would abhor today's retreat into narcissistic privacy that so characterizes the upper middle classes of this city."

At the time of this picture, Jeffers had already written his greatest works, including *Tamar*, heavy with biblical symbolism transferred to wild California landscape. Jeffers never loved the city. He built his house out of native stone in Carmel and retired more and more into his tower, so that an insurgent generation of writers arriving in Big Sur after World War II found him somewhat unapproachable.

The *Hesperian* magazine in 1931 had published a poem by Henry Ramsey apostrophizing Jeffers as a "son of stone." Today Jeffers is more of a monument of stone than he is a popular poet. His final "disgust with the human species in toto" (as Alfred Kazin said in *On Native Grounds*) hardly turned on new generations kicking over the traces of the eternal guilt-trip laid on the world by Christian dogma. ("Jesus died for your sins." But so did Janis Joplin.)

$\mathcal{J}$AMES D. HART standing next to
the bust of George Sterling by
Ralph Stackpole on the University of
California campus in Berkeley in 1979.
Professor Hart, as director of the Bancroft Library there, is in charge of the
Sterling archive and is the author of many
learned works on American literature.
In 1930–1931, Hart was editor of the
Hesperian, published at 1055 California
Street in the City. There were just two
issues, and the first thing in the first issue
was an attack by Theodore Dreiser on
money in America. It was called "Mooney
& America," and he castigated the ruling
class for victimizing the working class,
as symbolized by Tom Mooney in jail. It
was Money over Mooney all the way.
Other contributors to this bright little
magazine included Oscar Lewis, Clark-
son Crane, Else Gidlow, Norman Mac-
Leod, Carey McWilliams (biographer of
Ambrose Bierce), Charles Erskine
Scott Wood, Hildegarde Flanner, Yvor
Winters, and Henry Ramsey.

(The Bancroft Library was founded
upon the historical and literary collections of H. H. Bancroft, who sold them
to the University in 1905. By 1970, the
Bancroft Special Collections contained
over 250,000 printed works, twenty-six
million manuscripts, and over one million
pictures.)

$\mathcal{A}$MONG OTHER prominent English professors at the University of California
in Berkeley who have had much literary
contact with San Francisco, Mark Schorer
(center) stands out for his own fiction as
well as his literary criticism. His books
are: *The State of Mind* (thirty-two stories;
1947), *The Wars of Love* (a novel; 1954),
*Criticism: The Foundations of Modern
Literary Judgment* (edited with Josephine
Miles and Gordon McKenzie; 1948), and
[*D.H.*] *Lawrence in the War Years* (1968).
Of a later generation is Thomas Parkinson, poet and specialist in W. B. Yeats,
who has been an editor and friend of
many San Francisco poets since World
War II. He was among the witnesses for
the defense of Allen Ginsberg's *Howl*
in the infamous San Francisco obscenity
trial. In 1961 he edited *A Casebook on
the Beat.* City Lights Books later published
his *Protect the Earth.* He is also the author
of several books of poetry. He is married
to the painter Ariel Parkinson.

*L*ABOR BURIES ITS DEAD after "Bloody Thursday" in the great maritime strike of 1934. This lithograph by Bits Hayden is the frontispiece for Mike Quin's *The Big Strike* (not published until 1949). Forty thousand workers marched up Market Street. Mike Quin gives the background:

In San Francisco, July 1934, the laboring population laid down its tools in a General Strike.

An uncanny quiet settled over the acres of buildings. For all practical purposes not a wheel moved nor a lever budged. The din of commercial activity gave way to a murmur of voices in the streets.

Along the Embarcadero and in front of the National Guard Armory self-conscious-looking schoolboys wearing steel helmets and ill-fitting khaki uniforms paced up and down fingering heavy automatic rifles.

Highways leading out of the city bore a continuous stream of expensive cars carrying well-to-do refugees to distant sanctuaries. They were fleeing from bombs and rioting mobs.

There were no bombs.

There were no rioting mobs.

These existed only in the pages of the daily press which characterized the event as a Bolshevik revolution, and conjured up visions of tempestuous throngs sweeping, torch in hand, through the city streets.

The Hayden illustration had this poem (presumably by Quin) on the facing page:

Stop in your tracks, you passer-by;
Uncover your doubting head.
The workingmen are on their way
To bury their murdered dead.

The men who sowed their strength in work
And reaped a crop of lies
Are marching by. Oppression's doom
Is written in their eyes.

Pamphleteer, columnist, radio broadcaster, Quin became the authoritative voice for those thousands of workers. His writings were collected in 1940 under the title *Dangerous Thoughts*. Theodore Dreiser wrote him: "I fear I cannot convey to you the merit of your book, *Dangerous Thoughts*. It is so ripe in social and economic observation, so new in method, so vigorous, refreshing, and wholly true. And, considering the world old record of man's inhumanity to man, as well as our present social indecency and cruelty, it is wholly devastating. It should be laid before the eyes of the whole world, and I hope it will be." Quin died in 1947, and *On the Drumhead* (a further collection of his writings) was published the next year, with engravings by Victor Arnautoff.

The story of literary San Francisco in the 1930s cannot be divorced from its labor strife and power politics, much as literary critics would like to ignore them in our present revisionist times. While old genteel journals like *Argonaut* seemed to have gone into a deep dream, the West Coast bristled with radical periodicals. Lincoln Steffens edited the *Pacific Weekly* (1935–1937), with articles like "Revolt in the West" and "Decoding the Hearst Papers." In his own column Steffens wrote, "Stocks moved up on Monday at the prospect of war." The *Maritime Strike Pictorial* in 1937 printed a picture of Tom Mooney still behind bars with the caption: "Twenty-one years behind prison walls for a bombing he did not commit has not broken the fighting spirit of Tom Mooney. . . . Active as a union organizer, he was framed through perjured testimony paid by industrial barons." (Much later came books like William Martin Camp's *Port of Gold*, 1948; Harry Bridges's *Rise and Fall of Radical Labor in the U.S.*, 1972; and Walter Havighurst's *Pier 17*.)

As for literature itself in the 1930s, the *Pacific Weekly* carried the Marxist view of Karl Long in its March 8, 1935, issue:

We are watching history here on the rim of the San Francisco Bay, but we wait in vain for the writer who will catch up and immortalize this portentous moment. It requires no depth of thought to see the significance of the General Strike, the Sacramento trial, the battle on the Seattle waterfront; still less, perhaps, to perceive the widening circle of discontent spreading from San Diego to the Puget Sound; but literature is another matter.

We are really another nation here. There is the East, the Plains area, and the South; and fundamentally we have little to do with any of the three. As Marx said, history lies on the Pacific; but the difference is more immediate than that. I myself (to become personal for a moment) am an urban communist, with my inner life centered about metropolitan streets, and perhaps typical of my generation; nevertheless, I have hunted, fished, climbed a mountainside in a blinding rain, made fires from pine logs, listened to logging-camp yarns, ascended glaciers, and bailed out leaky boats. All of us can remember uncles who were Wobblies. Or men like one I know of, who once threw a scab bodily through a plate-glass window. We have grown up differently.

Where is the literature to come out of this magnificent life? It has, somehow, failed to emerge from the womb. The fate of the Pacific writer has been to emigrate to New York, or to remain in a sort of obscure splendor. Ambrose Bierce, Jack London, George Sterling—what have they in common with the Pacific coast except in relation to the things they were not? Whom have we now? Charles Erskine Scott Wood, Sara Bard Field, Robinson Jeffers, Marie Welch, all of whom, with the possible exception of Jeffers, might as well be writing anywhere else as here. Even Jeffers has, by his unfortunate preoccupation with one theme, almost completely uprooted himself. This is obviously not to say that they do not write well; on the contrary, we are more than fortunate in having greatness at our doorstep; but they are not writers of the Pacific. . . .

As for the very young writers, there is little that is not discouraging. Without wishing to dispraise Mr. Saroyan, it must be said that he manages to combine an incredible naiveté with, as Ella Winter has truly said, a disinclination to think; a situation not uncommon in California these days. But one does not become an artist in that fashion. As for Tillie Lerner, from whom one hopes so much, her article in No. 4 of the *Partisan Review* was most disappointing; hysteria is no substitute for creative work. And, concerning the innumerable young people who publish small poetry magazines, one can only remark that the time for Greenwich Village passed long ago.

This exhausts the list which springs immediately to mind. It is the more unfortunate in that one of the greatest stories in the world is now displaying itself in California; in California primarily, but also throughout the whole coast. A people is stirring into life, and will sooner or later find its artists. But how more important to grow with the revolution, as Gorki did, than merely to chronicle it afterwards!

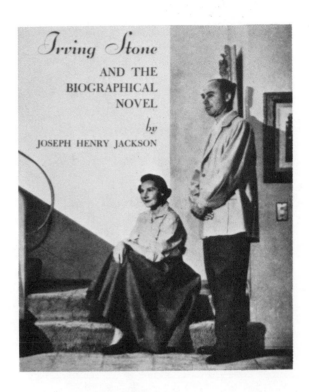

RVING STONE was born on Washington Square, San Francisco, in 1903. There is a plaque on a bench on the east side of the square to mark the place his house once stood. Joseph Henry Jackson, while he was book editor of the *San Francisco Chronicle*, pointed out that Stone was born on Bastille Day, July 14, a fact he took as symbolic of Stone's early political point of view.

Stone's early works include *Clarence Darrow for the Defense* and a novel based upon the life of Eugene V. Debbs. Jackson characterized Stone's writing as "fictionalized biographies about historical characters who have been falsely represented. . . . He found his great pleasure in saying 'But look! It wasn't like that at all! Here is what happened, and why. *This* is what it was really all about!' " In this genre was Stone's life of Jack London, *Sailor on Horseback* (1938). This picture of Stone and his wife probably was taken at his latter-day home in the area known as Los Angeles, that "instant megalopolis" where the American Dream came too true.

WILLIAM SAROYAN in San Francisco in the late 1930s. (Next page. Note Thomas Wolfe's *Look Homeward, Angel* in the stack of books.) He was born in Fresno of Armenian parents in 1908. Saroyan's first collection of stories, *The Daring Young Man on the Flying Trapeze,* brought him the beginnings of fame in 1934. His autobiographical *My Name Is Aram* (1940) vividly brought to life the Armenian children of his childhood in the San Joaquin Valley. His great play, *The Time of Your Life* (1939), is said to be based upon real-life characters at Izzy Gomez's saloon at 848 Pacific Street, San Francisco, a famous bohemian watering place. The bartender in the play is presumably based on Izzy himself (pictured here in a poster of the time). Saroyan refused a Pulitzer Prize for the play, considering the award a commercial banality.

In *Places Where I've Done Time*, Saroyan gives the places he lived in San Francisco in the late 1920s: 2378 Sutter Street, 1707A Divisidero Street, and 348 Carl Street. In those days, he frequented Breen's on Third Street, among other bars. ("Breen's was another of the foolish places I went to instead of college.") And he worked very briefly at places like the Steamer Division of the Southern Pacific at Embarcadero and Mission Street and the Postal Telegraph Branch Office at 405 Brannan. He also wrote of attending the Panama Pacific International Exhibition in 1915 at age seven: "We saw shining, almost imaginary buildings, full of unbelievable works of sculpture, painting, weaving, basketmaking, products of agriculture, and all kinds of mechanical inventions . . . a place that couldn't possibly be real." Saroyan's writing is marvelously characterized by James D. Hart in his Oxford *Companion to California*: ". . . an exuberant, sentimental, and rhapsodic exaltation of

diverse characters, all presented in radiant moments of revelation."

After many years of acclaim as a writer, Saroyan's fortunes declined (though not his wild Armenian imagination and great gusto for life). On February 20, 1959, the *San Francisco Chronicle* reported: "Saroyan Is Broke, Will Live Abroad." (Although he lived there many years, Saroyan remained so American that one could never think of him as an expatriate. So with Thomas Wolfe and Jack Kerouac.)

Saroyan's son, Aram (above), lives near San Francisco in Bolinas (a town populated with poets which some call Bolinas Free State). His most recent booklet is a "saga of Lew Welch & the Beat Generation" entitled *Genesis Angels* which the critic Garson Kanin said "does honor to the great American literary name of Saroyan." In the late 1970s, Aram Saroyan gave a poetry reading in a big auditorium in the City with Rod McKuen (who had experienced his *Stanyan Street and Other Sorrows* here). They added a joy and a sorrow or two to his San Francisco experience that night.

Twenty years before, McKuen wrote in "Stanyan Street,"

> I do not think
> me and San Francisco
> will be friends again

JOHN STEINBECK holds his baby Thom after his christening in Monterey (California) at the Little Russian Church in 1944. There are plenty of pictures of Steinbeck in the Monterey-Salinas-Big Sur area, but none in San Francisco. One would think, in reading his novels, that he'd had nothing to do with it. Yet in *Travels with Charley* (1962) we read:

> When I was a child growing up in Salinas we called San Francisco "the City." Of course it was the only city we knew, but I still think of it as the City, and so does everyone else who has ever associated with it. A strange and exclusive word is "city." Besides San Francisco, only small sections of London and Rome stay in the mind as the City. New Yorkers say they are going to town. Paris has no title but Paris. Mexico City is the Capital.
>
> Once I knew the City very well, spent my attic days there, while others were being a lost generation in Paris. I fledged in San Francisco, climbed its hills, slept in its parks, worked on its docks, marched and shouted in its revolts. In a way I felt I owned the City as much as it owned me.
>
> San Francisco put on a show for me. I saw her across the bay, from the great road that bypasses Sausalito and enters the Golden Gate Bridge. The afternoon sun painted her white and gold—rising on her hills like a noble city in a happy dream. A city on hills has it over flat-land places. New York makes its own hills with craning buildings, but this gold and white acropolis rising wave on wave against the blue of the Pacific sky was a stunning thing, a painted thing like a picture of a medieval Italian city which can never have existed. I stopped in a parking place to look at her and the necklace bridge over the entrance from the sea that led to her. Over the green higher hills to the south, the evening fog rolled like herds of sheep coming to cote in the golden city. I've never seen her more lovely. When I was a child and we were going to the City, I

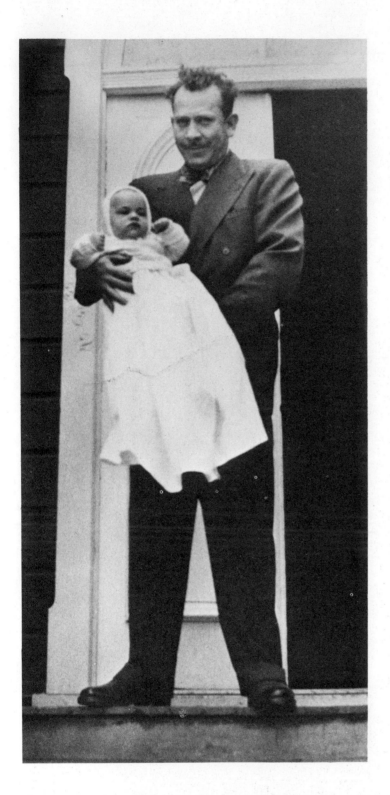

couldn't sleep for several nights before, out of bursting excitement. She leaves a mark.

$\mathcal{T}$HE BLACK CAT CAFE, 710 Montgomery Street, during World War II. Close to the old Montgomery Block, it was the most famous of bohemian hangouts in San Francisco, especially during the 1930s. A postcard advertised it as the seacoast of bohemia. Note the two doughboys in helmets at the back of the café. A sign out front proclaimed it off limits to military personnel, and the two soldiers were to keep them out. The Cat closed in 1963, and the location is now occupied by the Paule Anglim gallery, devoted to avant-garde painting and sculpture. (The fine printer, Jack Stauffacher of the Greenwood Press, had an exposition there in 1978, the first public showing of his deluxe letterpress edition of *Phaedrus*.)

Patrons of the Black Cat Cafe were depicted in an oil painting by Cornelius Sampson in 1938 (right). Among those in the painting who are still around today: Henri Lenoir, poet George Hitchcock, artist José Ramiz, and jeweler Peter Macchiarini.

$\mathcal{G}$ATHERING of resident writers in 1947 at the home of Joseph Henry Jackson, book editor of the *San Francisco Chronicle*. The photo was taken for publication in *The San Francisco Book* by Herb Caen with photographs by Max Yavno, and includes (from left to right): Wallace Stegner, William Saroyan, C. S. Forester, Joseph Henry Jackson, George Stewart, Kathryn Forbes, Oscar Lewis.

Stegner, born in Iowa in 1909, taught American literature and creative writing at Stanford University from 1945 to 1971. His best known novel is *The Big Rock Candy Mountain*, published four years before this picture was taken. He won a Pulitzer Prize in 1971.

C. S. Forester wrote the Hornblower saga, beginning with *Captain Horatio Hornblower* in 1939, *The African Queen*, and many other water-borne tales.

George Stewart was a professor at the University of California in Berkeley from 1923 to 1962 and now lives in an elegant San Francisco retirement home. Most of his writing deals with far western history. Best known: *Bret Harte* (1931), *Ordeal by Hunger* (1936), *Storm* (1941), *Fire* (1948), and *Names on the Land* (1945). He was between the storm and the fire when this picture was taken.

Kathryn Forbes, born in San Francisco in 1909, published *Mama's Bank Account* in 1943, stories of her Norwegian grandmother in San Francisco. (It was dramatized in 1944 as *I Remember Mama* and later televised.)

ℋERB CAEN, the *San Francisco Chronicle*'s Walter Winchell, at 12 Adler Place in 1948. (Twelve Adler, across the street from Henri Lenoir's Vesuvio, later became "Spec's" and inherited much of the literati trade when Lenoir retired.) The occasion of Caen's visit was a book party for Barnaby Conrad's new *Innocent Villa* (Random House). A bullfight buff, Conrad later founded El Matador, an afficionados' bar nearby on Broadway. Caen wrote of Conrad on May 26, 1948: "Barnaby is well on his way to becoming the new Saroyan." This turned out to be pure bull. (He went on to write pure bullfight stories and paint pure bullfight pictures.)

ℛOBERT FROST first saw light in San Francisco in 1874 and lived here until he was eleven. He lived in seven different houses, all east of Van Ness and north of Market Street. Frost's father, who had worked on the old *San Francisco Evening Bulletin* and the *Post*, died of tuberculosis at the age of thirty-five, and his widow took her son back East in 1885. In 1947, Frost returned to accept an honorary degree on Charter Day at the University of California. Four years after the hundredth anniversary of his birth, March 22, 1974, the City dedicated Robert Frost Plaza where California Street meets Market. A large bronze plaque was placed, with this verse on it:

> Such was life in the Golden Gate:
> Gold dusted all we drank and ate.
> And I was one of the children told
> We all must eat our peck of gold.

Aside from that, San Francisco played little part in the poetry for which Frost became famous. (The swingers here don't swing on birches.) Albert Bender in an introduction to *Continent's End: An Anthology of Contemporary California Poets*, wrote in 1925: "Robert Frost is indubitably a Native Son but it would be, of course, ridiculous to claim as Californian any part of the work of New Hampshire's most distinguished citizen." There is one poem that Bender missed. Frost called it "Once by the Pacific," and it contains some great rough lines, as prophetic as any written since Frost's death in 1963:

> It looked as if a night of dark intent
> Was coming, and not only a night, an age.
> Someone had better be prepared for rage.
> There would be more than ocean water broken
> Before God's last "Put out the light" was spoken.

The poem is not quoted on the Robert Frost monument in the City, its vision too dark and too prophetic for light-seeking San Franciscans. (The birches still are bright in his adopted New England.)

OSCAR LEWIS by San Francisco Bay in 1976. Born here in 1893, he started writing for boys' magazines about 1914 and, after a couple of years in the Ambulance Corps overseas in the first World War, wrote for *Smart Set, Atlantic, Harper's, Scribner's, New Republic*, and *Saturday Review*. In the early 1920s, he became secretary and editor of the Book Club of California, editing and writing introductions for many fine Book Club publications. He won a Book Club gold medal in 1942 for his San Francisco novel, *I Remember Christine*, which Lawrence Clark Powell in 1951 said was one of the two novels since Frank Norris that had any distinction in the West. (The other was Clarkson Crane's *The Western Shore*.) His memory of early San Francisco literary history, including some acquaintance with George Sterling and Ina Coolbrith, has been invaluable to the editors of this book.

CIRCLE MAGAZINE began publication in 1944 in Berkeley while World War II was still going on. (Some of its first contributors still bore military titles.) *Circle* lasted for ten issues, edited by George Leite, with Bern Porter in some issues. It went out of existence in 1948 but in that brief period began a new synthesis of the arts and literature on the West Coast, the center of what came to be called the Berkeley Renaissance. Various elements born of the war itself coalesced here in a new postwar sensibility. Generally, the contents of *Circle* expressed antiwar, anarchist or antiauthoritarian, civil libertarian attitudes, coupled with a new experimentation in the arts. (*Circle* was a natural predecessor to KPFA/FM radio in Berkeley, and some of its contributors later became regular participants in KPFA's programs.)

Circle had a definite international stance, looking to European avantgarde poets and painters, especially to French Surrealists in exile in New York during the war and former American expatriots.

Henry Miller (whose self-portrait from *Circle* is shown on the following page), recently arrived in California, led off the first issue. Anaïs Nin was soon to follow. (She lived briefly with Ruth Witt-Diamant on Fair Oaks Street in San Francisco during this period.) Philip Lamantia, sixteen years old, had made contact with André Breton and the Surrealists in New York in 1943 and appeared in the second issue of *Circle*. Others who gave it a true international base were Lawrence Durrell, C. F. MacIntyre (translator from German and French), Kenneth Rexroth, Greek artist Jean Varda, Wallace Fowlie, Max Jacob, W. S. Graham, Robert Duncan, Jacques Vaché, Giuseppe Ungaretti, Alex Comfort, Yvan Goll, Bezalel Schatz, experimental musician and composer Harry Partch, and French composer Darius Milhaud (then in residence at nearby Mills College). Kenneth Patchen (who did not come west until the 1950s), William Carlos Williams, Oscar Williams, and e. e. cummings were among the eastern avant-garde. There was William Everson, from a conscientious objectors camp in Waldport, Oregon. There was Douglas MacAgy, director of the California School of Fine Arts in San Francisco. There was Josephine Miles, professor and poet-in-residence at the University of California in Berkeley. There was Richard Moore, later a KPFA staffer and still later general manager of public television station KQED in San Francisco. There was Weldon Kees, Rosalie Moore, Jeanne McGahey, Lawrence Hart, Thomas Parkinson (later a senior professor at the university), Judson Crews, Gil Orlovitz, Harold Norse, Mary Fabilli (a poet then married to William Everson), Harry Roskolenko, Brewster Ghiselin, Robert Barlow, Marie Wells, George Barrows, George P. Elliott, Charles Howard, Glen Coffield, Leonard Wolf, Hamilton Tyler, Hubert Creekmore.

The last issue of *Circle* in 1948 bore the following editorial:

> *Circle* is breaking a two years' silence with this issue because no other current literary magazine is equipped to function in the new world. From Fascist Review to Coyote's Coccyx to Last Ditch, a picture with equal dimensions of reaction and confusion is presented. The old ground has been plowed so often that even the worms can hardly survive, and turn instead to more lucrative pastures and slicker covers.
>
> The Red Beast articles in *Partisan* are almost word for word like those that appeared in *Hound and Horn* during the period when Phillips and Rahv were whining at the door of the John Reed Club and barking at the intellectual reactionaries.

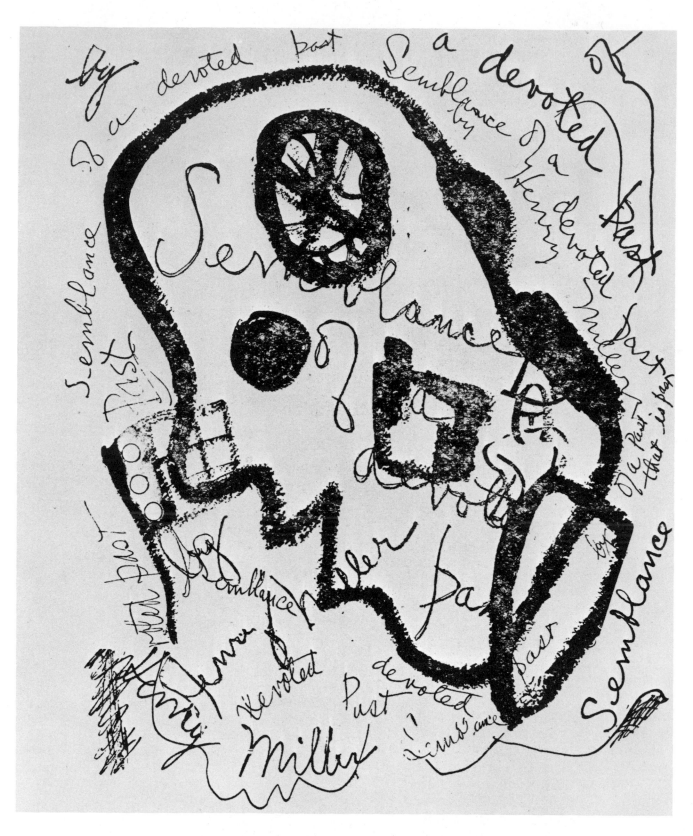

SELF-PORTRAIT BY HENRY MILLER

Tiger's Eye is blinded with last year's fashions and last century's functions. *Mainstream* unfortunately was too concerned and not discerning. And the only answer to *Now* is an equally vague and confused, how? *Horizon* is, was, and always will be the world as sensed by Cyril Connolly through a few rudimentary organs along the ventral side of the notochord (not to be confused biologically with the backbone, which develops much later). *View* went to Paris to lick its wounds. *Contour* and *Ark* are both segments of a *Circle*. Only *Circle* itself has lived through its past and continues to change, exploring the dynamic from art to zoology.

We might add, parenthetically, that in spite of the libelous mud thrown last year in *Harper's Magazine*, the Hearst press and a hundred other irresponsible sources: *Circle* is not the representative of Sex and Anarchy. If such a cult exists anywhere the most likely place would be San Simeon, where a library to go with it is already established. As for Henry Miller and "followers," Mr. and Mrs. Miller live at Big Sur with their daughter Valentine in a cabin on top of one of the steep Pacific Coast mountains. Mr. Miller is busy writing; he receives few visitors. George Leite is doing research in criminal psychology, is creatively married and is the father of two children. Kenneth Rexroth is enjoying a Guggenheim fellowship, and is not associated with *Circle*. Dr. Wilhelm Reich continues to practice psychiatry in New York. Mildred Brady, wife of a professor of economics at the University of California, is herself a serious student of sexual cults and aberrations, so has left Berkeley for England and greener pastures.

On one of the last pages of the last issue appeared an ad for a "New Writers' Group" in San Francisco:

WRITERS

There is a struggle going on for the minds of the American people. Every form of expression is subject to the attack of reaction. This attack comes in the shape of silence, persecution, and censorship: three names for fear. In the face of this fear, the writer can speak. We believe in the possibility of a culture which fights for its freedom, which protects the economic interests of its workers in all fields including the arts, and which can create for itself new forms and new voices, against reaction and the threat of war.

We are organized to strengthen independent expression and to defend writers and writing from censorship and persecution. We mean to develop new writers; to reinforce the work of writing; to broaden the relationship between writers and the public.

We will function politically; we will set up workshops and cooperate with labor organizations; we will work to open up new channels of expression; and we will act wherever necessary to give full strength to our voice as part of the progressive movement everywhere.

The future still lay to the west. On the last frontier, in San Francisco, an *Ark* had been launched. (The Bomb to End All Bombs had been dropped, and Apocalypse was tomorrow.) In 1947, the first issue of *Ark* magazine was printed on a small hand press. There was no formal connection but *Ark* (and KPFA/FM) carried on where *Circle* left off. Some of *Circle*'s writers were present, but in general *Ark*'s antiwar, antistate position was much more militant, more political, and less aesthetic than *Circle*. Its editorial for the spring 1947 issue began,

In direct opposition to the debasement of human values made flauntingly evident by the war, there is rising among writers in America, as elsewhere, a social consciousness which recognizes the integrity of the personality as the most substantial and considerable of values. . . .

Present-day society, which is becoming more and more subject to the State with its many forms of corrupt power and oppression, has become the real enemy of individual liberty. Because mutual aid and trust have been coldly, scientifically destroyed; because love, the well of being, has been methodically parched; because fear and greed have become the prime ethical movers, States and State-controlled societies continue to exist. Only the individual can cut himself free from this public evil. He can sever the forced relations between himself and the State, refuse to vote or go to war, refuse to accept the moral irresponsibility yoked onto him. Today, at this catastrophic point in time, the validity if not the future of the anarchist position is more than ever established. It has become a polished mirror in which the falsehoods of political modes stand naked. No honest person, if he has looked into this mirror, can morally support a government of any description, whether it be a State-capitalist Soviet Union, a capitalist America, a fascist Spain, or any considered society wherein an idea is woven into a blanket of law and cast over a living people from above. Any inorganic thing made authority over the organic is morally weakening and makes annihilating warfare inevitable.

Every small good a government performs is outweighed by a very real and really appalling evil. People who have had no experience in these matters tend to minimize the brutality of police, judiciary prejudice, the abuses of the polls, and the failure of the law to protect those in need of protection: on one hand those who exist in conditions of misery and neglect in State prisons, asylums and homes, and on the other the depressed groups who in their daily lives are subject to the forces of hatred and ignorance.

Therefore, we are concerned with a thorough revaluation of the relations between the individual and society. . . . We believe that social transformation must be the aim of any revolutionary viewpoint, but we recognize the organic, spontaneous revolt of individuals as presupposing

such a transformation. The vanguard of such a revolt is becoming a potent force in contemporary literature.

So were the intellectual seeds of future rebellious decades sown in the late 1940s in San Francisco.

Although the political position of those in the *Ark* (or thrashing about in the rising waters nearby) was generally one of "philosophical anarchism" (as Kenneth Rexroth defined it), they did not fit the public image of the anarchist as someone looking like Walt Whitman with a homemade bomb in his pocket or small angry men with dirty faces and dirty feet, creeps fiddling with moustaches in hopeless cellars. They were, rather, intellectuals, teachers, literate artists, and poets following in the best traditions of philosophical anarchism as espoused by Herbert Read and the Freedom Press in London. (The continuing presence of a lively group of old Italian anarchists in North Beach—ancient supporters of Sacco and Vanzetti—made that area a friendly landing place for the *Ark*. Its last issues were published there.)

A look at the contributors to *Ark*'s 1947 issue shows what a coalition was at work. Kenneth Patchen contributed an excerpt from *Sleepers Awake*: "I tell you that this is the age of anonymous man— that drear creature who will accept any guidance so long as he can submerge himself in a will stronger than his own. You are entering into that shadowed valley where the passionless submission of men shames the beasts of the steaming jungle." Others included Kenneth Rexroth (already a literary catalyst and translator of greater importance to younger generations than Ezra Pound), George Woodcock (the legendary British anarchist), Ammon Hennacy (of the militant, anarchist *Catholic Worker*), James Laughlin (publisher of New Directions Books), Lieutenant Commander Richard Eberhart (with a great antiwar poem), Robert Duncan (whose first book, *Heavenly City, Earthly City*, was just being published by Bern Porter), Paul Goodman (the New York poet, then an anarchist), Sanders Russell (an editor with Duncan of *Experimental Review* in Woodstock, New York, another anarchist center), Philip Lamantia, Thomas Parkinson, Richard Moore, Robert Stock, artist Ronald Bladen, and the great e. e. cummings.

In the face of the McCarthy Committee on Un-American Activities, this "little" magazine, printed by voluntary labor on a letterpress owned by the magazine, was the literary bridge between the 1940s of the Berkeley Renaissance and the Beat rebellion of the mid 1950s in San Francisco, as well as the very first stirring of a new ecological consciousness. By 1956 its title had been changed to *Ark II–Moby I*, edited by James Harmon and Michael McClure, the latter a new young arrival from the Midwest. Its editorial noted that the original *Ark* "was probably the first coherent expression of a new aesthetic and social freedom, which as the years have gone by is now seen to be the characteristic approach of the post War II generation." (The addition of the whale in the title—no doubt McClure's work, to judge by his later mammalian poetry—hinted at a new consciousness of *all* sentient beings. This

was linked to Buddhist conceptions of being, and from Moby Dick the line led eventually to the good ship Greenpeace and present-day ecological movements. McClure had sounded the future.)

Further bridging the 1940s and 1950s, three other radical literary little magazines sprang into strident existence: Horace Schwartz's *Goad* (1951–1953), Leslie Woolf Hedley's *Inferno*, and Richard Wirtz Emerson's *Golden Goose*, a strange rebellious bird flown in from Middle America. The final issue of *Inferno* (1956) ignored the others with this note: "This issue completes six years of active publishing by the only independent press functioning in California. In these years we have found ourselves censored, libeled & threatened by mccarthyite fascists. . . ." Thus these brave birds shook their burning wings and raised their voices defiantly upon the stage of the McCarthy era, and were gone.

Ark–Moby outlasted them, and in its 1956–1957 issues it was evident that the new Beat writers had joined forces with the East Coast's Black Mountain school of poets (Charles Olson, Robert Creeley, Louis Zukofsky, Cid Corman and his *Origin*) plus writers from southern California (Lawrence Lipton and "Venice West" flipsters and hipsters) to form a broad new national poetry front.

*T*HE LATE SAN FRANCISCO photographer Imogen Cunningham did quite a few literary portraits, including Muriel Rukeyser, Theodore Roethke, Upton Sinclair, Gertrude Stein, Sherwood Anderson, Jules Romains, William Rose Benét, Kenneth Rexroth, Marianne Moore, James Stephens, and Mark Schorer.

Poet Rukeyser (who died in February 1980) was photographed in San Francisco in the mid 1940s. She had first come to the City in 1937 for the opening of the Golden Gate Bridge. After unhappily working for the Office of War Information in Washington during World War II, she asked Josephine Miles at the university in Berkeley to recommend her for a teaching job. Miles demurred: "It is like a sailor wanting to have a farm." (Quite right. Rukeyser belonged with the crew of the *Ark*.) In 1945 she came to teach poetry at the California Labor School in San Francisco. And in the City her friends included Robert Duncan, Eric Berne, Ella Winter (Steffens), Donnan Jeffers

(son of Robinson Jeffers), Charles Olson, and Kenneth Rexroth. Besides going to soirées at Rexroth's, she also gave poetry readings sponsored by Pierre Salinger's mother. And during this period she wrote much of her *Life of Poetry, Orpheus*, and *The Green Wave*, as well as doing translations of Octavio Paz whom she met in Berkeley in 1944. When she died, the *New York Times* said her poetry "rang with strong protests against inhumanity wherever she saw it. . . . A lyric, feminist poet, Miss Rukeyser was socially and politically committed as few other American poets." In her own words, she was "Not Sappho, Sacco."

Northwest poet Roethke was caught by Cunningham when he was here for a reading at the San Francisco Museum of Art in 1959. There was a full house, but the poet had trouble with the microphone, treating it as if it had only recently been invented, or like a drunken stranger who was in the way. As a result, much of what he had to say was lost to the audience. In the Cunningham photo, the hand may be directing him out of town.

$\mathcal{K}$ PFA/FM (Pacifica Foundation, Berkeley.) In the early 1950s when television had yet to take over the mass consciousness of America, this small, listener-sponsored radio station, located on the fringes of the University of California, became an intellectual center perhaps of more temporary influence than the university itself. It earned a special place in the minds and hearts of Bay Area writers, artists, intellectuals and activists with regular programs by some of the most acute minds of their generation, including Alan Watts (philosophy East and West), Philip Elwood (jazz), Ralph Gleason (jazz), Kenneth Rexroth (book reviews on all subjects), Elsa Knight Thompson (public affairs), William Mandel (USSR), Pauline Kael (film), Jaime de Angulo (*Indian Tales*).

Dylan Thomas recorded special programs twice when he was in Berkeley; and other participants from elsewhere included Robert Frost, William Carlos Williams, Richard Eberhart, Robert Lowell, Marianne Moore, Theodore Roethke. Practically every important writer in the Bay Area appeared on

KPFA sooner or later. Visiting musicians and composers included many jazz greats as well as Darius Milhaud, Roger Sessions, and Virgil Thompson.

KPFA made its microphones available to myriad viewpoints, with a strong emphasis on pacifism. Founded by Lewis Hill (above, left) and other conscientious objectors and civil libertarians after World War II, the station was left-liberal, anti-war, humanist, philosophical, individualistic, and, in the tradition of Thoreau, anarchist rather than Communist. Despite this, and because of this, the station was often embroiled in censorship battles with the FCC and the Un-American Activities Committee.

This studio photo shows a group in the mid 1950s discussing censorship in the arts and literature. At far left is William Hogan, just beginning his many years as book editor of the *San Francisco Chronicle*. In the center is Ruth Witt-Diamant, founder of the San Francisco (State College) Poetry Center. On the far right is Alan Temko, architectural critic for the *Chronicle*.

*J*AIME DE ANGULO in Berkeley shortly before his death in 1950. Born of Spanish parents in Paris in 1887, he arrived in San Francisco just in time for the earthquake and fire in April 1906. Later he went back East and became an M.D. at Johns Hopkins University, then returned to California, where he worked on ranches, especially at Alturas. Here he came to know the Achumawi Indian ranch hands and eventually became known for his pioneering studies in their language. In the 1920s he settled in Berkeley, encouraged in his anthropological work by Alfred Kroeber and especially by George Boas at the University of California. David L. Olmsted, in his *Achumawi Dictionary*, wrote of Angulo:

During this time, he first became acquainted with Mabel Dodge Luhan and her entourage, while they were spending a brief period at Mill Valley, California. Angulo went originally to interview Tony Luhan, presumably on ethnographic and linguistic topics, and stayed to give a kind of Jungian psychotherapy to one of Mabel's young associates. This led to an invitation to Taos and also, to his first difference with D. H. Lawrence, to whom Mabel Dodge Luhan had written of Jaime. Lawrence, who himself wrote one of the most idiotic psychological tracts of all time (Fantasia of the Unconscious) was already jealous at long distance of Angulo, who had an M.D. and practical experience and had studied the subject at Ann Arbor and Zurich.

Later, in Taos, Angulo did his best to appease Lawrence, but the latter, who was to write so much nonsense about Indians, patronized the two men—Angulo and Luhan—from whom he could have learned about Indians. One objection to them, in the mind of the social-climbing, racist Lawrence, was that neither was Anglo-Saxon; in his scorn for "darkies" and democracy, he ruled them out of the "natural aristocracy" which, in his view, seemed to be composed largely of Anglo-Saxons who were rich and well-born. The other objection was that both were men. Lawrence, who basked in the idolatry of women, feared other men, particularly if they interrupted his monologues. Lawrence ridiculed Angulo's attempts to write fiction, and eventually drove him off.

Angulo, having homesteaded a ranch on the top of Partington Ridge, Big Sur, came to know Henry Miller when the latter moved there after World War II. Miller, in *A Devil in Paradise*, described him: "As usual, Jaime wore a bright headband around his forehead—his dirty snotrag probably. Brown as a walnut, gaunt, slightly bowlegged, he was still handsome, still very much the Spaniard—and still utterly unpredictable. With a feather in his headband, a little grease paint, a different costume, he might have passed for a Chippewa or a Shawnee Indian. He was definitely the outlaw." (Rather than the "devil" Moricand, Jaime and Miller's faithful friend Emil White, to whom the book is dedicated, are in a way the real heroes of it.)

In the late 1940s, Angulo recorded a series of programs on folktales of the American Indians for KPFA/FM, Berkeley, and they are still rebroadcast. His *Indian Tales* were published in 1953 by Hill & Wang. He also translated Lorca and had some contact with American poets, notably Jack Spicer and Robert Duncan. The latter lived with the Angulos in Berkeley during the last year of Jaime's life and typed his stories and texts on linguistics. Ezra Pound called Angulo the American Ovid.

*C*ROWD LISTENING TO MUSSOLINI BROADCAST, January 1, 1931, in front of Cavalli & Company, the Italian bookstore on the site of what is today the Vesuvio bar.

A. CAVALLI & COMPANY, the Italian bookstore, in 1915 was located on the present site of City Lights Bookstore, 261 Columbus Avenue (at Broadway). Cavalli's later moved across Adler Alley to 255 Columbus Avenue (above). It is now located at 1441 Stockton Street (at Columbus). Founded by Angelino Cavalli's father, Georgio, in 1880, it is presently owned by John Valentini.

THE ORIGINAL CITY LIGHTS
BOOKSHOP, 261 Columbus Avenue,
in the 1950s. (Vesuvio Café is off picture at
left. At far right is the Fratelli Forte
travel agency, advertising "Viaggi &
Excurzioni." In 1977, the Forte brothers
graciously moved to smaller quarters
next door, allowing City Lights to expand
in time for its twenty-fifth anniversary.)

City Lights was founded in June 1953
by Peter D. Martin and Lawrence
Ferlinghetti, the former an English
instructor at San Francisco State College.
It was Martin's brilliant idea to open the
first all-paperback bookstore in the
United States and thus pay the rent for
the second-floor editorial offices of his
magazine, *City Lights,* an early pop-
culture little magazine. *City Lights*
featured the first film criticism by Pauline
Kael plus pieces by Grover Sales and
others with titles like "The Sociological
Significance of Moon Mullins" and poems
by Robert Duncan, Philip Lamantia, and
Jack Spicer.

Martin, who now runs the New Yorker
Bookstore in Manhattan, is the son of
Carlo Tresca, Italian anarchist who was
assassinated in 1943. (City Lights itself
is generally in an anarchist, civil libertarian, antiauthoritarian tradition. Martin
named his magazine and the bookstore
after the film by Chaplin, whose Little
Man has always been a symbol of the
subjective man against the world. Some
of the bookstore's first customers were old
Italian anarchists in derbies buying
L'Adunata and *L'Humanità Nova.* One
was on the local garbage truck and
would run in to buy his anarchist paper
as the truck passed.)

Within a year of the bookstore's opening, Martin departed for New York, and
Shigeyoshi Murao became manager and
eventually co-owner with Ferlinghetti. In
the tradition of great literary bookstores

on the East Coast and especially in
Europe, City Lights began publishing its
own books in 1955 and now has about a
hundred books in print, none federally
financed by grants from the National
Endowment of the Arts. (Its editors, in
the Anarchist/Surrealist tradition, like
it that way.)

Shown in the photograph (from left
to right): Joanne Shedlov Joseph, Richard and Robert McBride (early City
Lights staff), Selden Kirby-Smith
Ferlinghetti, and Victor Wong (later a
KQED photographer and "Newsroom"
staffer). At the second-floor window are
Ferlinghetti and Shigeyoshi Murao. The
dog in front was listed annually in
Bowker's *Literary Market Place* as "Homer
Ferlinghetti, Publicity & Public Relations." He received mail regularly, although he expressed himself a bit too
candidly to be a success in that field. He
peed on a policeman's leg and was
immortalized for it in a poem.

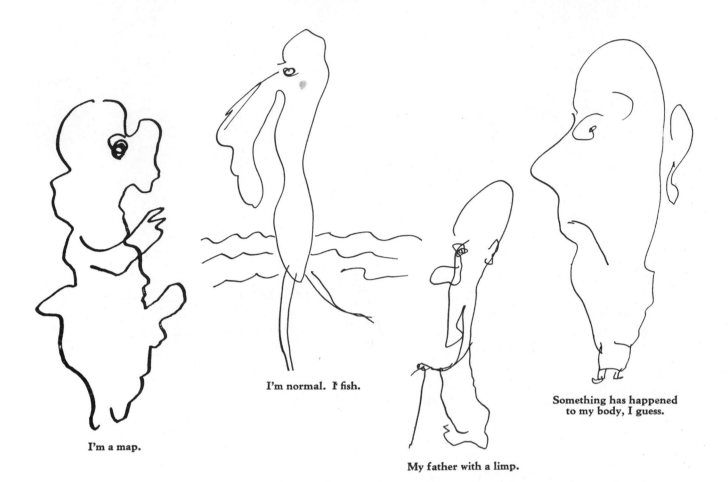

I'm a map.

I'm normal. I fish.

My father with a limp.

Something has happened
to my body, I guess.

"SIDE VIEW OF A POET" was the way *Counterpoint* magazine introduced these drawings by Dylan Thomas in its June 1952 issue. Here is its story of the drawings. (It was prescient. Dylan Thomas died the next year.)

When Dylan Thomas came to San Francisco this April it was his second visit to the United States. In New York he said he liked to think of poetry "as statements made on the way to the grave." And he proceeded about the country making these statements to museums and university audiences. The poetry he read at the San Francisco Museum of Art constituted, on the whole, one long meditation on

dying: a poem by W. H. Auden, a scene from Webster's *Duchess of Malfi*, "Death's Messenger" by Thomas Lovell Beddoes, Beddoes' suicide note, the last lines of Marlowe's *Faustus*, Yeats' "The Second Coming," his own "Ceremony After a Fire Raid" and his poem beginning

Do not go gentle into that good night,
Old age should burn and rave at close
   of day;
Rage, rage against the dying of the light.

Yet, in San Francisco two years before, Thomas had made other "statements" (a series of line-drawings tossed off in a bar one night while in the company of the painter Knute Stiles) which might well have

164

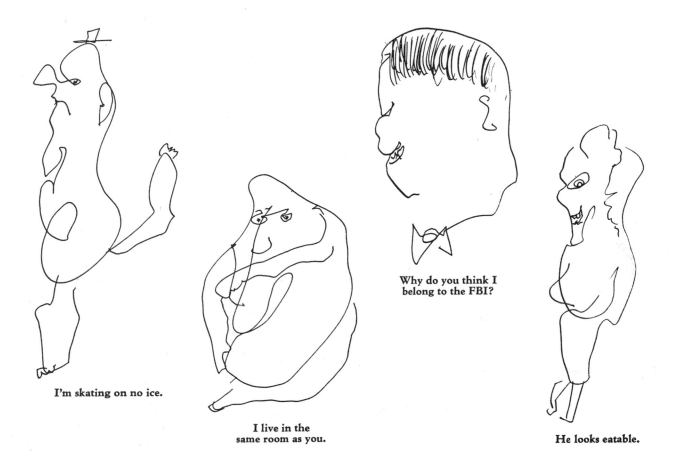

I'm skating on no ice.

**I live in the
same room as you.**

**Why do you think I
belong to the FBI?**

He looks eatable.

prepared his recent auditors for another,
different side of Thomas. The poet's asides,
between poems, to the gentry assembled to
hear him at the Museum partook of the
same salt as the drawings. We won't here
go into the Freudian relationship of his
drawing to his poetry, the relation of
several kinds of birds he drew to the
ubiquitous water-birds in his poetry, nor
into his aversion to tea-ladies. On the whole,
his remarks at the Museum were more
ascetic than acetic, and his reading voice
was strange and wild. Nevertheless, by the
end of his performance the audience (as
he paused to note) was "beautifully depleted."
And as he disappeared for the evening
behind the potted palms, one might have
parodied part of a T. S. Eliot poem to cover
the situation:

When Dylan Thomas visited the United
   States
His laughter hardly tinkled among
   the teacups.
I thought of Fragilion, that shy figure
   among the birch-trees,
And of Priapus in the shrubbery
Gaping at the ladies in the hall.
In the foyer of the Museum, at Professor
   Witt-Diamant's
I looked for the head of Mr. Thomas
   rolling under a chair
Or grinning over a screen
With seaweed in its hair . . .

$\mathcal{D}$YLAN THOMAS IN SAN FRANCISCO. The critic who described the Welsh poet in San Francisco's *Counterpoint* in 1952 also published a review of Thomas's *In Country Sleep* in the *San Francisco Chronicle* that began, "There is nothing like Dylan Thomas in poetry today. There is a wholeness, a harmony, a radiance about everything he has written which sets him apart." (The critic was one Lawrence Ferling.) Thomas's second tour of the United States in 1952 included a meeting with Henry Miller in Big Sur and with Alan Curnow, a writer from Christchurch, New Zealand, with whom Thomas felt some kinship. Here they are in San Francisco, possibly near the home of Ruth Witt-Diamant, with whom Thomas (left) was staying. It was Witt-Diamant who originally persuaded Thomas to come to the West Coast and read poetry. He gave big public readings twice, and he broadcast on KPFA. His voice had a singular beauty and richness, in the great Welsh oral tradition; and the excitement he generated was an early inspiration for a tradition of oral poetry here, the subsequent San Francisco poetry movement (from the mid 1950s to the present) being consistently centered on the performance of poetry in public.

Writing to his wife, Caitlin, after a brief detour to Canada on his first tour, Thomas said, "And thank God to be out of British Canada & back in the terrible United States." He described Los Angeles and Hollywood as "the nightmare zenith of my mad, lonely tour." (But he met Chaplin there, and a friend described the two of them in Chaplin's marble mansion: "They were roughly the same size, and both possessed this extremely fluid, rag-doll-like, quick motion, striding about the enormous drawing-room together, talking and chattering.") "But oh, San Francisco!" Thomas continued in his letter to Caitlin, "It is and has everything. . . . In Canada, five hours away by plane, you wouldn't think that such a place as San Francisco could exist. The wonderful sunlight there, the hills, the great bridges, the Pacific at your shoes. Beautiful Chinatown. Every race in the world."

$\mathcal{C}$ ERTAINLY THE MOST INTERNATIONAL
literary soirée in San Francisco in
the 1950s and early 1960s was that held
almost weekly at Kenneth Rexroth's
large second-floor flat at 250 Scott Street
above Jack's Record Cellar on the edge
of the mostly black Fillmore district. The
halls of the flat were lined to the ceiling
with apple boxes containing one of the
finest collections of literature (Western
and oriental, classical and modern, in
several languages), much of it review
copies in many fields (poetry, geology,
astronomy, art, sociology, philosophy,
political history, and radical thought in
general)—the vintage harvest of many
years of literary criticism for KPFA/FM,
the *Nation, Saturday Review*, and the
New York Times, among others.

Writers from many countries plus
migrant East Coast and Northwest poets
found their way to Rexroth's where they
encountered many of the resident San

Francisco radical community, the heart of
which was made up of World War II
conscientious objectors and poets active
in the Berkeley Renaissance of the late
1940s and published there, especially in
Circle magazine. A photograph taken on
February 5, 1957, shows (from left to
right) Ida Hodes, Eva Triem, an unidentified woman, Jack Spicer, James Broughton,
Philip Lamantia, Ariel Parkinson, Brother
Antoninus (William Everson), and Rexroth, reading.

In 1957, Rexroth wrote, "William Everson is probably the most profoundly
moving and durable of the poets of the
San Francisco Renaissance. . . . During
the War he was in a conscientious objec-
tor's camp in Oregon, where he was instrumental in setting off an off-time Arts
Program out of which have come many
still active people, projects and forces

167

which help give San Francisco culture its intensely libertarian character." Years later he expanded this view:

During the War there were a large number of concentration camps for conscientious objectors scattered through the mountains and forests of the West Coast. On their leaves these young men came to San Francisco, where they encountered the libertarian, pacifist group of intellectuals of the community. At Waldport, Oregon, . . . there was eventually established a conscientious objectors' camp of creative artists of all kinds who had been nothing but insoluble problems to the administration. After the War, possibly a majority of these people settled in the San Francisco Bay Area. Out of them came a radio station (KPFA), three or four theatres, several publishing enterprises, and a number of well-known musicians, painters and sculptors.

Taken perhaps a year earlier, this photo shows (from left to right) Kenneth Rexroth, an unidentified man (above Rexroth), L. Ferlinghetti (in back, on window seat), Dr. Leland Rather, two unidentified men (half hidden), a visiting Korean woman poet, Marthe Rexroth (standing in back) and Ruth Witt-Diamont (seated, with glasses).

THE ILLITERATI

PROPOSES:
CREATION, EXPERIMENT, AND REVOLUTION
TO BUILD A WARLESS, FREE SOCIETY;

SUSPECTS: TRADITION AS A STANDARD
AND ECLECTICISM AS A TECHNIQUE;
REJECTS: WAR
AND ANY OTHER FORM OF COERCION
BY PHYSICAL VIOLENCE
IN HUMAN ASSOCIATIONS.

NUMBER **4** SUMMER 1945

ILLITERATI #4 (SUMMER 1945) was the last issue of this militant resistance magazine printed at the C.O. camp in Waldport, Oregon. Its fine arts group also printed Martin Ponch's pacifist *Compass* and published antiwar books under the imprint of the Untide Press. Its first book was William Everson's *X War Elegies*, and its last was Kenneth Patchen's *An Astonished Eye Looks Out of the Air.* (One of the apprentice printers was Adrian Wilson who today has his fine press in Tuscany Alley, San Francisco.) In an interview in 1977, Everson recalled: "That whole San Francisco Renaissance had in some way a powerful inception in Waldport. First, the Interplayers, which was one of the leading theater groups in San Francisco in the postwar period, began at Waldport. And the rest of us who were writers there gravitated down to where Rexroth was pulling it together." Today San Francisco remains very much a literary center for conscientious objection to militarism in all its forms, as ever an island in a gun-toting country. Typical of the senti-

ments of many San Francisco writers is the following quote from Herman Melville which appeared here in the 1960s in a poster:

"There is something in the contemplation of the mode in which America has been settled, that, in a noble breast, should forever extinguish the prejudices of national dislikes. . . . Settled by the people of all nations, all nations may claim her for their own. You cannot spill a drop of American blood without spilling the blood of the whole world."

In the 1960s, the glossy New Left journal, *Ramparts*, was the most effective spokesman for the antiwar forces. *The New York Times* of July 18, 1968, reported:

FOUR RAMPARTS EDITORS FACING DRAFT CARD BURNING PROSECUTION

The Government is considering the prosecution of four top editors of *Ramparts* magazine for alleged violations of the Selective Service laws.

The editors were taken before a special Federal grand jury in New York last month to testify about the magazine's cover of December 1967, which depicted flaming draft cards bearing the names of four men. They were informed by the Government attorney that they were the "targets" of the investigation.

The four editors, who flew in from San Francisco on June 17 in response to the subpoenas, are Warren Hinckle III, president and editorial director; Robert Scheer, editor in chief; Dugald Stermer, art director, and Sol Stern, senior editor. . . .

Mr. Hinckle denounced the investigation as "harassment, pure and simple," and said it posed an "ominous threat to freedom of the press."

"An indictment of the *Ramparts* editors," the 29-year-old president said in an interview yesterday, "must be interpreted as a direct and unmistakable attempt to close down the leading organ of dissent in the American press."

*W*ILLIAM EVERSON, poet and fine
printer, during the period (1951–
1969) he was Brother Antoninus, a lay
brother in the Dominican order. This
picture was taken as he worked in the
bookbindery at the Dominican monastery
on Chabot Road, Oakland, in 1958. Born
in 1912, of Norwegian descent, he discovered Robinson Jeffers's pantheistic
poetry at Fresno State College and began
writing poems much influenced by

Jeffers's feeling for doom and death in a
brooding landscape, to which he later
added intense Christian exaltation
coupled with anguished sexual passion.
In 1969, he left his formal religious
order and married a young woman, Susanna
Rickson, who had originally come to him
for spiritual counseling. They moved
down the coast to the Swanton area
near Davenport, California, not far
away from the University of California
at Santa Cruz where he began teaching
poetry and printing.

*T*HE SAN FRANCISCO (STATE COLLEGE) Poetry Center was founded by Ruth Witt-Diamant in 1954 and dedicated by W. H. Auden, who gave his now-famous lecture on "The Hero in Modern Literature." The photo shows the bulletin board at the Center in about 1957. As director of the Center, Ruth Witt-Diamant, a native of Philadelphia, was instrumental in attracting most of the important contemporary American poets of the period, as well as some foreign ones, rising above the provincialism of the local poetry scene.

A break with that provincialism had indeed begun with the Berkeley Renaissance (and its *Circle* magazine) of the late 1940s. By the 1950s, writers from the East Coast and Middle America were beginning to arrive in considerable numbers, and San Francisco was ripe with a wider cultural ferment.

remember distinctly my first impression of him when we met in New York: it was of a powerful, sensitive being who moved on velvet pads. A sort of sincere assassin, I thought to myself, as we shook hands."

In 1952, Lawrence Ferling in *Counterpoint* reported on a poetry reading by Patchen at the San Francisco Museum of Art, sponsored by the Poetry Center, on November 13 of that year:

> He stood there for a long time, reading his poetry, his voice like the hush of concrete, his only gestures the words themselves. When he stopped reading it was 29 minutes to 11. The 163 people of San Francisco (who had preferred Patchen to mousetraps that cold night) clapped. He read two or three more poems. Then he edged out of the room, looking at the people, not smiling. Outside, Patchen stood still in the dim hallway, against a wall. He had a cigarette. He had a cane. He stood very quietly, very ungiantlike, in the hush of concrete, with his cigarette, with his cane, like a blind man waiting for something.

> But he saw everything.

Kenneth Patchen died in Palo Alto in 1972, and a Patchen memorial reading was held at the City Lights Poets Theater on Mason Street in the City, organized by poet and novelist Al Young. The overflow crowd listened to over twenty poets give their reactions, and they were long and loud. Some were eloquent, some labored, some lovely, others bathetic. In life, Patchen had inspired both love and hate but, whichever it was, one still respected his genius. Like Patchen's readers in general, the audience was very partisan, interjecting loud cries of approval or protest. (After one particularly harrowing poem, novelist Jerry Kamstra shouted, "Patchen would'a puked if he'd heard that!") Like a wake, it could have gone on all night. . . . Thus passed from the scene one of the most controversial (and uncompromising) giants of modern American poetry.

KENNETH PATCHEN in North Beach in the spring of 1955, on the roof of his Green Street apartment where he lived with his wife, Miriam Oikemus. Patchen is an example of the writer so much associated with the East Coast or Europe (in his case, Greenwich Village, New York) that it is forgotten he lived in the West a long time. Patchen lived and worked in the Bay Area the last twenty years of his life. In the 1940s, Henry Miller published a pamphlet about him called "Man of Anger and Light" in which he called Patchen "a sick giant consumed by the poisonous indifference of a world which has more use for mousetraps than for poets. . . . The first thing one would remark on meeting Kenneth Patchen is that he is the living symbol of protest. I

A "POETS' SEMINAR" sponsored by the Poetry Center in the mid 1950s, Robert Creeley reading. Typical of the small, intimate affairs held mostly in poets' houses, these evenings became less common as the excitement of big public poetry events took over. Listeners this evening included Helen Adam (at left) and Robert Duncan.

WHEN POETRY WENT PUBLIC in the City: Listening to poetry and jazz at The Cellar on Green Street in 1957. The contrast with the "Poets' Seminar" is striking. (Left to right down front): Michael McClure, Lenore Kandel (whose *Love Book* was seized by the police for alleged sexual obscenity a few years later), William Fritsch, Shigeyoshi Murao (later editor of *Shig's Review*) and Robert Briggs (later a literary agent).

Whereas Kenneth Patchen later performed poetry and jazz at the Black Hawk with formally scored music, sessions at The Cellar were done to loose "head" arrangements, mostly improvised, generally funky, slightly "stoned." This semi-spontaneous, semi-wild music (especially in numbers like Rexroth's "Thou Shalt Not Kill") was one source of the Rock sound of the 1960s. The "beat" was in the beatitude, and the beatitude was in the beat.

WHAT THEY WERE LISTENING TO in the preceding picture: Kenneth Rexroth performing with jazz at The Cellar. He is reading his ode on the death of Dylan Thomas, "Thou Shalt Not Kill," a powerful vituperative put-down of the Man in the Grey Flannel Suit as the slick personification of mammon and soulless modern civilization which Rexroth saw killing the poet everywhere:

> "You killed him, you son of a bitch,
> In your Brooks Brothers Suit. . . ."

No greater nor more ferocious castigation of modern society exists anywhere in contemporary literature. (On a smaller scale than Allen Ginsberg's "Howl," it was its direct forebear.)

Rexroth was a father figure for the Beats (even though he did not have reciprocal feelings). Many of his attitudes and interests were theirs, especially "disengagement" from materialist-militarist society, together with a turning to the

ISSUED AS A PUBLIC SERVICE BY THE CELLAR. 576 GREEN. YUKON 6-5812

Far East's literature and "Buddha consciousness." These elements, together with the Beats' early interest in ecology and in psychedelics as a means of liberation, became basic themes of the counterculture in the 1960s. It was not for nothing that the Beatles spelled their name with a Beat.

_T_HE POETS' FOLLIES. It was not until the mid 1950s that the new San Francisco poetry movement really came together. Partly as a result of that ferment of westward-migrating creative people after World War II and partly a continuance of the Berkeley Renaissance of the late 1940s, the new San Francisco excitement was caused not only by New York carpetbaggers like Allen Ginsberg, Gregory Corso, Peter Orlovsky, and Jack Kerouac but also by writers and musicians who had been here considerably longer. Emphasis on public performance of poetry was not restricted to the invading East Coast poets, although Allen Ginsberg's first public reading of "Howl" at the Six Gallery (on October 13, 1955) turned up the volume and became notorious as the real kick-off of the movement.

The first Poets' Follies was held in 1955, and the performers were generally the more indigenous people who, with one or two notable exceptions, had little to do with the Easterners. In this old snapshot we see a rehearsal for the first Follies on January 22, 1955 (left to right): the fine printer Adrian Wilson (on clarinet, partially hidden), Dick Martin (guitar), Carol Leigh (washboard vocals), and Weldon Kees (piano, wearing derby).

176

The second picture, taken on opening night the same year, shows (left to right): Michael Grieg, then a young anarchist poet, now an editor of the *San Francisco Chronicle*; Weldon Kees, who disappeared on July 20, 1955, leaving his car at the Golden Gate Bridge; Lily Ayres, who worked as a stripper in the El Rey Burlesque in Oakland, to pay for her husband's anatomy classes in medical school. (In the Follies, she read "Sarah Stripteasedale.")

The last Poets' Follies was held May 11, 1958, at Fugazi Hall in North Beach and was billed as a "bohemian revel" and as "another session of S.F.'s unique Institution of Lower Learning." "Beat Music" was on the bill—whatever that was—a variation of the poetry-and-jazz which,

starting in The Cellar on Green Street, became popular in various spots like the Coffee Gallery on Upper Grant Avenue. The original group at The Cellar (recorded on a Fantasy LP) included Bruce Lippincott on sax, Sonny Wayne on drums, Bill Weisjahns on piano. (One of the stellar performers in the Follies not pictured here was Vincent McHugh, a novelist and poet whose *I Am Thinking of My Darling* was a best-seller in the 1940s. Weldon Kees was also an abstract painter and was considered to be one of the most interesting and complex poets in town at the time. The story of his sudden disappearance is told in Robert Stock's "Disappearing Act.")

*N*EAL CASSADY (LEFT) AND JACK KEROUAC in the City in 1952. Kerouac portrayed Cassady as Dean Moriarty in *On The Road* and as Cody Pomeray in *The Dharma Bums, Desolation Angels*, and *Book of Dreams*—a prototype for a certain kind of great western hero lost among machines, racing his hotrod rather than his horse (not John Wayne but Paul Newman—Cassady, in fact, looked and moved like a young Newman in *The Hustler*). Cassady was a great nonstop talker, and he rapped as he ran. It was only when he sat down silent to write it all out in his autobiography, *The First Third*, that he became a bit tongue-tied, almost at times pedestrian. He was too fast with his tongue, too fast on his feet or on his wheels to sit still for long behind an old upright. He never stopped running and died in Mexico in 1968, four days short of his forty-fourth birthday, along a railroad track at San Miguel de Allende. In *The Electric Kool-Aid Acid Test*, Tom Wolfe wrote of Cassady's death: "Some local Americans said he had been going at top speed for two weeks and had headed off down the railroad tracks one night and his heart just gave out." Others said he "had made the mistake of drinking alcohol on top of barbiturates."

Sometime in the 1960s, Jack Kerouac had dropped out of Neal Cassady's speeding sights, and Cassady had gone on to drive Ken Kesey's Merry Prankster bus with its destination-sign reading FURTHER. (The whole story is tellingly retailed in Wolfe's *Electric Kool-Aid Acid Test*.) Kesey himself flew through San Francisco many times and roosted often in nearby retreats like Woodside but was never really a part of the San Francisco literary scene (not that he wanted to be). Kesey's novel, *One Flew Over the Cuckoo's Nest* (1962), dramatized what R. D. Laing was to say in psychology several years later (in *The Politics of Experience*): it was not the patient but the society that was sick and suffering a breakdown. (This view may be partially responsible for the simultaneous popularity of astrology—wherein one could believe that the fault was not in ourselves but in our stars.)

*C*AROLYN AND NEAL CASSADY in San Francisco, 1947, a few weeks before they were married. Carolyn Cassady years later wrote an account of her life with and without Neal and Jack. It was published as *Heart Beat* in 1976, and was schlepped into a Hollywood movie two years later, much to the mystification of those who had known the originals in real life. This is typical of movies made from books based on real people: the films become a kind of spurious documentary (or "pop doc").

ALLEN GINSBERG in San Francisco in 1956, pointing to the "Moloch Face of Sir Francis Drake" hotel on the corner of Powell and Sutter Streets. The vision is recorded in his *Howl and Other Poems* published by City Lights Books that year, a few months after Ginsberg's first public reading of it at the Six Gallery. (Copying Emerson's message to Whitman a century earlier, publisher Ferlinghetti had sent Ginsberg a wire the night of the reading:

"I greet you at the beginning of a great career.")

Printed in England for City Lights by Villiers Publications, Ltd., a second printing of it was seized by U.S. Customs in San Francisco on March 25, 1957, along with an issue of *Miscellaneous Man*, a little magazine edited by William Margolis. (The charges against the latter were dropped.) One newspaper reported, "Cops Don't Allow No Renaissance Here." The charge was obscenity. City

Lights defended itself in the *San Francisco Chronicle*: "It is not the poet but what he observes which is revealed as obscene. The great obscene wastes of *Howl* are the sad wastes of the mechanized world, lost among atom bombs and insane nationalisms. . . . Ginsberg chooses to walk on the wild side of this world, along with Nelson Algren, Henry Miller, Kenneth Rexroth, Kenneth Patchen, not to mention some great American dead, mostly in the tradition of philosophical anarchism." It was not exactly the tradition Ginsberg had in mind—citing William Blake and Walt Whitman would have been closer—but the American Civil Liberties Union was persuaded the book was not obscene, and the U.S. district attorney in San Francisco refused to institute condemnation proceedings. Customs released the printing.

The juvenile department of the local police then arrested publisher Lawrence Ferlinghetti and City Lights Bookstore manager Shigeyoshi Murao for selling obscene literature. The ACLU posted bail; and in a long court trial in the summer of 1957, the accused were defended free of charge by formidable legal talent: Jake ("Never Plead Guilty") Ehrlich, Lawrence Speiser, and Albert Bendich (counsels for the ACLU). The critical literary support for *Howl* was impressive. Poets, editors, critics, and university professors testified at the trial, including *Chronicle* book editor William Hogan, poet Robert Duncan, Ruth Witt-Diamant of the San Francisco Poetry Center, Professors Thomas Parkinson, Leo Lowenthal, and Mark Schorer of the University of California, James Laughlin of New Directions Books, novelist Eugene Burdick, Barney Rosset and Donald M. Allen of the Grove Press. Judge Clayton Horn ruled the book not obscene and set down the rule that if the material has *the slightest redeeming social importance,*

it is not obscene because it is protected by the First and Fourteenth Amendments of the United States Constitution and the California Constitution.

This established the legal precedent that in the next decade allowed Grove Press to proceed with the publication of D. H. Lawrence's *Lady Chatterley's Lover* and Henry Miller's *Tropic of Cancer,* books that had long been kept from U.S. readers. Censorship battles were to continue (including two other City Lights cases in the 1960s for the sale of Lenore Kandel's *Love Book* and for *Zap Comics*). But the floodgates were opened, and books like William S. Burroughs's *Naked Lunch* poured through. (Early chapters of the latter caused student editors of *The Chicago Review* to resign because the university would not allow publication. They published the work in *Big Table*, which, under the editorship of Paul Carroll in the 1960s, became a principal outlet for beat writing that couldn't get published anywhere else.)

Also in San Francisco were stand-up tragedians Lenny Bruce and Lord Buckley who were fighting their own censorship battles in the nightclubs. City Lights published Buckley's *Hiparama of the Classics* and distributed Bruce's *Stamp Help Out.*

On September 9, 1957, *Life* reported "Big Day for Bards at Bay: Trial over *Howl and Other Poems*." National publicity for Ginsberg in particular, and the continuing San Francisco poetry movement in general, kept up through most of the 1960s and 1970s. (The very first national notice was in a *New York Times Book Review* article on September 2, 1956, entitled "Richard Eberhart Discusses Group of Young Poets on West Coast.")

Ginsberg himself was not arrested or charged in the *Howl* trial. He was, in fact, in Tangier at the time.

Today, the Bank of America's new world headquarters looms symbolically in the sky near the place where "Howl" was tried, with its apocalyptic lines:

What sphinx of cement and aluminum bashed
    open their skulls and ate up their
    brains and imagination?
Moloch! Solitude! Filth! Ugliness! Ashcans
    and unobtainable dollars! Children
    screaming under the stairways! Boys
    sobbing in armies! Old men weeping
    in the parks!
Moloch! Moloch! Nightmare of Moloch!
    Moloch the loveless! Mental Moloch!
    Moloch the heavy judger of men!
Moloch the incomprehensible prison! Moloch
    the crossbone soulless jailhouse and
    Congress of sorrows! Moloch whose
    buildings are judgement! Moloch the
    vast stone of war! Moloch the
    stunned governments!
Moloch whose mind is pure machinery!
    Moloch whose blood is running money!
    Moloch whose fingers are ten armies!

Moloch whose breast is a cannibal
    dynamo! Moloch whose ear is a smok-
    ing tomb!
Moloch whose eyes are a thousand blind
    windows! Moloch whose skyscrapers
    stand in the long streets like endless
    Jehovahs! Moloch whose factories
    dream and croak in the fog! Moloch
    whose smokestacks and antennae
    crown the cities!
Moloch whose love is endless oil and stone!
    Moloch whose soul is electricity and
    banks!

This photograph is of the courtroom scene during the *Howl* trial in 1957 in the old Hall of Justice on Portsmouth Square. The defendants are seated in swivel chairs, Shigeyoshi Murao (who sold the book to police) with finger to lips (front, center). The court was crowded with local writers, critics, professors, and lawyers. In the front row (left, center) is Vincent McHugh, *New Yorker* writer, novelist, and translator, a witness for the defense. James Harmon, editor of the anarchist *Ark*, is in back row at right.

THE COVER OF LENNY BRUCE'S *Stamp Help Out* (published by the author) shows him in the act of destroying the source of some of his source materials. (Obviously, he's in the act of cleaning up his act.) Seriously, his satire went a great deal deeper than here indicated, and he couldn't be flushed away. *The New Columbia Encyclopedia* has since summed up his career in part as follows:

> Possessed of a cynical, surreal, and intensely comic view of the world, Bruce brutally satirized such sensitive areas of American life as sex, religion, and race relations. . . . Consequently Bruce was continually being arrested and tried for obscenity and forbidden to perform. He was also arrested for narcotics violations. In Aug. 1966, he died of an overdose of narcotics at the age of 41. After his death Bruce became a cult figure, considered by many to be a martyr to the cause of free speech. His autobiography, *How To Talk Dirty and Influence People* (1965) sold well. . . . After his cult popularity had diminished, he was still regarded as a seminal figure in American culture, whose influence could be seen in the work of important novelists, playwrights, and filmmakers of the 1970s.

In January 1963, Bruce sent a telegram to City Lights Bookstore, demanding that all copies of *Stamp Help Out* be immediately destroyed. His handwritten letter, itemizing his upcoming hassles with the law, followed the telegram:

> Im making my
> last farewell tour
> of the courts.
>   Did you see the
> new Confidential.
>   They will hang me
> if they catch any body
>   selling that book.

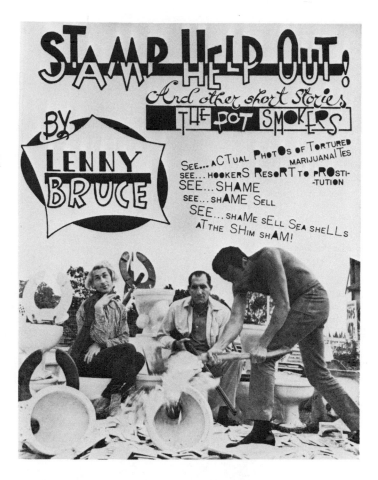

Feb 4 — VAN NUYS-ASSAULT
Feb 8 — OBSCENITY-Beverly Hills
Feb 14 — NARCOTICS, L.A.
Mar 4 — Obscenity-Chicago
March 15 — dropped charge
                    [part illegible]
So you see I can't
    stand another bust   Love-Lny

Ironically, the letter was written from the Hotel America, New York City. America was still not ready for his kind of freedom.

183

EVERGREEN REVIEW, No. 2, published by the Grove Press in 1957, edited by Donald M. Allen and Barney Rosset. Its back cover spoke of

the exciting phenomenon of a young group in the process of creating a new American culture. With what the *New Yorker* calls "a pervasive desire to get out into the open in order to breathe fresh, creative air . . . looking for some large poetic form that can accommodate anything and everything— including ordinarily rejected and suspect material," a vigorous new generation of writers, painters and musicians in the Bay Area is revolting against the sterility of American "academicians." Brought together here for the first time are the leading figures of the "San Francisco Renaissance."

Contributors included Kenneth Rexroth, Brother Antoninus (William Everson), Robert Duncan, Lawrence Ferlinghetti, Henry Miller, Michael McClure, Josephine Miles, Jack Spicer, Michael Rumaker, James Broughton, Gary Snyder, Philip Whalen, Jack Kerouac, and Allen Ginsberg. There were also critical articles by Ralph J. Gleason on the "San Francisco Jazz Scene" and New York art critic Dore Ashton's "Eastern View of the San Francisco School" (of painting).

This New York-oriented review made the eastern U.S. connection in painting and poetry. (Ginsberg, Kerouac, Ferlinghetti, Rumaker, and Gregory Corso on the set in San Francisco were all from the eastern seaboard.) It ignored some San Franciscans vital to the movement— notably Philip Lamantia (leading American Surrealist), black-Jewish poet Bob Kaufman (whose early broadsides were second only to Ginsberg's *Howl* as seminal influences), and figurative painter

James Weeks (whose paintings of jazz musicians in session were closer to San Francisco "jazz poetry" than any paintings mentioned by Ashton).

Ashton's essay, linking New York abstract expressionism to early non-objective paintings in San Francisco by Clyfford Still, Rothko, Hans Hoffman, and others associated with the California School of Fine Arts (Hassel Smith, Elmer Bischoff, Walter Kuhlman, Frank Lobdell, John Saccaro) made a connection in print with the San Francisco poets. In reality, such a liaison hardly existed. In New York some of the same poets, together with New Yorkers Frank O'Hara and Kenneth Koch, did indeed intimately associate with painters and art critics. In San Francisco this happened on only a very limited scale in the 1950s. James Weeks, John Saccaro, and Canadian Ronald Bladen were among the few who communicated directly with some poets or showed any awareness of the new poetry and its possible affinities with what the painters were doing. (Hubert Crehan, as editor of *Arts Digest* in New York, hired Ferlinghetti to write a monthly San Francisco Letter in which he reviewed Hassel Smith, Ronald Bladen, Jay DeFeo, and William Wulf. Sculptor Beniamino Buffano collaborated in print with Ferlinghetti on one later occasion.)

It was some time later that younger artists like Wallace Berman, Bruce Conner, George Herms, and Jordan Belson began to work with poets and "jumped around from painting to collage and film to poetry" (as art critic Thomas Albright later described them). Separate from them in North Beach in the 1970s were the powerful young visionary painters Michael Bowen, Michael McCracken, Arthur Monroe, and Wilfried Satty. And Peter Leblanc began a career of portraying poets and Buddhist themes in silkscreen and etching. In 1979 Wallace Berman had a posthumous show at the University Art Museum in Berkeley, including a poetry reading by his old friends Michael McClure, David Meltzer, and Diane di Prima.

Including Henry Miller among the San Francisco insurgent writers was gratuitous. (Given the New Yorker's mental map of what lay beyond the Hudson, it was natural to assume Miller's Big Sur was a part of San Francisco.) A hundred and seventy miles to the south, Miller remained aloof from the beat in San Francisco, even though his *Tropics* were underground classics for most poets and he was their immediate forebear as a dissident writer. (The title of Ferlinghetti's *Coney Island of the Mind* was taken from a Miller book.) When the young Allen Ginsberg wrote to Miller asking if he could drop in while visiting Big Sur, Miller wrote back a card: "Dear Friend— Please do not drop in." The dissident sound of San Francisco writers found no answering echo in Miller until the publication of Kerouac's *Subterraneans*.

Miller later invited Kerouac for dinner at Ephraim Doner's house in Carmel Highlands. Kerouac never made it, having delayed leaving Vesuvio's bar in North Beach until well past dinnertime, with at least a three-hour drive down the coast. He finally did arrive in a wilder part of Big Sur in the dark hours of the morning, in a taxi. It was a canyon where Ferlinghetti had a cabin. Kerouac, weaving about with his brakeman's lantern, couldn't find the cabin and fell asleep in a meadow, where Ferlinghetti found him at dawn. (The event is documented in Kerouac's *Big Sur* and in various Kerouac biographies.) Kerouac and Miller never did meet.

𝒫OET BOB KAUFMAN fending off police in the Co-Existence Bagel Shop, Grant Avenue and Green Street, in about 1956. The Bagel Shop (founded by J. Hoppe) co-existed for a very few years in the mid 1950s and was a central gathering place for what columnist Herb Caen dubbed "beatniks." Soviet Sputniks were much in the news, and beatnik was taken as a slick put-down. It was the height of the McCarthy era; and San Francisco police, among others, were not interested in co-existence with any kind of niks. (One Officer Bigarini became the butt of many caustic poems.) Bob Kaufman's early vituperative visionary broadsides were published by City Lights, and he became a symbol of poetic resistance. Eventually, he was published by the leading New York avant-garde publisher, New Directions, and by many foreign publishers. In France, he became known as the black American Rimbaud, even though he is half Jewish.

Two or three other establishments in North Beach had frequent poetry read-ings. The Place on Upper Grant had its Blabbermouth Night once a week. Poets included Richard Brautigan, Jack Spicer, John Wieners, and others who generally hung out in Gino & Carlo's bar on Green Street. The Cellar, also on Green, near Columbus, went out of existence in the early 1960s. The Coffee Gallery, across from the Bagel Shop, was the only one of these to last until 1980. By then there were regular poetry series in bookstores and coffeehouses all over town: the Intersection on Union Street and Cody's in Berkeley have the two longest-running series at the moment, according to *Poetry Flash*, a periodical calendar and review of literary events and publications edited by Steve Abbott and Joyce Jenkins. Some of the other poetry reading places around town: Kush's Cloud House, Cortland Corners Cafe, El Mundo Surdo, New College, La Pena, Mission Cultural Center, Panjandrum, Grand Piano, City Lights Bookstore, Bay Area Poets Coalition, Berkeley Poets Co-op, Café Strand, the San Francisco Art Institute, and Keystone Korners.

CHARLES OLSON, that whale of a poet,
stands off an admiring harpooner at
the San Francisco Museum of Art after
his Poetry Center reading in 1957. At
right is Robert Duncan.

BEATITUDE MAGAZINE'S first issue was printed at the Bread and Wine Mission, Greenwich and Grant Avenue, April 1959. (Left to right): William J. Margolis (later editor of *Miscellaneous Man* magazine), Eileen and Bob Kaufman. *Beatitude*, its title embodying Kerouac's original definition of beat, has been like a floating crapgame during the twenty years of its funky existence, edited by whatever resident visionary happened to want to do an issue. "Edited & produced on a kick or miss basis" by anarchists, "neo-existentialists, beggars, winos, freuds, wordmen, brushmen, axemen & other habitués & gawkers of the North Beach scene," the production was generally Xerox or mimeo, limited in run by the durability of the paper plates.

While big literary magazines like *Contact* and *Evergreen Review* came and went, *Beatitude* survived, and an extraordinary twentieth-anniversary issue was published in late 1979, edited by Neeli Cherkovski and Raymond Foye. Solid with new work by new and old writers (as well as unknown texts by Edgar Allan Poe, Fernando Pessoa, and Samuel Greenberg), this issue showed *Beatitude* to be still more alive than most big quarterlies, moribund in academe, and Little Magazines, breast-fed by the National Endowment of the Arts and Humanities, a far cry indeed from the rambunctious independence of the early *Argonaut* and *Overland Monthly*.

$\mathcal{G}$UI DE ANGULO, daughter of Jaime de Angulo, caught these four poets early in their careers on Varennes Street in North Beach in 1958. (From left to right): Michael McClure, Philip Lamantia, John Wieners (later of Boston), David Meltzer. McClure was soon to write his play *The Beard* (a shocker at the time, an early production of which was closed by the police, only to push it toward international fame). Lamantia, born in San Francisco, had already become known in the international Surrealist movement. Wieners wrote *The Hotel Wentley Poems* while living in the building on the northeast corner of Sutter and Polk Streets, a third-class hotel to which some writers and artists moved when the Montgomery Block was torn down in 1959. David Meltzer is the prolific poet and editor of *Journal for the Protection of All Beings*, *The San Francisco Poets* (Ballantine Books), *The Secret Garden: Anthology of the Classic Kabbalah* (Continuum Books), and *Tree* (an irregular journal devoted to aspects of Jewish mysticism and the creative tradition).

RICHARD BRAUTIGAN in the Co-Existence Bagel Shop in the 1950s (in the center, in white). Born in 1935 in the Pacific Northwest, he arrived in San Francisco quite young and became active as a poet in North Beach in the 1950s, reading at Blabbermouth Night at the Place and other literary haunts. It is a time he later seemed to want to forget, refusing interviews about the beat period on the grounds he was not one of them or, indeed, ever a "local" poet. He preferred his later reputation made in the 1960s, when his first prose books (*A Con-* *federate General from Big Sur,* 1964, and *Trout Fishing in America*, 1967) became national best-sellers.

A long-haired generation tuned to rock found Brautigan's fine whimsy to be all it needed in the way of prose literature. His uncommitted, musing protagonists helped fill the hippies' need for antiheroes. Recently, he has spent much time in Japan and on his ranch in Montana. (Returned to San Francisco one day in 1978 and noting a display in the window of City Lights Bookstore showing some recently picked "Leaves of Grass from Whitman's Grave," Brautigan snorted, "A good argument for cremation!")

THE VESUVIO BAR at 255 Columbus Avenue was founded by Henri Lenoir in 1949, after having lent his convivial artistic talents to other successful bohemian hangouts along the avenue—the Iron Pot and 12 Adler Place. Vesuvio's soon became the most popular bohemian watering place in North Beach. Lenoir retired from it in 1969 and later said,

I seem to have the knack, which I can't quite explain, of creating the kind of atmosphere which in a very subtle way attracts the creative talent in the population, be it artists, poets, writers or musicians. Though I have no particular creative talent myself, I feel an affinity for them and treat them with respect, whether broke or unknown or widely acclaimed and affluent. . . . For instance, at the Iron Pot, I met Artie Shaw, Dr. Oppenheimer, Harry Bridges, Jose Iturbi, Yehudi Menuhin and Theodore Dreiser. In the Vesuvio I was patronized by Kerouac, Philip Whalen, Michael McClure, Robert Duncan, Dylan Thomas, Varda, Dong Kingman, Philip Lamantia, Rock Hudson, Hassel Smith, Allen Ginsberg, Don Carpenter, Curt Gentry, Richard Brautigan, Walter Landor, Erskine Caldwell, Ferlinghetti, Herb Gold, Bob Dylan. . . .

These kinds of people were attracted by the non-bourgeois atmosphere created by the avant-garde paintings I hung on the walls, and the better educated segment of the public was in turn attracted by their presence. . . . From the Vesuvio tentacles spread out and in time spawned the Hungry I, the Coffee Gallery (which was first known as Miss Smith's Tea Room), the Place, the Anxious Asp, the Co-Existence Bagel Shop; and then the topless boys took advantage of all the tourists looking for beatniks, and decided to give them some sex."

At the bar at Vesuvio in September 1963 (left to right): Henri Lenoir, Richard Harrity (journalist), Sargent Johnson (sculptor), William Ryan (publisher and editor of *Contact*, an important conservative literary quarterly then published in Sausalito), Wing (artist), Allen Ginsberg (poet), Evan S. Connell (novelist and editor of *Contact*), Florence Allen (entertainer), Jean Varda (painter, collagist, and general bon vivant), Sally Stanford (restaurateur, madam, and sometime mayor of Sausalito). The photo was taken for *Cosmopolitan*.

JACK KEROUAC on Grant Avenue, Chinatown, San Francisco, in 1963, with painter William Morris (center) and poet Philip Whalen (right). Kerouac's ever-present spiral notebook is visible in his shirt pocket. This photo was taken about a year after Kerouac's *Big Sur* was published and a couple of years after he finished writing *Desolation Angels*. He was already spending much time with his mother living in Florida, as he did increasingly until his death in St. Petersburg in 1969. His *wanderjahr*, so lustily delineated in *On The Road* and in stories like "October in the Railroad Earth," was mostly over. (A superficial parallel with Jack London's *The Road* may be made; but London's life at the time of his *Road* was energized by belief in socialism and a political activism Kerouac never embraced. Kerouac's most direct literary forebear was the Thomas Wolfe of *Look Homeward, Angel*. Kerouac's sweeping vision of America was truly Wolfian. Wolfe's view was from a train window; Kerouac's, from a speeding car.)

His *Subterraneans* is the novel most often associated with San Francisco, though the *Dharma Bums* also passed through town. *The Subterraneans* actually happened in New York in the summer of 1953. In shifting the action to San Francisco, Kerouac said he was afraid of a lawsuit. According to Ann Charters in her biography, "he was also aware of the widespread interest in San Francisco after the publicity given the scene by journalists writing up the 'San Francisco Renaissance,' describing the Bohemian community in North Beach."

In an earlier picture, we see Kerouac
on the San Francisco waterfront, probably
near China Basin and the Southern Pacific
railroad yards, where he worked briefly in
the 1950s at the time of "October in the
Railroad Earth," his notebook full of San
Francisco blues.

$\mathcal{G}$ROUP GATHERED for a photo to be used on the cover of *City Lights Journal* (No. 3) in front of City Lights Bookstore on December 5, 1965. A fire alarm was turned in, and several engines sirened up to the store during the picture taking. Everyone in the photo was either a published poet, scholar, editor, artist, or entertainer. (Left to right): Stella Levy (City Lights editor), Lawrence Ferlinghetti (in hooded jalaba). Standing are Donald Schenker, David Schaff, Michael Grieg, Stan Persky, David Meltzer, Michael McClure, Allen Ginsberg, Daniel J. Langton, Burton Watson, "Stephen," Richard Brautigan, Gary Goodrow (of the original satirical theatre group, The Committee), unidentified man in moustache, Andrew Hoyem and son. Seated: Robert LaVigne (painter), Shigeyoshi Murao (City Lights manager and co-owner), Lew Welch with left hand on Larry Fagan, Peter Orlovsky. Lying down: Lee Meyerzove.

MICHAEL MCCLURE, BOB DYLAN, AND ALLEN GINSBERG together in Adler Alley between City Lights Bookstore and Vesuvio's at the time of the group meeting at City Lights, December 5, 1965.

The presence of Bob Dylan among the poets was not accidental. His early songs (such as "Bob Dylan's 115th Dream," "Subterranean Homesick Blues," "On the Road Again," "Gates of Eden") were considered by many poets of the 1960s subculture to be truly on their wavelength.

On the road, they were on the road with him and his guitar, as much as with Jack Kerouac.

Today, in the sad Born Again lyrics of Dylan's latest "You Gotta Serve Somebody," he has left many poets behind. Not that they wanted to keep up. Anarchist poets in particular still don't want to serve any gods or gurus, feeling that a motto like "You gotta serve somebody" leads too often to führers and Jonestowns.

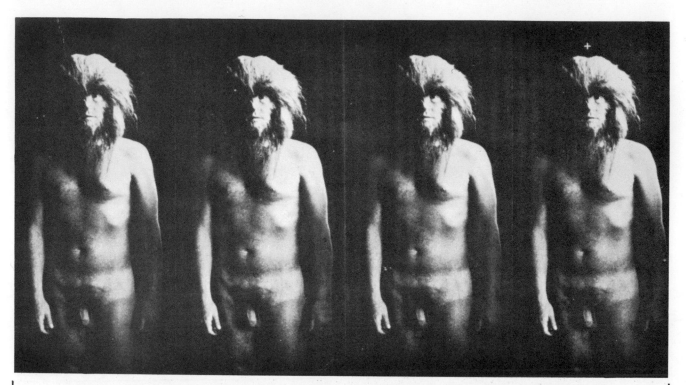

Poetry is a muscular principle and a revolution for the body-spirit and intellect and ear. Making images and pictures, even when speaking with melody, is not enough. There must be a poetry of pure beauty and energy that does not mimic but joins and exhorts reality and states the daily higher vision. To dim the senses and listen to inner energies a-roar is sometimes called the religious experience. It does not matter what it is called. Laughter as well as love is passion. The loveliness the nose snuffs in air may be translated to sound by interior perceptive organs. The touch of velvet on the fingertips may become a cry when time is stopped. Speed like calmness may become a pleasure or gentle muffled sound. A dahlia or fern might become pure speech in meditation. A woman's body might become the sound of worship. A goddess lies coiled at the base of man's body, and pure tantric sound might awaken her. There are no laws but living changing ones, and any system is a touch of death.

My eyes are intense dark brown and sometimes insane. I believe in LIBERTY, BEAUTY, FREEDOM, AND THE CREATION OF MY SOUL AND HELPING OTHERS IN THE CREATION OF THEIRS through poetry. —Michael McClure.

A flyer for a poetry reading by Michael McClure in the 1960s. The photo of the poet is by conceptual artist Wallace Berman.

*G*AVIN ARTHUR, grandson of President Chester Arthur, was a gay astrologer who wrote *The Circle of Sex* (1966) and died in 1972. He was a close friend to some beat poets in Japan town (Post and Buchanan Streets) in the 1950s. Some of the poets (Philip Whalen and Gary Snyder among them) had come together there in an old wooden building they called the East-West House, symbolizing a turning to the East and especially to Buddhist consciousness. (Philip Whalen later became a monk at the San Francisco Zen Center.) Gavin Arthur's occultism made him a natural ally. On his door was a calling card that read "Spiritual Counselor."

*D*ANIEL MOORE readied for press the final version of his extraordinary *Dawn Visions* (1962) while living in the Kent Cottage on the waterfront in Bolinas, some years before that Land's End town became a popular outpost for writers. In 1971, Glide Publication's *Mark in Time* printed Moore's photo with this autobiographical note:

Born July 30, 1940, 5:20 A.M., Alameda, California. Growing up and school in Oakland, Berkeley, Mexico City, San Francisco. Personal epic *Dawn Visions* written in Mexico and purple San Francisco apartment in 1962, published by City Lights. Manuscripts piled up thru travels and flights, painted books, zazen with Master Suzuki, those golden quiet afternoons! Boston bricks peripheried my vision in 1965 for a year Romance, then return to a dark time finally to Mexico and car-crash, two months flat-on-back monastery. Return to Berkeley to create and direct the Floating Lotus Magic Opera Company for visceral manifestation and expansion of poetic vision for human figures and real voices and orchestra, torchlighting nights open with the dance-rhythm'd Word. Now momentarily dissolved, the Floating Lotus enters the Invisible.

By the time this was printed, however, Moore had become a Sufi and, like Rimbaud, renounced written poetry.

CLAUDE PELIEU (later Claude Washburn) in drag in San Francisco, 1968. A refugee from Gaullist France, Pelieu collaborated with Mary Beach (a distant relative of Sylvia Beach) on many outstanding translations into French of the San Francisco poets, including practically all of Allen Ginsberg's work, mostly published in France by Christian Bourgois. They also translated William Burroughs and poets of the New York school in the 1960s. They lived in North Beach in the 1960s, and in Mill Valley (briefly) in the late 1970s. (He never was a priest.)

THE CITY OF SAN FRANCISCO *ORACLE*, the Haight-Ashbury community's newspaper, celebrated the new age of the Flower Children with this issue in the spring of 1967. Pictured in composite are (left to right) Timothy Leary, Allen Ginsberg, Alan Watts, and Gary Snyder. The psychedelic graphics in the *Oracle*, sometimes employing the same poster artists doing rock posters for Bill Graham's Fillmore Auditorium, revolutionized media graphics on a scale far beyond its modest circulation and set up the style for a whole generation of counterculture publications, including *Rolling Stone* and fugitive underground newspapers across the country and in Europe, wherever psychedelic consciousness spread.

The main elements of this graphic style were eventually absorbed into middle-class culture in general, as were most other characteristics of the hippy life-style, in dress, long hair, music and dope. The new consciousness itself, with its definitely Buddhist foundations, was also eventually ingested into middle-class culture. "Widen the area of consciousness" was Allen Ginsberg's phrase for it; and the generation did just that, some with psychedelics, some solely by natural, nondrug means. A revolution in consciousness did take place; and the breakthrough resulted in scores of consciousness-raising institutions from Esalen Institute to the San Francisco Zen Center and further second- and third-generation spin-offs (like est), thoroughly assimilated into bourgeois culture. This followed the pattern outlined by Herbert Marcuse, Marxist philosopher, who noted the enormous capacity of the dominant society "to ingest its own most dissident elements." A revolution in consciousness did truly come about, but was ingested

by the bourgeois culture which was thus able to abort any true political revolution.

Not pictured in the *Oracle* photo is one who should have been—Emmett Grogan—who had more to do with the daily life of the Haight-Ashbury community than any of the above. He organized the Diggers, a turned-on self-help group that stole food from markets and served it free to all, printed free visionary broadsides (*The Digger Papers*), and were socially and politically active on a street-gang level. He later wrote two books: *Ringolevio: A Life Played for Keeps* and *Final Score*. He died young, a victim of his own lifestyle, and one Marcuse would have recognized.

It is not generally known that Emmett Grogan was the one who arranged for San Francisco poets to appear in Bob Dylan's film, *The Last Waltz*, which was shot at Bill Graham's Winterland on Thanksgiving, 1976, with all the guests invited to an all-night superbanquet and dance. The film itself gave the impression that it all took place on a New York based tour of The Band, missing the entire San Francisco Winterland feeling. The event was in fact a kind of postmortem celebration of the euphoric 60s. (One poet prayed: "Thy kingdom come and gone, thy will will be undone, on earth, as it isn't heaven. . . .)

AT THE "HUMAN BE-IN" in Golden Gate Park, February 14, 1967 (left to right): Allen Ginsberg, Maretta Greer, and Gary Snyder, chanting "om sri maitreya" in face of setting sun. The small stage was crowded with other chanters, folk guitarists, Haight-Ashbury leaders, and assorted psychedelic visionaries and spokesmen (including Timothy Leary). A vast audience participated in this mass articulation of the new consciousness. At least ten thousand were spread out in the huge meadow in front of the stage. The climax of the event came when a parachutist floated down directly into the last rays of the setting sun, and a great "ah" went up. To the participants it truly seemed a new age had arrived, with a new vision of life and love on earth. Allen Ginsberg, turning to Lawrence Ferlinghetti, who was also on stage, whispered, "What if we're all wrong?"

The political (or New Left) part of the counterculture did not think they were all wrong. The new consciousness was seen as a fusion of Eros and reason, a new "reality principle" necessary for the transformation of society in the face of capitalist materialism. Herbert Marcuse (ideologue of the New Left) spoke of "the persistent demand for a new subjectivity" and later analyzed the situation as follows:

> The movement took the form, then, of a cultural revolution from the very beginning; it conceived of the revolution of the 20th century as one in which not only political and economic demands, but also radically other desires and hopes would be articulated: the desire for a new moral sense, for a more human environment, for a complete "emancipation of the senses" (Marx), in other words, a liberation of the senses from the compulsion to perceive people and things as objects of exchange. "Power to the Imagination!"

*T*OTEM CEREMONY at Grace Cathedral in 1971 was one of those bridges between the counterculture of the 1960s and the ecological consciousness of the 1970s. Former Bishop James Pike of Grace Cathedral had been in touch with that consciousness, especially through his friendly association with Alan Watts, a former Anglican minister who became a leading interpreter of Zen in books such as *Philosophy East and West* and in his program on KPFA/FM, Berkeley.

The lotus positions are a reflection of that particular grafting of Buddhism and Christianity that flowered in San Francisco and elsewhere in the West in the 1960s, the liberation of the spirit being often linked to expanded consciousness or consciousness-raising techniques, some psychedelic, some not. The San Francisco Zen Center (with its organic farm at Green Gulch Ranch near Muir Beach) is another connection with the Buddhist-oriented counterculture. Through Richard Baker-Roshi, the Zen Center in the 1970s remained in touch with the literary community, sponsoring readings by poets often versed in various forms of Buddhist practice (not necessarily Zen), including Philip Whalen, a monk at the Zen Center. Baker-Roshi was instrumental in the publication by City Lights Books in 1975 of *Insights & Poems* by Huey Newton and Ericka Huggins. (He introduced the authors to the editors and wrote an introduction to the book.) The Zen Center's own publication, *Wind Bell*, also makes crosscultural connections.

Shown here are Gary Snyder, reading from scroll, Allen Ginsberg in deer mask (being his usual vatic self), and Janine Pommy-Vega (author of *Poems to Fernando*).

ALAN WATTS, as pictured in his autobiography, *In My Own Way* (1972), in which he said:

I have no idea how I came to be so weird, but never for a moment have I regretted that I forgetfully reincarnated myself as the child of Laurence Wilson Watts and Emily Nary Buchan, at Rowan Tree Cottage in Holbrook Lane, in the village of Cheslehurst, Kent, England, almost due south of Greenwich, on the morning of January 6, 1915, at about twenty minutes after six, with the sun in Capricorn, conjuncted with Mars and Mercury and in trine to a Moon in Virgo, with Sagittarius rising, and under bombardment in the midst of the First World War.

The jacket blurb of his autobiography said of him in 1972,

One can hardly think of another man who has been so sympathetically associated, both in his personal lifestyle and in his intellectual activity, with such new movements in contemporary life since the early fifties as Zen, the "beat generation," the psychedelic adventure, the "hippie" culture, and the emergence of Growth Centers (such as Esalen in Big Sur), right up to the more recent interest in ecology and the practice of meditation.

Over the past twenty-five years, Alan Watts has become widely recognized as the most penetrating, and above all readable, interpreter of Eastern religions for Western readers. His role in creating the Zen "boom" in this country is undisputed, and his writings and lectures have become a byword on campuses from New York to California. The author of some twenty books, he is considered one of the outstanding philosophical writers of our day.

He was a brilliant speaker, a casuist who could take either side of an argument and win. He was also known for his wild laughter and was a friend of many poets. His Zen spirit still lives on his old houseboat in Sausalito (which he once shared with artist Jean Varda) and in the high woods on Mount Tamalpais, where he had a retreat for many years, cloud-hidden.

George Oppen

Joanne Kyger

MARK IN TIME, an extraordinary album of portraits by Christa Fleischmann, was published in 1971 by Glide Publications. It contained eighty poets who (the editors said) "have, for different reasons and various lengths of time, been described as belonging to or associated with the San Francisco community of poets."

Here are some of the faces in the book:

George Oppen: Objectivist poet published by New Directions who won a Pulitzer Prize in 1968.

Joanne Kyger: A Virginia Woolf among poets, though with considerably more wit in person than the lady of Bloomsbury.

Lew Welch: A roommate of Gary Snyder and Philip Whalen at Reed College, he later worked and drank around the waterfront in the City. In 1971, he disappeared in the wilderness near Gary Snyder's house north of Nevada City, California.

George Hitchcock: Poet and publisher of Kayak Books, once an actor and theater director in the City, he now lives in Santa Cruz and teaches at the University of California there.

Josephine Miles: Born in 1911 in Chicago, she wrote her first poem in joy at the armistice and the end of war. She was associated with the Berkeley Renaissance in the 1940s. She teaches language and literature at the University of California in Berkeley.

Madeline Gleason: Poet, playwright, and painter, she presented the first poetry festivals in San Francisco in the late 1940s.

Lew Welch

Josephine Miles

George Hitchcock

Madeline Gleason

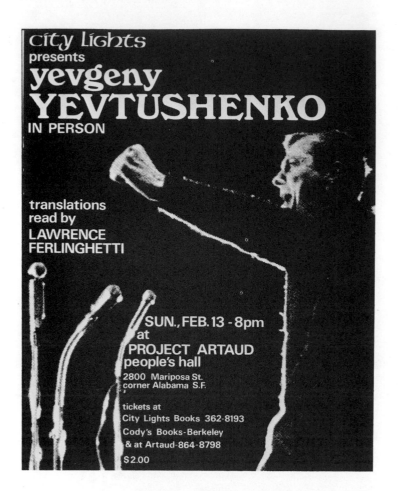

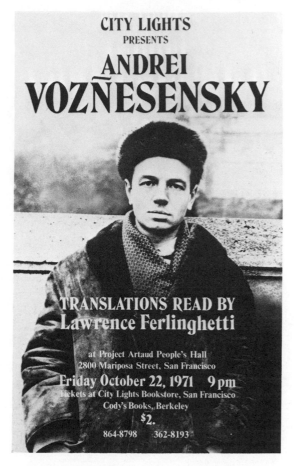

$\mathscr{P}$OSTERS from some of the bigger literary events in the first years of the 1970s. These events were produced by the City Lights Poets Theatre in various locations around town capable of holding large audiences. The Ezra Pound Memorial came a few weeks after the poet's death in 1972. The benefit for the Greek Resistance was a broad coalition of activist writers from several countries, especially Greece, Chile, and the United States.

The Russian poets each drew a crowd of about two thousand in a converted warehouse at the edge of the Mission district, Project Artaud People's Hall. The Yevtushenko reading was followed by a party at the City Lights Poets Theatre, 420 Mason Street, at which the picture of Allen Ginsberg, Yevtushenko, and Lawrence Ferlinghetti was taken (page 208). This was in 1972. The great proletarian poet from Siberia was staying at the Hotel Saint Francis, Union Square. Both Yevtushenko and Voznesensky returned to San Francisco for further readings later in the decade. (As on the earlier trips, they came separately, a literary feud having developed between them that at last report had still not been settled.) Voznesensky had been the first to appear here, back in 1966 at the old Fillmore Auditorium, sponsored by impresario Bill Graham and City Lights, on a double bill with the Jefferson Airplane.

Performing in the heroic oral tradition of Mayakovsky, the Russians belted out their poems at the top of their voices (and yet could impart great intimacy in quiet passages). They stood like athletes used to performing in huge stadia and gestured dramatically. (One local critic was in fact moved to describe Yevtushenko as "the discus-thrower from Smolensk." And John Russell in a 1979 *New York Times* review of Voznesensky spoke of how his "consonants had the ring of cavalry on cobblestones" and "even silence had its heartbeat.")

These Russian poets never *sat* in the manner of academic and parlor poets. They were in direct contrast to American poets influenced by Buddhism who adopted a reading style in the lotus position, sitting on the platform cross-legged. (At some group readings in San Francisco at this time practically all the poets would be sitting or lying on stage.)

The two styles showed off the difference between the activist and the "quietist," the political and the apolitical poet. (One exception was Allen Ginsberg, who sometimes read activist poems in the lotus position.) In general, the influence of the Russians upon poets here (who have their own loud-and-clear oral tradition) was considerable. There was collaboration in translation, and new poems by the Russians written here (or shortly thereafter) sometimes sounded much like the "wide open" poetry of the San Francisco school. It was felt that more human contact was made, in addition to the cross-fertilization of poetry, than in most official cultural exchange programs.

CITY LIGHTS PRESENTS A BENEFIT POETRY READING

FOR THE GREEK RESISTANCE

with hElen kazantzakis, Fernando Allegria, Kay Boyle John Chioles, Andrei Codrescu, Diane di Prima, Lawrence Ferlinghetti, George Hitchcock, Paul Mariah, Thanassis Mascaleris Janice Masja, Thulane Nkabinde, Harold Norse, Dino Siotis, Soter Torregian, Nanos Valaoritis, Roberto Vargas, Paul Xadvier

APRIL 20 — FUGAZI HALL 678 Green St.- 8:30 donation $2 & 1.50
TICKETS AT CITY LIGHTS BOOK STORE - 362-8193 & CODY'S IN BERKELEY

city lights presents
EZRA POUND MEMORIAL POETRY READING
dave bromige·lennart bruce gail chiarrello·tom clark andre codrescu·robert creeley·mike davidson·william everson·lawrence ferlinghetti·susan griffin·thom gunn·joanne kyger· ron loewinsohn·gerard malanga·harold norse·michael palmer·tom parkinson·stan rice·jack shoemaker·john simon·sotere torregian

FRI. DEC. 8 8:30pm
tel hi gym $1.
555 chestnut, s.f.

tickets at City Lights & Cody's in Brkly.

$\mathcal{T}$HE PHOTO THAT SUMMED UP AN ERA was taken by Walter Chappell in the spring of 1971 to be used on the cover of *The Frisco Kid*, a novel by Jerry Kamstra about beats and bohemians in North Beach during the 1950s and 1960s. Vesuvio's is on the left, City Lights Bookstore on the right, and Kamstra's story of the photo went like this:

It is no mean feat convincing 150 poets, oddballs, café loungers, wanderers, walkers, dreamers, winos, writers, bohemians, beats, boppers and bamboozlers to show up at ten in the morning to pose for a photograph that's to be the dust jacket of a novel that most of them are characters in. . . . I hired Johnny Woodrose (Shoeshine Devine in the book) to sweep North Beach with a pocketful of invitations. . . . I expected 30 or 40 people to come; more than 170 people, most of whom never arise before noon, actually got up and staggered down to Adler Alley.

CHARLES BUKOWSKI, longtime resident of the underside of Los Angeles, ventured up to San Francisco for his first poetry reading, sponsored by the City Lights Poets Theatre at the Telegraph Hill Neighborhood Center in North Beach on September 4, 1973. During the course of the event, he drank all the beer in the refrigerator onstage, read pugilistically from his works, and roused the huge audience to cheers, sneers, and insults, all of which bounced off him as off an old boozer in a skid row saloon.

City Lights had just published his *Erections, Ejaculations, Exhibitions and General Tales of Ordinary Madness*, followed by *Notes of a Dirty Old Man*. Bukowski was born in Andernach, Germany, in 1920, but was brought to this country at a very tender age. After fifty years in the United States, he wasn't so tender anymore. The tale of his touching and raucous return to Germany in 1978 is recorded in his *Shakespeare Never Did This* (1970).

NANOS VALAORITIS reading at the benefit for Greek Resistance at Fugazi Hall in North Beach in 1972. Kay Boyle is seated behind him. Born in Switzerland of Greek parents, Valaoritis had been associated with the avant-garde in Paris and with some French Surrealists. From 1963 to 1967 he edited the Greek review, *Pali*, publishing those who later were forced into exile by the 1967 coup and who became the literary leaders of the Greek Resistance. Since then Valaoritis has taught at San Francisco State University.

$\mathcal{K}$AY BOYLE, certainly one of the most important women writers living in San Francisco today, was originally associated with the American expatriates in Paris in the 1920s. Written in the 1930s and 1940s in Europe, her *Thirty Stories* (published by New Directions) remains a major work of the period, as well as her *Three Short Novels* (Beacon Press). On May 16, 1979, Herb Caen reported in the *San Francisco Chronicle* that she "asked Atty. Jerome Garchik to get her files from the FBI—and learned therefrom that 'she had a clandestine affair with Ezra Pound prior to the First World War.' Kay would have been about 12 at that time, but since some children are more precocious than others, I felt free to enquire: 'Well, did you?' 'I didn't meet him till the 1920's' she laughs, 'and I didn't like him then.' "

The photo shows her between Joan Baez, Sr., on her right, and Jacqueline McGuckin among Cesar Chavez's United Farm Worker marchers in Modesto, California, in 1974.

$\mathcal{D}$AVID FECHHEIMER, a modern-day private eye who edited *City*'s Dashiell Hammett feature, stands in front of the house at 2151 Sacramento Street with its plaque reading, "This house, built in 1881, was once occupied by Sir Arthur Conan Doyle." (How long he occupied it only the Shadow knows. It was a high-class bordello in the 1950s.) Doyle visited San Francisco in 1923 on his second and last trip to the United States.

In *Our Second American Adventure*, this Lord of Mystery described San Francisco rather like a British viceroy making a foray into aboriginal territories, though he liked the place better than gung-ho Kipling had. While he was here Doyle spoke much of spiritualism and of "working to the downfall of materialism," which he saw everywhere about him. His effect on San Francisco reminded him of "an ants' nest stirred up with a stick. Every one of the papers, and they were many, was filled with every kind of challenge, argument, denunciation, and protest, with an occasional whisper of agreement. . . . Public opinion, especially the more educated public opinion, seemed reactionary and ill-informed." And he concluded,

> Our visit to San Francisco with its very material atmosphere had left a sad impression upon our minds—and I can well say "our," for the whole of our party were conscious of the same strong psychic reaction. It was only on the last day that a gleam came through the clouds which brought great peace and joy into my soul, for it seemed to me that I saw better things ahead, and some hope that this dark place of the earth might in truth become the mother of future light. It is hardly fair to blame America for the state of San Francisco, for its population is cosmopolitan and its seaport attracts the floating vice of the Pacific; but be the cause what it may, there is much room for spiritual betterment.

And he recorded his final glimpse of the City: "It was midnight after my last lecture when we crossed the bay in the ferry to get our Portland train. Looking back we saw the league-long field of lights, the great twinkling sky-signs, all beating upwards against an overhanging cloud. A burning house flared on the sea-front. The whole effect was sinister and terrible in the extreme."

The "sinister and terrible" may have had something to do with so many mystery writers or detective novelists settling in or about the City or using it as the setting for their mysterious works. Among the contemporary mystery, detective, or "macabre" writers here, one may on some dark nights back into Joe Gores (author of *Hammett*), Collin Wilcox (*The Third Victim, Twospot* with Bill Pronzini), Bill Pronzini (*Blowback, Midnight Specials, The Snatch*), Fritz Leiber (whose *Our Lady of Darkness* was set at 811 Geary Street, the flat where Dashiell Hammett wrote *The Maltese Falcon*), Leonard Wolf (*Bluebeard*), Poul Anderson (*Murder in Black Letter* and *Perish by the Sword*). And there is Danielle Steele, who writes all those super-popular gushy Gothic romances.

Also in the area is Anne Rice (*Interview with a Vampire*) although she is not exactly in this genre, her "interview" really being with cancer. Another writer whose work is ironically connected with his own life is Dean Lipton: in 1970 he published *Faces of Crime & Genius*, a study of the faces of criminals and of geniuses who were also criminals; in 1978 he published *Malpractice: Autobiography of a Victim*, which is the story of his own face, disfigured by a surgeon's negligence.

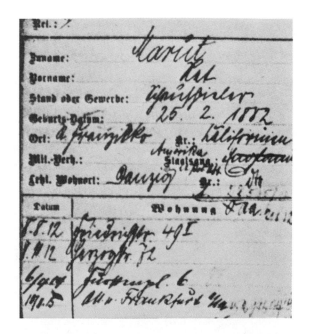

Der "Underground" ist der "Overground"

THE MYSTERY of the true identity of B. Traven (paranoid author of *The Death Ship* and other novels, as well as *The Treasure of Sierra Madre*) was deepened a few years ago by the discovery of an alien-registration form in Düsseldorf, Germany, filled out in 1912 under the name of Ret Marut (one of his aliases) and giving "S. Franzisko" as his place of birth. He claimed Chicago as birthplace another time, and among other aliases he used "Hal Croves"—the name by which the film company shooting *Treasure of Sierra Madre* knew him. In Mexico, where he became a naturalized citizen, he was buried in 1969 under the name of "Traven Torsvan." Judy Stone of the *San Francisco Chronicle* interviewed him in Mexico and wrote *The Mystery of B. Traven.*

A GERMAN GUIDEBOOK to San Francisco, edited by Hartmut Gerdes (a North Beach resident) and published by Verlag Schauberg in 1976, illustrated the San Francisco literary scene with the above poster by Gilbert Shelton.

The guidebook was heavy on North Beach scenes, with photos of leading literary coffeehouses such as the Caffé Trieste. Also included was Francis Ford Coppola's Columbus Towers, not a coffeehouse but a fertile film hive not generally recognized as an integral part of the intellectual life of North Beach. Among the projects on Coppola's back burner is a writers' club to be established in the neighborhood, as well as rumored plans to move the Pacific Film Archive to Coppola's Little Fox Theatre.

In the guidebook there was also a photo of the Transamerica Pyramid taking off like a rocket into space. The fact that the Transamerica bank was built on the site of the old Montgomery Block—the single most important structure in the literary history of San Francisco—symbolizes the present state of affairs: it's still Money over the Mooneys of our intellectual life.

ERNEST J. GAINES at the San Francisco Civic Center in 1972. Mickey Friedman, writing in the *San Francisco Examiner* (September 3, 1979), said Gaines's *Autobiography of Miss Jane Pittman* "has as much chance as any book I can think of to become a classic." Gaines has lived on Divisadero Street in San Francisco since 1963. He is now working on *The Revenge of Old Men*, set in Louisiana, as are all of his published works. He returns often to his boyhood home on a Louisiana plantation, which he uses as the major setting for his novels.

According to Friedman, Gaines "has friends who are writers, but he doesn't see them regularly: 'I just don't like to be around writers every week and talk about writing.'" This is typical of many San Francisco authors these days, despite the public image of the city as a picturesque hangout for picturesque writers who both love and hate to publicize themselves. Literary New Yorkers especially turn up here frequently, looking for the literary "scene," and often find nothing "happening." The writers are holed up on their hills, or blissed-out in their alleys. Or living in hot-tub suburbs like Mill Valley, working on hot books for New York publishers, rather like successful writers retreated to Long Island. (Don Carpenter, author of *Hard Rain Falling*, comes first to mind in Mill Valley, probably the brightest writer there.)

FRANK CHIN, novelist and playwright, was born in Berkeley in 1940 and grew up in the Chinatowns of Oakland and San Francisco. His writing has been centered on the Asian American experience, demolishing many Asian stereotypes. Some typical titles, with descriptions furnished by the author: *Bus to America*, "a discussion of San Francisco Chinatown's being against busing for the sake of preserving white supremacy, not, as has been supposed, 'preserving Chinese culture'"; *Racist Love* (with Jeffery Paul Chan), "an anatomy of the white racist positive stereotype of the Asian American minority as the 'good, lovable and assimilated' minority"; and *Don't Pen Us Up in Chinatown*, "an answer to racist idiocies penned by Jules Irving, director of the Lincoln Repertory Theater, *Times* staffer Ralph Blumenthal, and Tom Wolfe in the *New York Times*."

In a letter to the editors of this book, Chin said, "I write in the tradition of Wong Sam and Assistants, and Sui Sin Far, not the Christian Science fiction tradition of the Christian Chinese American autobiography practiced by Yung Wing, Leong Gor Yun, Pardee Lowe, Jade

215

Snow Wong, Calvin Lee, and Maxine Hong Kingston, sucking white fantasy and telling lies for a buck and a pat on the head." He was the first Chinese American brakeman on the Southern Pacific Railroad, "the first Chinaman to ride the engines." He gave that up to begin his writing career with a job at KING/TV in Seattle. This snapshot was taken in a house on Nob Hill Avenue North on top of Seattle's Queen Anne Hill in 1968.

Nellie Wong of the Women's Writer's Union wrote in *Poetry Flash* in November 1979 that Frank Chin is "probably Asian America's most talked about unpublished writer," though he is far from unpublished and his plays have been produced by some of the best experimental groups in the country, including the American Place Theatre in New York. Nellie Wong also pointed out the lively Asian American organizations in the Bay Area: the Japanese Art and Media Workshop, Asian American Theatre Workshop, Asian American Writers Workshop, and the Justice Hotel Basement Playwrights. And she went on to list some two dozen Asian American writers here who "have had to scrap around for a place to read, a place to be heard, and a place to be published."

Chin's far-out style no doubt shocks the pants off the straight Asian community here, as it must the older writers like Toshio Mori, whom William Saroyan hailed in 1949 as "one of the most important new writers in the country at the moment, the first real Japanese-American writer." Yet Mori's *Yokohama, California* grew out of his being made to feel like an alien in the promised land (during World War II), and Chin's work also springs from alienation, but of a slightly different sort. The deep difference would seem to be that Chin is alienated from his own ethnic community as well, except for those of his own long-haired generation who are with him.

HERBERT GOLD with William Saroyan near Gold's flat on Nob Hill in 1979. He was interviewing Saroyan for the *New York Times* upon publication of Saroyan's *Obituaries*. (The subtitle should have been "Rumors of Death Greatly Exaggerated.")

Gold, born in Cleveland, Ohio, was the first of four sons of a Russian immigrant. He has lived in San Francisco since 1960, where he arrived after a European *wanderjahr*. He has published more than a dozen books—quasi-autobiographical novels and stories—plus innumerable articles in big periodicals ranging from *The Nation* to *Esquire*. His deepest books are perhaps *The Man Who Was Not With It* (1956) and his beautiful *Fathers* (1967); but he may be remembered more for *Waiting For Cordelia* (1977) about a prostitutes' union in San Francisco. In 1979 he won the San Francisco Art Commission's annual Award of Honor, not necessarily for the last work.

He might also be enshrined for his early characterization of the Beat writers as "a pack of unleashed zazous." His review in *The Nation* (November 16, 1957) began, " 'WHOEE, I told my soul.' This urgent message from Jack Kerouac to his soul contains most of the sense which emerges from his frantic tirade in the form of a novel, *On the Road*." He referred to Allen Ginsberg's major poem as "his blathering *Howl*"; and he ended with the plea "Hipster, Go Home."

At least Gold was concerned with what was happening here at that time and eventually became an active part of the community, which is more than can be said for many itinerant writers who have lost their roots. Erskine Caldwell, who moved to San Francisco in 1956, is a good example. In a big suburban-type house on Twin Peaks, he wrote *Certain Women*. But he never came down from the heights, except for newspaper interviews and a public library lecture in 1964 called "Fodder and Fondue in Fiction."

He was quoted as having a disgust for city intellectuals. "Intellectual life is synthetic life," he said, sounding synthetic.

San Francisco book reviewers like Luther Nichols, Don Stanley, and Michael Grieg treated Caldwell's new book very badly, as had the *Chronicle*'s Joseph Henry Jackson back in 1948 when he called Caldwell's latest "pretty dreary." At that time, in fact, Caldwell staged "a one-man revolution against critics in general and literary critics in particular" at the Mark Hopkins Hotel. Caldwell left San Francisco late in the 1960s but returned for a celebration of his seventy-fifth birthday at Trader Vic's in January 1979. Herb Caen reported it in the *Chronicle* and noted that Caldwell had given up tobacco, among other things. He was a long, long way from Tobacco Road.

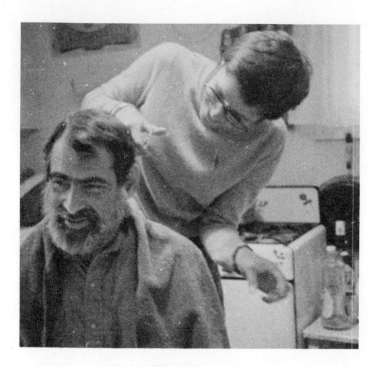

$\int$ TEPHEN SCHNECK having his hair
cut recently by the noted Swiss
equestrian, Hadwig Stadelman. This
action had nothing to do with his having
won the Prix Formentor for his novel
The Nightclerk, or with his *Nocturnal
Vaudeville*, a novel that didn't win any
prizes, or with a screenplay he wrote
recently that won the best script award
at a Paris film festival. As with many
other San Francisco writers, he seems
better recognized abroad than on his home
turf, attesting to the persistent Babbittry
of the local media (with some notable
exceptions).

Other writers here who may be said to
have suffered the same treatment: Mark
Harris (*Something About a Soldier* and
Bang the Drum Slowly), Leo Litvak
(*Waiting for the News* and *College Days
in Earthquake Country*), Charles Reich
(*The Greening of America*), Leonard
Gardner (*Fat City*), Gina Berriault (*The
Mistress and Other Stories, Descent,
Conference of Victims*, and *The Son*),
Tillie Olsen (*Tell Me a Riddle, Yonnon-
dio*, and *Silences*), Maya Angelou (*I

Know Why the Caged Bird Sings), Alice
Adams (*Beautiful Girl, Careless Love*,
and *Families and Survivors*), Ella Lefland
(*Mrs. Munck* and *Rumors of Peace*),
Maxine Hong Kingston (*The Woman
Warrior*), Susan Griffin (*Woman &
Nature: The Roaring Inside Her*), and
Curt Gentry (*The Last Days of the Great
State of California*).

That there are no group pictures of
these prose writers points up the fact
that, unlike the poets, they haven't hung
out together, remaining mostly isolated
in their separate worlds. In the 1960s
one of the few continuing literary salons
was Kenneth Rexroth's, but that was very
largely poets. Publisher Jack Vietor did
regularly bring writers together for
great conversational dinners at Trader
Vic's during that period, but that was an
invitational affair at the Captain's Table.

All of which is not to say San Francisco
is like James Joyce's Dublin, where the
artist survived only by silence, exile, and
cunning. For instance, the City of San
Francisco officially celebrated the 60th
birthday of poet Robert Duncan on May
7th, 1979, presenting him with a plaque
honoring him for his contributions to the
intellectual life of the City. In a review
of it in *Poetry Flash* (June, 1979), Lewis
MacAdams reported:

Halfway through the brief ceremony . . .
an aide of Mayor Dianne Feinstein's burst
in with a whereas-filled proclamation de-
claring May 7th Robert Duncan Day in
the City. . . . A crowd of fifty or so well-
wishers and Duncan fans rose and
applauded as Duncan beamed, and accepted
the congrats of Scott Beach of the Art
Commission, who M.C.'d the event. The
Art Commission adjourned for a few minutes as the crowd happily filed past, con-
gratulating Duncan and reading the three
beautiful lines of Duncan's calligraphed on
the plaque:
*Often I am permitted to Return
to a Meadow
as if it were a scene made-up by the mind.*

THE THIRD SAN FRANCISCO INTER-
NATIONAL POETRY FESTIVAL sponsored by City Lights Books, University
of San Francisco, San Francisco State
University Poetry Center, Intersection,
and Poetry Flash, was held at the Palace
of Fine Arts on November 4 and 5, 1978.
This group of participants and friends
gathered backstage. (Left to right):
L. Ferlinghetti, Ishmael Reed, Slovak poet
Max Bazovsky, Jr. (in glasses), Michael
McClure, Thom Gunn, John Montgomery (in glasses), William Seward Burroughs (in hat), unidentified man (in back),

Jim Gustafson, the Swedish poet Bruno
Oijer, and (sitting in front) Mei-mei
Berssenbrugge with Carol Lee Sanchez.
Others performing in the festival but
not in the photo were Jack Hirschman,
Gregory Corso, Anne Waldman, David
Meltzer, the Chilean Enrique Lihn,
Ntozake Shange, Simon Ortiz, Paul
Vane, Erica Jong, Kate Millet, Robin
Morgan, Audre Lorde, Marge Piercy,
Kathleen Fraser, and Madeline Gleason
(who died six months later).

$\int$OME OF THE PARTICIPANTS in the
Sunday afternoon program of the
Third International Poetry Festival at
the Palace of Fine Arts, November 5,
1978, were (left to right) Kathleen Fraser,
Robin Morgan, Kate Millet, Carol Murray, and Marge Piercy.

STREET POETS of the late 1970s in front of the Coffee Gallery, 1353 Grant Avenue (left to right): Jack Micheline (author of *North of Manhattan* and *River of Red Wine*), Bob Kaufman (*Golden Sardine* and *Solitudes Crowded With Loneliness*), Janis Blue, and David Moe (behind Blue; editor of *Love Lights*, a poetry newspaper masquerading as porno sold mostly to tourists wearing white shoes). The occasion of this photo was one of the many open poetry readings held at the Coffee Gallery since the mid 1950s, some with music, mostly guitar, and heavy on the juice.

The publication of Blue's poetry book, *In Good Old No Man's Land*, was here being celebrated. (The turbaned para-lady on the right did not reveal her identity, except by dubious proximity to Moe.) Poet and short-story writer Micheline is sometimes described as a precursor of Charles Bukowski, having been estab-lished in the latter's wild genre before Bukowski escaped from the post office.

Blue, who wears nothing but blue and drives a blue VW bus, in 1978 organized a series of open-mike poetry readings with free soul food on Sunday afternoons at Peta's Bar and Restaurant, Columbus and Union Street. It was a great place to hear famous street poets like Ruth Weiss and Eugene Ruggles. Now and then a bearded New York Jewish taxi driver would park his cab in a yellow zone out front, rush in, and read poems. Street poets who couldn't get a hearing anywhere else were allowed to vent their talents by the hour, including one "Hobo," an old Wobbly with a long white beard looking like Greenwich Village's Jay Gould. Hobo's unpublished oral history of the world was longer than Gould's and twice as raunchy.

*B*EFORE AND AFTER two decades of poetic fire: Gregory Corso in San Francisco at the Poets Follies in the 1950s and at Coit Tower with son Max Orfeo in 1978. His *Gasoline* (City Lights, 1958) helped ignite the Beat flame. His later books were all published by New Direc-tions in New York. His collected short plays are being published this year by City Lights. The major part of his time has not been spent in San Francisco (although he lived in North Beach for extended periods—in the late 1960s at the Southeast corner of Chestnut and Powell Streets, in 1979 in an alley near Chestnut and Columbus). He has been married several times and fathered three children. He has lived in Europe for long years yet remains in his language a true American primitive of the Lower East Side. Living Shelley's vision of the pure poet, he burns up life, his every act a flame-out. On the back of *Gasoline*, Jack Kerouac wrote "Gregory was a tough young kid from the Lower East Side who rose like an angel over the rooftops and sang Italian songs as sweet as Caruso and Sinatra, but in *words*. 'Sweet Milanese hills' brood in his Renaissance soul, evening is coming on the hills. Amazing and beautiful Gregory Corso, the one & only Gregory the Herald. . . ."

$\mathcal{A}$ T THE SAVOY TIVOLI on upper Grant
Avenue in 1978 (left to right): Bob
Kaufman, Gregory Corso, Harold Norse,
and Neeli Cherkovski, the last an editor
of *Beatitude*, poet, and biographer. Harold
Norse was for a long time an expatriate
(mostly in France and Greece) but re-
turned to the United States in the early
1970s and became a hot gay poet in San
Francisco following publication of his
Hotel Nirvana and Other Poems and
Carnivorous Saint.

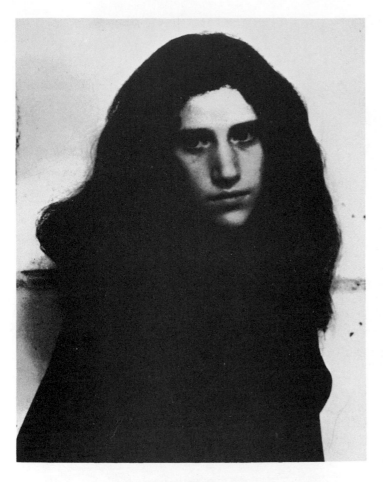

*D*IANE DI PRIMA, a power on the poetry scene for many years as editor and publisher of *Floating Bear* and the Poets Press, came west in the 1960s. Her major poetry work in the last few years in San Francisco has been *Loba*, which Adrienne Rich described as "an epic act of language, a great geography of the female imagination." Muriel Rukeyser said the *Loba* poems are "old incantations made new in our living flesh."

Diane di Prima was one of the San Francisco poets who participated in the City of Rome's International Poetry Festival in June 1979. The Communist government of Rome backed the Roman *Teatro Beat* in inviting dissident writers from capitalist countries and establishment poets from the USSR. (They were the only ones who could get out.)

*W*OMAN'S GROUP in Bolinas in 1979 including painters, poets, and journalists. (There was a bookstore affair across the street at the Blue Heron.) The individuals of this power group inspired many a male writer (as well as themselves) on this very last frontier—a wooden sidewalk, dirt road hamlet an hour northwest of the Golden Gate. Among writers who have lived there for at least a month since 1969, the better known are Bill Berkson, Tom Clark, Lewis Warsh, Richard Brautigan, Joanne Kyger, Robert Creeley, Ted Berrigan, David Meltzer, Ebbe Borregaard, Aram Saroyan, Gerard Malanga, Lewis MacAdams, Philip Whalen, Peter Warshall, Orville Schell, Kenneth Lamott, Bobbie Louise Hawkins, Alice Notley, Jim Carroll, Jim Koller, Margot Patterson Doss, Duncan Mac-Naughton, Charles Fox.

Although city slickers in their urbanity have been known to refer to the "Bolinas bucolics," writers there are for the most part fugitives from pathogenic industrial civilization and/or from old bourgeois life-styles (as was the Carmel group early in the century and the Southern Agrarians who called themselves Fugitives in the 1930s). The town is full of ecologists and counterculture—if not countercapitalist—activists and quietists, including writers and editors who made it big elsewhere and dropped out or spaced out in the psychedelic 1960s and never came back. There are part-time editors of *CoEvolution Quarterly* and erstwhile Rolling Stone writers. There are "New York school" poets associated with *Big Sky* magazine once published in Bolinas. There is Donald M. Allen, an early Grove Press editor who put together the San Francisco issue of *Evergreen Review* and *The New American Poetry* anthology— books which brought into focus a new

national poetry front, largely based in San Francisco. Today it remains the principal non-academic poetry scene in the country.

As this book goes to press, Donald Allen is moving back to the City, where his Grey Fox Press will undoubtedly continue to publish important seminal texts. Just published: Allen Ginsberg's *Composed On the Tongue*, including "Improvised Poetics," and "Encounters with Ezra Pound," reprinted from *City Lights Journal*. Among others in the Grey Fox's lair are Philip Whalen, Edward Dorn, Charles Olson, Robert Creeley, Michael McClure, Gary Snyder, Jack Spicer, and Lew Welch.

(In the Bibliography will be found contributions of other San Francisco little presses, too numerous to catalog here. These small work-horses of the continuing San Francisco movement deserve a separate book.)

SURREALISTS CELEBRATING the birthday of "The Splendid Bird of Sabotage" jazz great Charlie Parker, with a poetry reading in 1979 (left to right): Philip Lamantia, Nancy Joyce Peters, and Ted Joans.

As a fifteen-year-old high school student, Lamantia had his first poems published in 1943 by André Breton in *VVV*. The next year Lamantia left home (San Francisco's outer Mission district) and joined the Surrealists in exile in New York. He subsequently researched indigenous cultures, historic transmutations, magic and the *poetic marvelous* in Mexico, Morocco, Greece, Spain, and—since 1970—in San Francisco. For him, "Surrealism is a vital myth through which a permanent revelation of humanity shall become a *new way of life*." He is a contributing editor of *Arsenal: Surrealist Subversion* and writes for *Cultural Correspondence*. His books of poetry include *Touch of the Marvelous, Blood of the Air*, and *Selected Poems*.

After nearly a decade of international adventure and intrigue, mostly in Europe and the Middle East (looking into esoteric Egypt), Nancy Joyce Peters (Lamantia) did a year as a librarian at the Library of Congress before landing in San Francisco (1971) where she is an editor-director of City Lights Books, poet (*It's In the Wind*), and contributor to *Arsenal* and *Cultural Correspondence*.

At the right is Ted Joans, genuine and original jazz poet who chose Surrealism as a weapon to defend himself against the "abject vicissitudes" of racist society. Joans has been active with the New York hipsters, Beats, and black poets everywhere. His poetic trajectory propels him around the world, and he lights longest and brightest in Timbuktu and Paris. Among his scattered works are *Funky Jazz Poems, The Hipsters, Afrodisia, Black Pow-Wow, Jazz Is Our Religion*, and *Flying Piranha* (with Joyce Mansour).

$\mathcal{T}$HE MISSION CULTURAL CENTER in San Francisco continues to be the vortex of swirling Latin American activism in the arts. Situated in the heart of the Mission district, with its enormous Latino population, the center has been the host for many militant literary events, usually supporting liberation movements in one or another Latin American or Caribbean country. Further support has been evident in new mural painting (in the tradition of Diego Rivera and Siqueros) upon public walls all over the Mission district.

In close touch with Newyorican writers in lower Manhattan (particularly at the Newyorican Café), San Francisco Latino writers were much more active politically in the 1970s, and in fact more effective, than their Anglo counterparts in town. Two years before the Sandinista victories in Nicaragua, poet and Catholic priest Ernesto Cardenal (at left, at microphone) was presented to an enthusiastic audience at the center, introduced by Roberto Vargas (on the left), resident Nicaraguan writer. With the victory of the popular revolutionary forces in Nicaragua, Cardenal has become Minister of Culture in the new government. At another event about the same time (1977), Fernando Alegria reads from his poetry as Vargas listens. Alegria, senior professor at Stanford University and a leading Chilean (pro-Allende) poet, is also editor of a quarterly of Chilean literature in exile.

*W*ATERFRONT WRITERS AND ARTISTS gathered on the docks at the time of the publication of their *Waterfront Writers: The Literature of Work* issued in San Francisco by Harper & Row in September 1979. (Left to right): (in front) Mike Vawter, George Benet, Norm Young, Herb Mills, Ken Fox, Gene Dennis, Brian Nelson, and Bob Carson. In back Charley Hansen (in visor; not one of the writers) and Max Mallia (eyes closed). Edited by Robert Carson, longshoreman and founder of the group, the collection included poetry and (as the jacket blurb put it) "fictional writing, sociology, oral history, and philosophical enquiry by workers who stand at the juncture of a colorful past and a mechanized, routine future." The blurb further allied these writers with Studs Terkel (Chicago author of *Working*) and Eric Hoffer. The latter, a San Francisco waterfront worker of an earlier generation now in his late seventies, also indulged in philosophical enquiry, notably in *The True Believer*, published by Harper & Row in 1951. This was followed by *The Ordeal of Change* in 1963, and the title reveals its bias: To Hoffer, change was an ordeal, not an opportunity for revolution.

Many of the present waterfront writers would probably not count themselves as true believers in Hoffer's homespun philosophy. In a caustic and hilarious 1979 review of Hoffer's *Before the Sabbath* in the *San Francisco Chronicle*, Grover Sales began,

> In the late 40's San Francisco's longshoreman-pundit Eric Hoffer got media-whooped as a Deep Thinker for a pastiche of contradictory aphorisms, crochets, and high-flown-wind called "The True Believer," reputed to be Dwight Eisenhower's favorite reading, along with pulp Westerns. In a rare flash of unarguable lucidity, Hoffer wrote, "Eisenhower mastered the art of saying nothing at great length." The same applies to Hoffer's most recent book, his tenth. . . .
>
> The recurrent abuse of "intellectuals" and "professors" may endear Hoffer's junk food-for-thought to a vast audience of impressionables who mistake snap philosophy and off-the-wall history for self-improvement. . . . Eric Hoffer is to philosophy what Rod McKuen is to poetry.

*C*ONTRIBUTORS TO *Y'BIRD* (1979): (Left to right): (standing) Lawson Inada, Joe Bruchac, Victor Cruz, Alex Kuo, James Welch, Al Young, Neil Parsons, Mei-mei Berssenbrugge; (sitting) Frank Chin, Phil George, Ishmael Reed. Ishmael Reed, in his Preface to Grove Press's *Yardbird Reader*, says:

The American multicultural renaissance, still ignored by the major book reviewers, precipitated the decline of the powerful Eastern cultural establishment. Due to its limiting Eastern vantage point, it was incapable of assaying the true national culture. . . . As the ethnic phase of American literature ends—counter-culture ethnic, black ethnic, red ethnic, feminist ethnic, academic ethnic, beat ethnic, New York school ethnic, and all of the other churches who believe their choir sings the best— the National poetry begins."

Founded in 1972, *Yardbird* published five issues between 1972 and 1976. The editors were Ishmael Reed, Al Young, Shawn Wong, and William Lawson. (Ishmael Reed and Al Young are the most potent novelists writing in the San Francisco area today and certainly among the best in America. Books like Ishmael Reed's *Mumbo Jumbo* put the latest masterpieces of Philip Roth, Saul Bellow, John Fowles, and other university novelists in the deep shade.)

*J*N THAT UNIQUE RUSHING TOGETHER of cultures which has become more and more evident on the West Coast since World War II, the Before Columbus Foundation is a literary catalyst. The Before Columbus Foundation in Berkeley is Pre-Columbian only in a symbolic sense, as is evident in this multi-ethnic picture which itself exemplifies what the Foundation is all about. Started in about 1974, the Foundation is a wholesaler and distributor of American multicultural writings. It functions as a forum for the dissemination of information on all of America's varied ethnic and cultural traditions, and it acts as agent in scheduling writers' readings and selling their books across the country. It works (in the words of Ishmael Reed) "to expand the horizons of the multi-cultural literary experience."

(Left to right): Shawn Wong, Simon Ortiz, Robert Callahan, Victor Cruz, David Meltzer, Ishmael Reed.

The shape of the future may possibly be discerned in such unifying literary forces as the Before Columbus coalition. In the wake of "tune in, turn on, drop out" life styles and the collapse of the New Left in the fragmented 1970s, many embryonic coalitions across the world today (from West Coast multi-cultural groups to One World Poetry Festivals in Europe) seem in effect to be rejoining old radical traditions calling for a new free society transcending the special interests of isolated minority groups, and beyond nations.

THE EAGLE CAFE, opposite Pier 43 on the Embarcadero, in 1975. The occasion was the arrival of the S.S. *Pacific Queen*, and this composite photo by Clem Albers was "augmented" by Joe Rosenthal, *San Francisco Chronicle* photographer famous for his shot of the Iwo Jima flag raising in World War II. The Eagle, much-loved hangout for longshoremen, beltline railroadmen, waterfront writers, and waterfront buffs, was moved intact to the first floor of nearby Pier 39 three years after this picture was taken.

Nineteenth-century log books preserved aboard the *Balclutha* (the square-rigged sailing ship in the photo) record the lashes meted out before the mast to rebellious seamen. It wasn't Richard Henry Dana but Andrew Furuseth (the personification of all the Sailors' Union stood for years later) who said this for the crews: "You can put me in jail. But you cannot give me narrower quarters than as a seaman I have always had. You cannot give me worse food than I have always eaten. You cannot make me lonelier than I have always been." These words, as close to poetry as prose can get, are recorded on Furuseth's monument on Market Street.

Life remains realer than literature here on the Embarcadero, which is one side of the inner city (seen in the map below), its other boundaries being Market Street and Van Ness Avenue. North Beach—about the size of Greenwich Village—from the old Montgomery Block to the Embarcadero, has always been the center of the literary life of the City. The *New York Times Magazine* (in a recent feature on "The Poetry Boom") called it "North Beach, California."

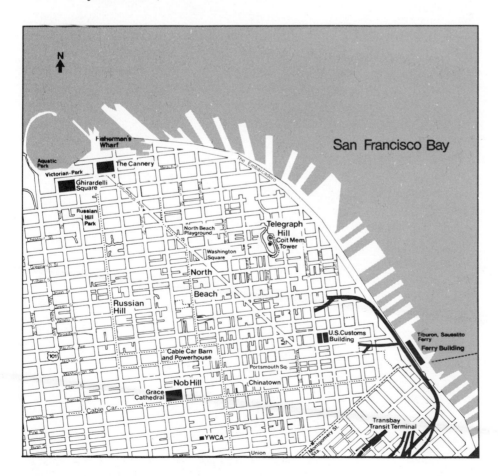

Afterword

We tracked *Literary San Francisco* through the years from opposite ends of its history. I began at the beginning and moved forward chronologically, while Ferlinghetti set off from the contemporary period back through the twentieth century. Like the transcontinental railroad, we met at midpoint. But it wasn't easy to cover so elusive a territory, for San Francisco area writers are as restless as they are numerous. They've always been on the road—that road (from Twain to London to Kerouac) running through the American literary imagination as if it would tie together a vast, unruly continent. Some who were born here, like Robert Frost or Gertrude Stein, left home to put down roots in other places; some, like Stevenson, Steinbeck, or Henry Miller, stayed only briefly. Many famous native sons and daughters were not natives at all. And from the gold rush, myriad innocents abroad (or children of empire) have been moving in and out of town at a prodigious pace.

When we put the two parts of this book together, it was clear that other things haven't changed much over the years. Nineteenth century recitations and oratory go on now in poetry readings; the popular broadsides grew into a flourishing small press tradition. San Francisco, though perhaps not "the most infernal hole on the face of the earth," as Horace Greeley thought, is still isolated, with a provincial enthusiasm for illustrious foreign visitors. The literary wars rage just as they did in the mid-1860s; bohemian and eccentric spiritual communities sprout like poppies in the golden hills.

Familiar figures and themes thread through both centuries: wilderness writers, prophesying bearded bards, humorists in dead earnest, novelists of the road (with their comrades and muses), women writers struggling to be heard. Drug fiends, geographers of inner and outer space; tracers of lost persons and the dark intricacies of the human heart. Visionary mystics and poets of apocalyptic or hermetic illumination. Realists, reformers, feminists enragées, and radicals. Wits and gossips; playful, satiric, and muckraking journalists; populist poets and sentimental favorites; hard-drinking Wild West macho poets, and queens of Bohemia. The scandalous, the invisible, the anguished, the suicides.

Earthquakes, dank fogs, and strong winds roaring in off the Pacific are still part of this beautiful place; and so are injustice, greed, and the gross misuse of money—Mammon and Molloch loom larger than ever. Lionel Trilling lamented that no first-rate American writer had dealt with the great ideas of progress, social legislation, planning, and international cooperation in a great literary way. Few literary San Franciscans pass muster, I suppose, before the academic mandarins. As it happens, most of the writers pictured in this book have not been satisfied with the rationalist, bourgeois mystique; they've always moved on out beyond the liberal imagination. There is in them a tendency to excess, wild innovation, and often a blazing moral energy. Think of those early dreamers of radical equality and harmonian democracy, of new writers from ethnic and marginal populations, so long muted by the dominant culture, now bursting into bright prominence. And think of the explosive contemporary underground that opts for eros over death—returning passion to the body, re-thinking humanity's relation to nature, and standing against war.

The coast's continuing vitality comes partly from that tension here at continent's end, the land of first and last chance. A pervading sense of impermanence, of mortality, urges renewed awareness of *being*. It not only impels life to overcome literature, but our best writers to make a conscious stab at the impossible, to invent a high existence. That old Terrestrial Paradise haunts the imagination yet. They're still out here, dancing on the brink of the world.

—NANCY J. PETERS

Abbott, Keith. *Rhino Ritz: An American Mystery*. Berkeley, Calif.: Blue Wind Press, 1979.

Adam, Helen, and Adam, Pat. *San Francisco's Burning*. Berkeley, Calif.: Oannes Press, 1963.

Adams, Alice. *Beautiful Girl*. New York: Knopf, 1978.

Alegria, Fernando. *Instructions for Undressing the Human Race*. San Francisco: Kayak Books, 1968.

Allen, Donald M., ed. *The New American Poetry*. New York: Grove Press, 1960.

Allen, Donald M., ed. *The Poetics of the New American Poetry*. New York: Grove Press, 1973.

Allen, Judith. "The Life and Writings of Nora May French." Unpublished Master's thesis, Mills College, Oakland, 1963.

Anagogic and Paideumic Review no. 1 (September 1959). Edited by Sheri Martinelli. San Francisco.

Anderson, Margaret, ed. *The Little Review*, September 1916. San Francisco.

Anderson, Poul. *Brain Wave*. New York: Ballantine, 1954.

Angelou, Maya. *I Know Why the Caged Bird Sings*. New York: Random House, 1969.

Angulo, Jaime de. *Indian Tales*. New York: A. A. Wyn, 1953.

Anthony, Gene. *The Summer of Love: Haight-Ashbury at Its Highest*. Millbrae, Calif.: Celestial Arts, 1980.

Argonaut, 1877–1958. San Francisco.

Ark Nos. 1 (1947), 2 (1956–1957), 3 (1957). San Francisco.

Arthur, Gavin. *The Circle of Sex*. San Francisco: privately printed, 1966.

Asher, Don. *Blood Summer*. New York: Putnam, 1977.

Atherton, Gertrude. *Adventures of a Novelist*. New York: Liveright, 1932.

Atherton, Gertrude. *Patience Sparhawk and Her Times*. New York and London: J. Lane, 1897.

Austin, Mary. *The American Rhythm*. New York: Harpers, 1923.

Austin, Mary. *Earth Horizon*. Boston: Houghton Mifflin, 1932.

Austin, Mary [Gordon Stairs, pseud.] *Outland*. London: J. Murray, 1910.

Badé, William F. *The Life and Letters of John Muir*. Boston and New York: Houghton Mifflin, 1924.

Baird, Joseph A. *California's Pictorial Letter Sheets 1849–1869*. San Francisco: David Magee, 1967.

Bancroft, Hubert Howe. *The Works of Hubert Howe Bancroft*. Vols. 38 and 39. San Francisco: A. L. Bancroft, 1882–1890.

Bancroft Scraps. "California Authors." Scrapbook in Bancroft Library, Berkeley, Calif.

Barker, Charles A. "Henry George and the California Background of Progress and Poverty."

California Historical Society Quarterly 24, no. 2 (June 1945)

Barker, Eric. *The Planetary Heart*. Mill Valley, Calif.: Wings Press, 1942.

Beasley, Delilah. *The Negro Trail Blazers of California*. San Francisco: California Historical Society and San Francisco Negro Historical and Cultural Society, 1919.

Beatitude, 1959–1980. San Francisco.

Bechdolt, Frederick, and Hopper, James. *9009*. New York: McClure, 1908.

Bell, James Madison. *The Day and the War*. San Francisco: Agnew and Deffenbach, 1864.

Benson, Ivan. *Mark Twain's Western Years*. Stanford, Calif.: Stanford University Press, 1938.

Berkson, Bill. *Parts of the Body*. Bolinas, Calif.: Tombouctou Books, 1980.

Berriault, Gina. *The Mistress and Other Stories*. New York: Dutton, 1965.

Bierce, Ambrose. *The Ambrose Bierce Satanic Reader: Selections from the Invective Journalism of the Great Satirist*. Edited by Ernest Jerome Hopkins. Garden City, N.Y.: Doubleday, 1968.

Bierce, Ambrose. *The Collected Works of Ambrose Bierce*. New York: W. Neale, 1909–1912.

Bierce, Ambrose. *The Enlarged Devil's Dictionary*. Garden City, N.Y.: Doubleday, 1967.

Bierce, Ambrose. *The Letters of Ambrose Bierce*. Edited by Bertha Clark Pope. New York: Gordian Press, 1967.

Big Sky nos. 1–9 (1971–1975). Edited by Bill Berkson et al. Bolinas, Calif.

Blazek, Douglas. *Zany Typhoons*. Sacramento, Calif.: Open Skull Press, 1970.

Blazer, Robin. *Cups*. San Francisco: Four Seasons Foundation, 1968.

Blue, Janice. *In Good Old No-Man's Land*. San Francisco: Green Light Press, 1978.

Bolton, Herbert E. *Anza's California Expeditions*. Berkeley, Calif.: University of California Press, 1930.

Borthwick, J. D. *Three Years in California 1851–1854*. Oakland, Calif.: Biobooks, 1948.

Boyle, Kay. *Fifty Stories*. New York: Doubleday, 1980.

Boyle, Kay. *The Long Walk at San Francisco State and Other Essays*. New York: Grove Press, 1970.

Brautigan, Richard. *Confederate General from Big Sur*. New York: Grove Press, 1964.

Brautigan, Richard. *Trout Fishing in America*. San Francisco: Four Seasons Foundation, 1967.

Brawley, Ernest. *The Rap*. New York: Atheneum, 1974.

Brewer, William. *Up and Down California in 1860–1864*. New Haven, Conn.: Yale University Press, 1931.

Brooks, Van Wyck. *Scenes and Portraits*. New York: Dutton, 1954.

Brooks, Van Wyck. *The Times of Melville and Whitman*. New York: Dutton, 1947.

Broughton, James. *Seeing the Light*. San Francisco: City Lights Books, 1977.

Broughton, James. *True and False Unicorn*. New York: Grove Press, 1957.

Brown, Cecil. *Life and Loves of Mr. Jiveass Nigger*. Farrar, Straus & Giroux, 1970.

Brown, John Henry. *Reminiscences and Incidents of the Early Days of San Francisco*. San Francisco: Mission Journal, 1886.

Brown, William. *The Way to the Uncle Sam Hotel*. San Francisco: Coyote Books, 1964.

Browne, J. Ross. *Crusoe's Island: A Ramble in the Footsteps of Alexander Selkirk, with Sketches of Adventure in California and Washoe*. New York: Harper and Brothers, 1864.

Browne, J. Ross. *J. Ross Browne: His Letters, Journals, and Writings*. Albuquerque, N.M.: University of New Mexico Press, 1969.

Bruce, Lennart. *Making the Rounds*. San Francisco: Kayak Press, 1967.

Bruce, Lenny. *How to Talk Dirty and Influence People*. Chicago: Playboy Press, 1965.

Bruce, Lenny. *Stamp Help Out*. San Francisco: privately printed, 1963.

Buckley, Lord. *Hiparama of the Classics*. San Francisco: City Lights Books, 1960.

Bukowski, Charles. *Erections, Ejaculations, Exhibitions, and General Tales of Ordinary Madness*. San Francisco: City Lights Books, 1972.

Bukowski, Charles. *Notes of a Dirty Old Man*. San Francisco: City Lights Books, 1973.

Burdick, Eugene, and Wheeler, Harvey. *Fail-Safe*. New York: McGraw-Hill, 1962.

Burgess, Gelett. *Bayside Bohemia: Fin de Siècle San Francisco and Its Little Magazines*. San Francisco: Book Club of California, 1954.

Burgess, Gelett. *The Heart Line*. Indianapolis: Bobbs-Merrill, 1907.

Busch, Niven. *California Street*. New York: Simon & Schuster, 1959.

Busch, Niven. *The San Franciscans*. New York: Simon & Schuster, 1962.

Caen, Herb. *Baghdad-by-the-Bay*. Garden City, N.Y.: Doubleday, 1949.

Caen, Herb. *The San Francisco Book*. Photographs by Max Yavno. Boston: Houghton Mifflin, 1948.

Californian, 1864–1866. Edited by Charles Henry Webb and Bret Harte. San Francisco.

Caputo, Thomas H. *Fifty Selected Poems*. San Francisco: Thorp Springs Press, 1977.

Carpenter, Don. *Hard Rain Falling*. New York: Harcourt, Brace & World, 1966.

Carson, Robert, ed. *Waterfront Writers*. San Francisco: Harper & Row, 1979.

Cassady, Carolyn. *Heart Beat: My Life with Neal and Jack*. Berkeley, Calif.: Creative Arts, 1976.

Cassady, Neal. *The First Third and Other Writings*. San Francisco: City Lights Books, 1971.

Chamisso, Adelbert von. *A Sojourn at San Francisco Bay, 1816*. San Francisco: Book Club of California, 1936.

Change no. 1 (1963). Edited by Ron Loewinsohn and Richard Brautigan. San Francisco.

Chapman, Charles Edward. *A History of California: The Spanish Period*. New York: Macmillan, 1930.

Cherkovski, Neeli. *Ferlinghetti: A Biography*. Garden City, N.Y.: Doubleday, 1979.

Cherkovski, Neeli. *Public Notice*. San Francisco: Beatitude Press, 1976.

Chiarrello, Gail. *Bhangra Dance*. Berkeley, Calif.: Oyez Press, 1970.

Chin, Frank, and Inada, Lawson Fusao, eds. *Aiiieeeee: An Anthology of Asian American Writers*. Washington, D.C.: Howard University Press, 1974.

Chinn, Thomas W. *A History of the Chinese in California*. San Francisco: Chinese Historical Society of America, 1969.

Choris, Ludovik [Louis]. *Voyage Pittoresque Autour du Monde*. Paris: Firmon Didot, 1822.

Circle nos. 1–10 (1944–1948). Edited by George Leite and Bern Porter. Berkeley, Calif.

City Lights Anthology. San Francisco: City Lights Books, 1974.

City Lights Journal nos. 1 (1961), 2 (1964), 3 (1966), 4 (1978). San Francisco.

Clappe, Louise Amelia Knapp Smith. *California in 1851–1852: The Letters of Dame Shirley*. Introduction by Carl Wheat. San Francisco: Grabhorn Press, 1933.

Clark, Tom. *How I Broke In*. Bolinas, Calif.: Tombouctou Books, 1977.

Clemens, Samuel L. *Mark Twain's Autobiography*. Introduction by Albert Bigelow Paine. New York: Collier, 1925.

Clemens, Samuel L. *Mark Twain's Letters*. Edited by Albert Bigelow Paine. New York: Harper and Brothers, 1917.

Clemens, Samuel L. *Mark Twain's Notebook*. Edited by Albert Bigelow Paine. New York: Harper and Brothers, 1935.

Clemens, Samuel L. *Roughing It*. Hartford, Conn.: American Publishing, 1872.

Clemens, Samuel L., and Harte, Bret. *Sketches of the Sixties*. San Francisco: John Howell, 1926.

Codrescu, Andrei. *The Life and Times of an Involuntary Genius*. New York: Braziller, 1975.

Collins, Robert. *John Halsey, the Anti-Monopolist*. San Francisco: G. F. Neal, 1881.

Connell, Evan S., Jr., *Mrs. Bridge*. New York: Viking, 1959.

Conrad, Barnaby. *Matador*. New York: Houghton Mifflin, 1952.

Contact, 1958–1965. Sausalito, Calif.

Coolbrith, Ina. *Songs from the Golden Gate.* Boston: Houghton Mifflin, 1895.

Corso, Gregory. *Gasoline.* San Francisco: City Lights Books, 1958.

Creeley, Robert. *A Form of Women.* New York: Jargon/Corinth, 1959.

Creeley, Robert. *Selected Poems.* New York: Charles Scribner's Sons, 1976.

Cummins (Mighels), Ella Sterling. *Literary California: Poetry, Prose, and Portraits.* San Francisco: Harr Wagner, 1918.

Cummins (Mighels), Ella Sterling. *The Story of the Files.* San Francisco: Cooperative Printing Co., 1893.

Cutter, Donald C., ed. *The California Coast: A Bilingual Edition of Documents from the Sutro Collection.* Norman, Okla.: University of Oklahoma Press, 1969.

Daggett, Rollin Mallory. *Braxton's Bar.* New York: G. W. Carleton, 1882.

Dahlen, Beverly. *Out of the Third.* San Francisco: Momo's Press, 1974.

Dana, Richard Henry. *Two Years Before the Mast.* New York: Harpers, 1840.

Dawson, Emma Frances. *An Itinerant House and Other Stories.* San Francisco: William Doxey, 1897.

De Ford, Miriam Allen. *They Were San Franciscans.* Caldwell, Idaho: Caxton, 1947.

Delano, Alonzo. *A Live Woman in the Mines.* New York: Samuel French, 1857.

Delano, Alonzo. *Pen-Knife Sketches; or, Chips of the Old Block.* San Francisco: Union Office, 1853.

Derby, George Horatio. *Phoenixiana; or, Sketches and Burlesques.* New York: Appleton, 1856.

Di Prima, Diane. *Revolutionary Letters.* San Francisco: City Lights Books, 1974.

Di Prima, Diane. *War Poems.* New York: Poets Press, 1968.

Domhoff, G. William. *The Bohemian Grove and Other Retreats.* New York: Harper & Row, 1974.

Dorn, Edward. *The Collected Poems 1956–1974.* Bolinas, Calif.: Four Seasons Foundation, 1975.

Doss, Margo Patterson. *San Francisco at Your Feet.* New York: Grove Press, 1964.

Doyle, Arthur Conan. *Our Second American Adventure.* London: Hodder and Stoughton, 1924.

Doyle, Kirby. *Sapphobones.* New York: Poets Press, 1966.

Drinnon, Richard. *Rebel in Paradise: A Biography of Emma Goldman.* Chicago: University of Chicago Press, 1961.

Duerden, Richard. *The Air's Nearly Perfect Elasticity.* Bolinas, Calif.: Tombouctou Books, 1979.

Duncan, Isadora. *My Life.* New York: Boni and Liveright, 1927.

Duncan, Robert. *Bending the Bow.* New York: New Directions, 1968.

Duncan, Robert. *Heavenly City, Earthly City.* Drawings by Mary Fabilli. Berkeley, Calif.: Bern Porter, 1947.

Dumas, Alexandre. *Un Gil Blas en Californie.* Paris: M. Levy, 1851.

Emrich, Duncan. *Comstock Bonanza: Western Americana of J. Ross Browne, Mark Twain, Sam Davis, Bret Harte, James N. Galley, Dan de Quille, Joseph T. Goodman, Fred Hart.* New York: Vanguard Press, 1950.

Erlich, J. W., ed. *Howl of the Censor.* San Carlos, Calif.: Nourse, 1961.

Evergreen Review 1, no. 2 (1957). New York.

Everson, William [Brother Antoninus]. *Archetype West: The Pacific Coast as a Literary Region.* Berkeley, Calif.: Oyez Press, 1976.

Everson, William. *The Residual Years.* New York: New Directions, 1958.

Ferling, Lawrence, pseud. *La Cité: Symbôle dans la Poésie Moderne de Langue Anglaise.* Unpublished doctoral thesis, University of Paris, 1951.

Ferlinghetti, Lawrence. *A Coney Island of the Mind.* New York: New Directions, 1958.

Ferlinghetti, Lawrence. *Landscapes of Living & Dying.* New York: New Directions, 1979.

Field, Sara Bard. *Darkling Plain.* New York: Random House, 1936.

Forbes, Kathryn. *Mama's Bank Account.* New York: Harcourt Brace, 1943.

Fixel, Lawrence. *The Scale of Silence: Parables.* Santa Cruz, Calif.: Kayak Books, 1970.

Fleischmann, Christa. *Mark in Time.* San Francisco: Glide Publications, 1971.

Forrey, Carolyn. "Gertrude Atherton and the New Woman." *California Historical Society Quarterly* 55, no. 3 (Fall 1976).

Fox, Charles. *The Noble Enemy.* New York: Doubleday, 1980.

French, Nora May. *Poems.* San Francisco: The Strange Company, 1910.

Gaines, Ernest J. *The Autobiography of Miss Jane Pittman.* New York: Dial Press, 1971.

Gardner, Leonard. *Fat City.* New York: Farrar, Straus & Giroux, 1969.

Garnett, Porter. *The Bohemian Jinks.* San Francisco: The Bohemian Club, 1908.

Garnett, Porter. Collection of articles from the *Pacific Monthly*, 1907–1909. Bancroft Library, Berkeley, Calif.

Genthe, Arnold. *As I Remember.* New York: Reynal and Hitchcock, 1936.

Gentry, Curt. *Frame Up: The Incredible Case of Tom Mooney and Warren Billings.* New York: Norton, 1967.

George, Henry. *Progress and Poverty.* New York: J. W. Lovell, 1879.

George, Henry, Jr. *The Life of Henry George.* New York: Doubleday, 1900.

Gilman, Charlotte Perkins. *In This Our World and Other Poems.* San Francisco: Barry and Marble, 1895.

Gilman, Charlotte Perkins. *The Living of Charlotte Perkins Gilman.* New York: Appleton-Century, 1935.

Ginsberg, Allen. *Howl and Other Poems.* San Francisco: City Lights Books, 1956.

Ginsberg, Allen. *Kaddish and Other Poems, 1958–1960.* San Francisco: City Lights Books, 1961.

Gleason, Madeline. *Poems 1944.* San Francisco: Grabhorn Press, 1945.

Goad, 1951–1953. Edited by Horace Schwartz. Sausalito, Calif.

Gold, Herbert. *Fathers.* New York: Random House, 1966.

Gold, Herbert. *Salt.* New York: Dial Press, 1963.

Golden Era, 1852–1893. San Francisco.

Grieg, Michael. *A Fire In His Hand.* New York: Tower Books, 1963.

Griffin, Susan. *Woman and Nature: The Roaring Inside Her.* New York: Harper & Row, 1978.

Gunn, Thom. *Jack Straw's Castle and Other Poems.* New York: Farrar, Straus & Giroux, 1976.

Gustafson, Jim. *Tales of Virtue & Transformation.* San Francisco: Coyote Books, 1964.

Hagedorn, Jessica Tarahata. *Dangerous Muse.* San Francisco: Momo's Press, 1975.

Hall, Carol B. *The Bierce-Poe Hoax.* San Francisco: Book Club of California, 1939.

Hammett, Dashiell. *The Maltese Falcon.* New York: A. A. Knopf, 1930.

Hammett, Dashiell. *The Thin Man.* New York: A. A. Knopf, 1932.

Hansen, Harvey J., and Miller, Jeanne Thurlow. *Wild Oats in Eden: Sonoma County in the 19th Century.* Santa Rosa, Calif.: privately published, 1962.

Harris, Mark. *Something About a Soldier.* New York: Macmillan, 1957.

Harris, Thomas Lake. *The New Republic.* Santa Rosa, Calif.: Fountain Grove Press, 1891.

Hart, James D. *American Images of Spanish California.* Berkeley, Calif.: Friends of the Bancroft Library, 1960.

Hart, James D. "Bohemia, Hubert Howe Bancroft, and the Bancroft Library." *Bohemian Club Library Notes* 37 (New Year, 1977).

Hart, James D. *A Companion to California.* New York: Oxford University Press, 1978.

Hart, James D. *My First Publication.* San Francisco: Book Club of California, 1961.

Hart, James D. *Robert Louis Stevenson: From Scotland to Silverado.* Cambridge, England: Cambridge University Press, 1966.

Hart, Jerome A. *In Our Second Century.* San Francisco: Pioneer Press, 1931.

Harte, Bret. *Condensed Novels and Other Papers.* New York: Carleton, 1867.

Harte, Bret. *The Complete Works of Bret Harte in Prose and Poetry.* London: J. C. Hotten, 1873.

Harte, Bret. *The Letters of Bret Harte.* Edited by Geoffrey Bret Harte. Boston and New York: Houghton Mifflin, 1926.

Harte, Bred, ed. *Outcroppings.* San Francisco: A. Roman, 1865.

Hartmann, Sadakichi. *My Rubaiyat.* San Francisco: privately published, 1916.

Haskell, Burnett, G. *What Nationalism Is, the American Cure for Monopoly and Anarchy.* San Francisco: privately published, 1889?

Hawkins, Bobbie, Louise. *Frenchy and Cuban Pete.* Bolinas, Calif.: Tombouctou Books, 1977.

Heizer, Robert, and Almquist, Alan F. *The Other Californians: Prejudice and Discrimination under Spain, Mexico, and the United States to 1920.* Berkeley, Calif.: University of California Press, 1971.

Henderson, David. *Felix of the Silent Forest.* Introduction by Leroi Jones. New York: Poets Press, 1967.

Henderson, David. *Jimi Hendrix: Voodoo Child of the Aquarian Age.* New York: Doubleday, 1978.

Herd, Dale. *Early Morning Wind and Other Stories.* Bolinas, Calif.: Four Seasons Foundation, 1972.

Hernandez-Cruz, Victor. *Tropicalizations.* Berkeley, Calif.: Reed and Cannon, 1976.

Hesperian, 1858–1863. [later *Pacific Monthly*], San Francisco.

Hesperian no. 1 (1930). Edited by James D. Hart. San Francisco.

Hinckle III, Warren, and Turner, William. *The Cuba Project.* Boston: Houghton Mifflin, 1980.

Hine, Robert V. *California's Utopian Colonies.* New Haven, Conn.: Yale University Press, 1969.

Hirschman, Jack. *Lyripol.* San Francisco: City Lights Books, 1976.

Hitchcock, George. *Tactics of Survival and Other Poems.* San Francisco: Bindweed Press, 1964.

Hoffer, Eric. *The True Believer: Thoughts on the Nature of Mass Movements.* New York: Harper & Row, 1951.

Hoffer, Eric. *Working and Thinking on the Waterfront: A Journal.* New York: Harper & Row, 1969.

Hopper, James M. *Caybigan.* New York: McClure, Phillips, 1906.

Hopper, James M. Magazine Stories. (7 volumes, 1896–1956). Bancroft Library Collection, Berkeley, Calif.

Hoyem, Andrew. *The Wake.* San Francisco: Auerhahn Press, 1963.

Inferno, 1950–1956. Edited by Leslie Woolf Hedley. San Francisco.

Irwin, Inez. *Angels and Amazons.* Garden City, N.Y.: Doubleday, Doran, 1933.

Irwin, Wallace. *The Love Sonnets of a Hoodlum.* San Francisco: Elder and Shepard, 1902.

Irwin, Will. *The City that Was: A Requiem of Old San Francisco.* New York: B. W. Huebsch, 1906.

Issler, Anne (Roller). *Happier for His Presence: San Francisco and Robert Louis Stevenson.* Stanford, Calif.: Stanford University Press, 1949.

Jackson, Joseph Henry. *Irving Stone and the Biographical Novel.* Garden City, N.Y.: Country Life Press, 1954.

Jeffers, Robinson, *Selected Poems.* New York: Random House, 1965.

Joans, Ted. *A Black Manifesto in Jazz Poetry and Prose.* London: Calder and Boyars, 1971.

Johnson, Diane. *The Shadow Knows.* New York: A. A. Knopf, 1974.

Jones, Idwall. *Ark of Empire: San Francisco's Montgomery Block.* Garden City, N.Y.: Doubleday, 1951.

Journal for the Protection of All Beings no. 1. Edited by Lawrence Ferlinghetti, David Meltzer, and Michael McClure. San Francisco: City Lights Books, 1961.

Journal for the Protection of All Beings no. 4. Edited by Lawrence Ferlinghetti, David Meltzer, Michael McClure, and Gary Snyder. San Francisco and Sausalito: City Lights Books and Co-Evolution Quarterly, 1978.

Kamstra, Jerry. *The Frisco Kid.* New York: Harper & Row, 1972.

Kandel, Lenore. *The Love Book.* San Francisco: privately printed, 1966.

Kaplan, Justin. *Lincoln Steffens: A Biography.* New York: Simon & Schuster, 1974.

Kaufman, Bob. *Golden Sardine.* San Francisco: City Lights Books, 1967.

Kaufman, Bob. *Solitudes Crowded with Loneliness.* New York: New Directions, 1965.

Kayak nos. 1–12 (1964–1967). Edited by George Hitchcock. San Francisco.

Kazin, Alfred. *On Native Grounds.* New York: Reynal and Hitchcock, 1942.

Keeler, Ralph. *Vagabond Adventures.* Boston: Fields, Osgood, 1870.

Kees, Weldon. *Poems, 1947–1954.* San Francisco: Adrian Wilson, 1954.

Kemble, Edward Cleveland. *A Kemble Reader: Stories of California 1846–1848 . . .* San Francisco: California Historical Society, 1963.

Kerouac, Jack. *Big Sur.* New York: Farrar, Straus and Cudahy, 1962.

Kerouac, Jack. *Book of Dreams.* New York: Viking, 1961.

Kerouac, Jack. *On the Road.* New York: Viking, 1957.

Kertesz, Louise. *The Poetic Vision of Muriel Rukeyser.* Baton Rouge: Louisiana State University Press, 1980.

Kherdian, David. *Six Poets of the San Francisco Renaissance.* Introduction by William Saroyan. Fresno: Giligia Press, 1967.

King, Clarence. *Mountaineering in the Sierra Nevada.* Boston: J. R. Osgood, 1872.

Kingston, Maxine Hong. *The Woman Warrior.* New York: A. A. Knopf, 1976.

Kipling, Rudyard. *Letters from San Francisco.* San Francisco: Colt Press, 1949.

Kizer, Carolyn. *Midnight Was My Cry.* New York: Doubleday, 1971.

Koller, James. *Poems for the Blue Sky.* Santa Barbara, Calif.: Black Sparrow Press, 1976.

Kotzebue, Otto von. *Voyage of Discovery in the South Seas and to Behring's Straits.* London: printed for Sir Richard Phillips, 1821.

Kroeber, A. L. *Handbook of the Indians of California.* BAE Bulletin 78, Smithsonian Institution. Washington, D.C.: Government Printing Office, 1925.

Kroeber, Theodora. *Ishi in Two Worlds: A Biography of the Last Wild Indian in North America.* Berkeley, Calif.: University of California Press, 1968.

Kush. *How to Turn Your Living Room into Walden Pond.* San Francisco: Sleeping Gypsy Press, 1977.

Kyger, Joanne. *The Tapestry and the Web.* San Francisco: Four Seasons Foundation, 1965.

Lai, Him Mark; Lim, Genny; and Yung, Judy. *Island: Poems Written by Chinese Immigrants on Angel Island, 1910–1940.* San Francisco: HOC-DOI Project, 1980.

Laing, R. D. *The Politics of Experience.* New York: Ballantine Books, 1967.

Lamantia, Philip. *The Blood of the Air.* San Francisco: Four Seasons Foundation, 1970.

Lamantia, Philip. "Poetic Matters." *Arsenal: Surrealist Subversion* no. 3 (1976).

Lamantia, Philip. *Selected Poems, 1943–1966.* San Francisco: City Lights Books, 1967.

Langsdorf, Georg Heinrich. *Voyages and Travels in Various Parts of the World.* London: H. Colburn, 1812.

Lark, 1895–1897. Edited by Gelett Burgess. San Francisco.

Lawson, Todd S. J. *Patriotic Poems of Amerikkka.* San Francisco: Peace and Pieces Books, 1971.

Lefland, Ella. *Love Out of Season.* New York: Atheneum, 1974.

Leiber, Fritz. *The Best of Fritz Leiber.* Introduction by Poul Anderson. New York: Ballantine, 1974.

Leiber, Fritz. *Our Lady of Darkness.* New York: Berkeley Publishers, 1978.

Lewis, Grover. *I'll Be There in the Morning If I Live.* San Francisco: Straight Arrow, 1973.

Lewis, Oscar. *Bay Window Bohemia.* Garden City, N.Y.: Doubleday, 1956.

Lewis, Oscar. *San Francisco Since 1872: A Pictorial History of Seven Decades.* San Francisco, privately published, 1946.

Linenthal, Mark. *Growing Light.* San Francisco: Black Thumb Press, 1979.

Litvak, Leo. *College Days in Earthquake Country.* New York: Random House, 1971.

Lloyd, Benjamin E. *Lights and Shades in San Francisco.* San Francisco: A. L. Bancroft, 1876.

London, Charmian Kittredge. *The Book of Jack London.* New York: Century, 1921.

London, Charmian Kittredge. "George Sterling—As I Knew Him," *Overland Monthly* 86 (March 1927).

London, Jack. *Essays of Revolt.* New York: Vanguard Press, 1926.

London, Jack. *The Iron Heel.* New York: Macmillan, 1908.

London, Jack, and Strunsky, Anna. *The Kempton-Wace Letters.* New York: Macmillan, 1903.

London, Jack. *Martin Eden.* New York: Macmillan, 1908.

London, Jack. *The Road.* New York: Macmillan, 1907.

London, Jack. *The Valley of the Moon.* New York: Macmillan, 1913.

London, Joan. *Jack London and His Times.* Seattle, Wash.: University of Washington Press, 1939.

Lovecraft, Howard Phillips. *Supernatural Horror in Literature.* New York: Dover, 1973.

Ludlow, Fitz Hugh. *The Hasheesh Eater: Being Passages from the Life of a Pythagorean.* San Francisco: City Lights Books, 1979.

Lukas, Susan. *Stereopticon.* New York: Stein & Day, 1975.

MacAdams, Lewis. *The Poetry Room.* New York: Harper & Row, 1970.

McClure, Michael. *The Beard.* San Francisco: privately printed, 1965.

McClure, Michael. *Meat Science Essays.* San Francisco: City Lights Books, 1963.

McCunn, Ruthanne Lum. *An Illustrated History of the Chinese in America.* San Francisco: Design Enterprises, 1979.

McDevitt, William. *Ambrose Bierce on Richard Realf.* San Francisco: W. McDevitt, 1948.

McEwen, Arthur. *The Life and Times of the Virginia City Territorial Enterprise: Being Reminiscences of Five Distinguished Comstock Journalists.* Ashland, Ore.: Osborne, 1971.

McGettigan, Francisca Carillo Vallejo. *Along the Highway of the King.* Oakland and San Francisco: Howell-North, 1943.

McHugh, Vincent. *I Am Thinking of My Darling.* New York: Simon & Schuster, 1943.

McHugh, Vincent, and Kwock, C. H., trans. *Why I Live on the Mountain: Thirty Poems from the Chinese.* San Francisco: Golden Mountain Press, 1958.

McKuen, Rod. *Stanyan Street and Other Sorrows.* New York: Random House, 1967.

McWilliams, Carey, *Ambrose Bierce, a Biography.* New York: A. and C. Boni, 1929.

Marberry, M. Marion. *Splendid Poseur: A Biography of Joaquin Miller.* New York: Crowell, 1953.

Markham, Edwin. *The Man with the Hoe and Other Poems.* New York: Doubleday and McClure, 1899.

Meltzer, David, ed. *The San Francisco Poets.* New York: Ballantine, 1971.

Meltzer, David. *Tens: Selected Poems.* New York: McGraw-Hill, 1973.

Meltzer, Milton. *Mark Twain Himself.* New York: Crowell, 1960.

Mencken, H. L. *Prejudices: First Series.* New York: Knopf, 1919.

Menken, Adah Isaacs. *Infelicia.* Edited by John Thompson. Philadelphia: Lippincott, 1868.

Micheline, Jack. *North of Manhattan: Collected Poems.* Introduction by Jack Kerouac. San Francisco: Manroot, 1976.

Miles, Josephine. *To All Appearances: Poems New and Selected.* Urbana, Ill.: University of Illinois Press, 1974.

Miles, Josephine. *Coming to Terms.* Urbana, Ill.: University of Illinois Press, 1979.

Miller, Henry. *Patchen: Man of Anger and Light.* New York: Padell, 1946.

Miller, Joaquin. *Joaquin Miller: His California Diary 1855–1857.* Seattle: Dogwood Press, 1936.

Miller, Joaquin. *The Poetical Works.* New York: Putnam, 1923.

Miller, Joaquin. *Selected Writings.* Eugene, Ore.: Union, 1977.

Miller, Richard. *Bohemia: The Proto-Culture, Then and Now.* Chicago: Nelson-Hall, 1977.

Miscellaneous Man nos. 1–15 (1954–1959). Edited by William J. Margolis. San Francisco and Berkeley, Calif.

Modjeska, Helena. *Memories and Impressions of Helena Modjeska: An Autobiography.* New York: B. Blom, 1969.

Moe, David. *Plug in the Electric Dictionary.* San Francisco: Community Press, 1973.

Moore, Daniel. *Dawn Visions.* San Francisco: City Lights Books, 1963.

Mori, Toshio. *Yokohama California.* Introduction by William Saroyan. Caldwell, Idaho: Caxton, 1949.

Morris, Wright. *A Reader.* New York: Harper & Row, 1970.

Muir, John. *The Mountains of California.* New York: Century, 1894.

Mukherjee, Sujit. *Passage to America: The Reception of Rabindranath Tagore in the United States, 1912–1941.* Calcutta: Bookland, 1964.

Mulford, Prentice. *Prentice Mulford's California Sketches.* Edited by Franklin Walker. San Francisco: Book Club of California, 1935.

Mulford, Prentice. *Prentice Mulford's Story: Life by Land and Sea.* New York: F. J. Needham, 1889.

Muscatine, Doris. *Old San Francisco.* New York: Putnam, 1975.

Nasatir, A. P. "Alexandre Dumas fils and the Lottery of the Golden Ingots." *California Historical Society Quarterly* 33, no. 2 (June 1954).

Neale, Walter. *Life of Ambrose Bierce.* New York: W. Neale, 1929.

News Letter, 1856–1928. San Francisco.

Noguchi, Yone. *Seen and Unseen: Or Monologues of a Homeless Snail.* San Francisco: Gelett Burgess and Porter Garnett, 1897.

Noguchi, Yone. *The Story of Yone Noguchi: Told by Himself.* Philadelphia: G. W. Jacobs, 1915.

Norris, Frank. *Frank Norris of "The Wave": Stories and Sketches . . . 1893-1897.* San Francisco: Westgate Press, 1931.

Norris, Frank. *Blix.* New York: Doubleday, McClure, 1899.

Norris, Frank. *Letters.* Edited by Franklin Walker. San Francisco: Book Club of California, 1956.

Norris, Frank. *McTeague: A Story of San Francisco.* New York: Doubleday, McClure, 1899.

Norris, Frank. *The Octopus: A Story of California.* New York: Doubleday, Page, 1901.

Norris, Kathleen. *My San Francisco.* Garden City, N.Y.: Doubleday, Doran, 1932.

Norse, Harold. *Hotel Nirvana: Selected Poems, 1953-1973.* San Francisco: City Lights Books, 1974.

Nowinski, Ira. *Café Society: Photographs and Poetry from San Francisco's North Beach.* San Francisco: Bean, 1978.

Nye, Russel. *The Unembarrassed Muse: The Popular Arts in America.* New York: Dial, 1970.

O'Connor, Richard. *Jack London: A Biography.* Boston: Little, Brown, 1964.

Olmsted, David L. Biographical Sketch of Jaime de Angulo in *Achumawi Dictionary.* Berkeley, Calif.: University of California Press, 1966.

Olmsted, Roger R. *Scenes of Wonder and Curiosity from Hutchings' California Magazine, 1856-1861.* Berkeley, Calif.: Howell-North, 1962.

Olsen, Tillie. *Silences.* New York: Delacorte, 1978.

Olsen, Tillie. *Tell Me a Riddle.* New York: Dell, 1961.

Olson, Charles. *Call Me Ishmael.* San Francisco: City Lights Books, 1958.

Oppen, George. *Of Being Numerous.* New York: New Directions, 1967.

Oppen, Mary. *Meaning of a Life: An Autobiography.* Santa Barbara, Calif.: Black Sparrow Press, 1978.

Orlovsky, Peter. *Clean Asshole Poems and Smileing Vegetable Songs.* San Francisco: City Lights Books, 1978.

Ortiz, Simon. *Going for the Rain.* New York: Harper & Row, 1976.

Overland Monthly, 1868-1875 and 1883-1935. San Francisco.

Palou, Francisco. *Historical Memoirs of New California,* 4 vols. Edited by Herbert Eugene Bolton. Berkeley, Calif.: University of California Press, 1926.

Palou, Francisco. *Palou's Life of Serra.* Translated by Maynard Geiger. Washington, D.C.: Academy of American History, 1955.

Parker, Elizabeth, and Abajian, James. *A Walking Tour of the Black Presence in San Francisco During the 19th Century.* San Francisco: African American Historical and Cultural Society, 1974.

Parker, William Belmont. *Edward Rowland Sill: His Life and Work.* Boston: Houghton Mifflin, 1915.

Parkinson, Thomas. *A Beat Casebook.* New York: Crowell, 1961.

Parkinson, Thomas. *Protect the Earth.* San Francisco: City Lights Books, 1969.

Parry, Albert. *Garrets and Pretenders: A History of Bohemianism in America.* New York: Coviche, Friede, 1933.

Patchen, Kenneth. *Poems of Humor and Protest.* San Francisco: City Lights Books, 1956.

Patchen, Kenneth. *Love Poems.* San Francisco: City Lights Books, 1960.

Paul, Rodman Wilson. "In Search of Dame Shirley." *Pacific Historical Review* 33, no. 2 (May 1964).

Pearsall, Robert, and Erickson, Ursula Spier. *The Californians: Writings of Their Past and Present.* San Francisco: Hesperian House, 1961.

Peck, George Washington. *Aurifodena: Or Adventures in the Gold Region.* New York: Baker and Scribner, 1849. (New Edition, James D. Hart, ed. San Francisco: Book Club of California, 1974.)

Pelieu, Claude. *Automatic Pilot.* Translated by Mary Beach. San Francisco: City Lights Books, 1964.

Peters, Harry T. *California on Stone.* Garden City, N.Y.: Doubleday, Doran, 1935.

Peters (Lamantia), Nancy Joyce. *It's in the Wind.* Chicago: Black Swan Press, 1977.

Le Petit Journal de Refusées, 1897. Edited by Gelett Burgess. San Francisco.

Pioneer, 1854-1855. San Francisco.

Pitt, Leonard. *The Decline of the Californios.* Berkeley, Calif.: University of California Press, 1966.

Pittsinger, Eliza. *Bugle Peals: Or Songs of Warning for the American People.* San Francisco: Weed, 1882.

Plymell, Charles. *The Last of the Moccasins.* San Francisco: City Lights Books, 1971.

Poets of the Cities: New York and San Francisco 1950-1965. Dallas: Dallas Museum of Fine Arts, 1974.

Powers, Stephen. "Tribes of California." *Contributions to North American Ethnology* 3. Washington, D.C.: Government Printing Office, 1877.

Pronzini, Bill, and Wilcox, Collin. *Twospot.* New York: Putnam, 1978.

Putnam, Ruth. *California: The Name.* University of California Publications in History, no. 4 (1917).

Read, Herbert. *Poetry and Anarchism.* London: Freedom Press, 1938.

Realf, Richard. *Poems by Richard Realf: Poet, Soldier, Workman.* New York and London, Funk & Wagnalls, 1898.

Reed, Ishmael, ed. *Calafia: The California Poetry.* Berkeley, Calif.: Y'Bird Books, 1979.

Reed, Ishmael. *Mumbo Jumbo.* Garden City, N.Y.: Doubleday, 1972.

Reed, Ishmael, and Young, Al, eds. *Yardbird Lives!* New York: Grove Press, 1978.

Reich, Charles. *The Greening of America*. New York: Random House, 1970.

Renaissance [later merged with *Notes from Underground*], July 1961–1962. Edited by John Bryan.

Rexroth, Kenneth. "Disengagement and the Art of the Beat Generation." *Evergreen Review* 1, no. 2 (1957).

Rexroth, Kenneth. *Thou Shalt Not Kill*. Sunnyvale, Calif.: Horace Schwartz, 1955.

Rexroth, Kenneth, and Ferlinghetti, Lawrence. "Poetry Readings in the Cellar" [LP 7002]. Fantasy Records, 1957.

Rhodehamel, Josephine De Witt, and Wood, R. F. *Ina Coolbrith: Librarian and Laureate of California*. Provo, Utah: Brigham Young University Press, 1973.

Rice, Ann. *Interview with the Vampire*. New York: Knopf, 1976.

Richards, Janet. *Common Soldiers*. San Francisco: Archer Press, 1979.

Ridge, John Rollin [Yellow Bird, pseud.] *The Life and Adventures of Joaquin Murieta, the Celebrated California Bandit*. Introduction by Joseph Henry Jackson. Norman, Okla.: University of Oklahoma Press, 1955.

Rock, Francis J. *J. Ross Browne: A Biography*. Washington, D.C.: Catholic University of America, 1929.

Roethke, Theodore. *Collected Poems*. New York: Doubleday, 1966.

Rolling Renaissance: San Francisco Underground Art in Celebration, 1945–1968. San Francisco: Intersection, 1975.

Ruggles, Eugene. *The Lifeguard in the Snow*. Pittsburgh: University of Pittsburgh Press, 1977.

Royce, Josiah. *California from the Conquest in 1846 to the Second Vigilance Committee in San Francisco: A Study of American Character*. New York and Boston: Houghton Mifflin, 1886.

Royce, Sarah. *A Frontier Lady*. New Haven, Conn.: Yale University Press, 1932.

Rukeyser, Muriel. *Body of Waking*. New York: Harper & Brothers, 1958.

Rukeyser, Muriel. *The Life of Poetry*. New York: Current Books, 1949.

Sachs, Emanie. *The Terrible Siren: Victoria Woodhull*. New York: Harper & Row, 1928.

San Francisco Earthquake nos. 1–5 (1965–1968). Edited by Jan Herman, Gail Chiarrello Dusenberg, et al. San Francisco.

Sanchez, Nellie van de Grift. *Spanish Arcadia*. Los Angeles: Powell, 1929.

Saroyan, Aram. *Genesis Angels: The Saga of Lew Welch and the Beat Generation*. New York: William Morrow, 1979.

Saroyan, William. *Places Where I've Done Time*. New York: Prager, 1972.

Saroyan, William. *The Time of Your Life*. New York: Harcourt Brace, 1940.

Satty, Wilfried. *The Illustrated Edgar Allan Poe*. New York: Warner Books, 1976.

Schaff, David. *The Moon by Day*. San Francisco: Four Seasons Foundation, 1973.

Scheffauer, Herman. *Of Both Worlds*. San Francisco: A. M. Robertson, 1903.

Schevill, James. *Violence and Glory: Poems 1962–1969*. Chicago: Swallow Press, 1969.

Schneck, Stephen. *The Nightclerk*. New York: Grove Press, 1965.

Schorer, Mark. *Sinclair Lewis: An American Life*. New York: McGraw-Hill, 1961.

Schorer, Mark. *The State of Mind: Thirty-Two Stories*. Boston: Houghton Mifflin, 1947.

Schutzman, Steve. *Smoke the Burning Body Makes*. San Francisco: Panjandrum Press, 1978.

Schwartz, Stephen. *Hidden Locks*. Chicago: Black Swan Press, 1972.

Shaw, William. *Golden Dreams and Waking Realities*. London: Smith-Elder, 1851.

Sidney-Fryer, Donald. *Emperor of Dreams: A Clark Ashton Smith Bibliography*. West Kingston, R.I.: D. M. Grant, 1978.

Sienkiewicz, Henry. *Portrait of America: Letters*. Edited by Charles Morley. New York: Columbia University Press, 1959.

Sill, Edward Roland [pseud.] *Poems*. Boston and New York: Houghton Mifflin, 1888.

Simon, Linda. *The Biography of Alice B. Toklas*. Garden City, N.Y.: Doubleday, 1977.

Sinclair, Upton. *The Autobiography of Upton Sinclair*. New York: Harcourt, Brace & World, 1962.

Sinclair, Upton. *Mammonart*. Pasadena: privately published, 1925.

Smith, Clark Ashton. *The Star-Treader and Other Poems*. San Francisco: A. M. Robertson, 1912.

Smith, Nora Archibald. *Kate Douglas Wiggin as Her Sister Knew Her*. Boston: Houghton Mifflin, 1925.

Smith, Henry Nash. *Virgin Land: The American West as Symbol and Myth*. New York: Vintage, 1957.

Snyder, Gary. *The Old Ways: Six Essays*. San Francisco: City Lights Books, 1978.

Snyder, Gary. *Turtle Island*. New York: New Directions, 1974.

Soulé, Frank; Gihon, John H.; and Nisbet, James. *The Annals of San Francisco*. New York: Appleton, 1855.

Spicer, Jack. *After Lorca*. San Francisco: White Rabbit Press, 1957.

Spicer, Jack. *Billy the Kid*. Stinson Beach, Calif.: Enkidu Surrogate, 1959.

Starr, Kevin. *Americans and the California Dream*. New York: Oxford University Press, 1976.

Steffens, Lincoln. *The Autobiography of Lincoln Steffens*. New York: Harcourt, Brace, 1931.

Stein, Gertrude. *The Autobiography of Alice B. Toklas*. New York: Random House, 1933.

Steinbeck, John. *Travels with Charley in Search of America*. New York: Viking, 1962.

Sterling, George; Taggard, Genevieve; and Rorty, James, eds. *Continent's End*. San Francisco: Book Club of California, 1925.

Sterling, George. *The Triumph of Bohemia: A Forest Play*. San Francisco: Bohemian Club, 1907.

Sterling, George. *The Wine of Wizardry*. San Francisco: A. M. Robertson, 1909.

Stevenson, Robert Louis. *The Amateur Immigrant: From the Clyde to Sandy Hook*. Chicago: Stone and Kimball, 1895.

Stevenson, Robert Louis. *The Silverado Squatters*. London: Chattus and Windus, 1883.

Stevenson, Robert Louis, and Osbourne, Lloyd. *The Wrecker*. London: Cassell, 1892.

Stewart, George R. *Bret Harte: Argonaut and Exile*. Boston and New York: Houghton Mifflin, 1931.

Stewart, George R. *John Phoenix, Esq: The Veritable Squibob*. New York: Henry Holt, 1937.

Stewart, George R. *Storm*. New York: Random House, 1941.

Stock, Robert. "Disappearing Act" [about Weldon Kees]. *Ponchartrain Review* (1970).

Stoddard, Charles Warren. *Exits and Entrances*. Boston: Lathrop, 1903.

Stoddard, Charles Warren. *For the Pleasure of His Company: An Affair with the Misty City Thrice Told*. San Francisco: A. M. Robertson, 1903.

Stone, Irving. *Adversary in the House: Eugene V. Debs*. Garden City, N.Y.: Doubleday, 1947.

Stone, Irving. *Sailor on Horseback: The Biography of Jack London*. Boston: Houghton Mifflin, 1938.

Swift, John Franklin. *Robert Greathouse*. New York: Carleton, 1870.

Switzer, Linda Stevens. "An Ethnohistory of the Costanoans of San Francisco Bay." in *The Costanoan Indians*, Robert Heizer, ed. Local History Studies 18. Cupertino, Calif.: De Anza College, 1974.

Taber, Louise A. "Black Bart, Poetic Bandit, and His Strange Career." *California Gold Rush Days*. San Francisco: privately published, 1936.

Taggard, Genevieve. *Slow Music*. New York: Harper & Brothers, 1946.

Tagore, Rabindranath. *Nationalism*. San Francisco: Book Club of California, 1917.

Taper, Bernard. *Mark Twain's San Francisco*. New York: McGraw Hill, 1963.

Taylor, Bayard. *Eldorado; or Adventures in the Path of Empire*. New York: Putnam, 1850.

Thorpe, John. *Cargo Cult*. Bolinas, Calif.: Big Sky Press, 1972.

Time to Greez! Incantations from the Third World. Edited by Buriel Clay II, Janice Mirikitani, et al. Introduction by Maya Angelou. San Francisco: Glide Publications and Third World Communications, 1975.

Toklas, Alice B. *What Is Remembered*. New York: Holt, Rinehart, and Winston, 1963.

Tooley, Ronald Vere. *California as an Island*. London: Map Collector's Circle, 1964.

Trilling, Lionel. *The Liberal Imagination*. New York: Viking, 1950.

Twain, Mark. See Clemens, Samuel L.

Unna, Warren. *The Coppa Murals: A Pageant of Bohemian Life in San Francisco at the Turn-of-the-Century*. San Francisco: Book Club of California, 1952.

Upton, Charles. *Panic Grass*. San Francisco: City Lights Books, 1968.

Valaoritis, Nanos. *Flash Bloom*. Illustrated by Marie Wilson. San Francisco: Wire Press, 1980.

Vallejo, Mariano Guadalupe. *História de California*. Ms, Bancroft Library, Berkeley, Calif.

Van Alstyne, Richard W. *The Rising American Empire*. New York: Norton, 1960.

Van der Zee, John. *The Imagined City: San Francisco in the Minds of Its Writers*. San Francisco: San Francisco Public Library, 1979.

Van der Zee. *The Greatest Men's Party on Earth: Inside the Bohemian Grove*. New York: Harcourt, Brace, 1974.

Vargas, Roberto. *Primeros Cantos*. San Francisco: Ediciones Pocho Che, 1972.

Victor, Frances Fuller. *The New Penelope and Other Sketches*. San Francisco: A. L. Bancroft, 1877.

Vincent, Peter. *Sanglorians Run*. New York: Delacorte, 1971.

Vose, Julia. *Moved Out on the Inside*. San Francisco: Figures, 1976.

Voznesensky, Andre. *Antiworlds*. Translated by W. H. Auden and others. Edited by Patricia Blake and Max Hayward. New York: Basic Books, 1966.

Wagner, Henry R. *Spanish Voyages to the Northwest Coast of America in the Sixteenth Century*. San Francisco: California Historical Society, 1929.

Walker, Franklin D. *Ambrose Bierce: The Wickedest Man in San Francisco*. San Francisco: Colt Press, 1941.

Walker, Franklin D. "Diogenes of the Tuolumne." *Westways* (June 1935).

Walker, Franklin D. "Fitz Hugh Ludlow: The Hasheesh Eater Among the Argonauts." *Westways* (August 1935).

Walker, Franklin D. *Frank Norris: A Biography*. New York: Doubleday, 1932.

Walker, Franklin D. *San Francisco's Literary Frontier*. New York: Knopf, 1939.

Walker, Franklin D. *The Seacoast of Bohemia: An Account of Early Carmel*. San Francisco: Book Club of California, 1966.

Wasp, 1868–1928. San Francisco.

Watts, Alan. *In My Own Way*. New York: Pantheon Books, 1972.

Wave, 1890–1900. San Francisco.

Webb, Charles Henry. *John Paul's Book.* Hartford, Conn., and Chicago: Columbia Book Company, 1874.

Wecter, Dixon. *Literary Lodestone.* Stanford, Calif.: Stanford University Press, 1950.

Weiss, Ruth. *Light and Other Poems.* San Francisco: Peace and Pieces, 1976.

Welch, Lou. *Wobbly Rock.* San Francisco: Auerhahn Press, 1960.

Welch, Lou. *Ring of Bone: Collected Poems, 1950–1971.* Bolinas, Calif.: Grey Fox Press, 1973.

Wentworth, May, ed. *Poetry of the Pacific.* San Francisco: Pacific Publishing, 1867.

Whalen, Philip. *Decompressions: Selected Poems.* Bolinas, Calif.: Grey Fox Press, 1978.

Whalen, Philip. *Self-Portrait from Another Direction.* San Francisco: Auerhahn Press, 1959.

Whitfield, James M. *Emancipation Oration . . .* San Francisco: The Elevator, 1867.

Wieners, John. *The Hotel Wentley Poems.* San Francisco: Auerhahn Press, 1958.

Wierzbicki, Felix P. *California As It is, and As It May Be.* San Francisco: W. Bartlett, 1849.

Wiggin, Kate Douglas. *Love By Express.* Hollis and Buxton, Maine: Dorcas Society, 1924.

Wilde, Oscar. *Irish Poets and Poetry of the Nineteenth Century.* Introduction by Robert D. Pepper. San Francisco: Book Club of California, 1972.

Wilner, Herbert. *Dovisch in the Wilderness.* New York: Bobbs-Merrill, 1968.

Wilson, Harry Leon. *Ruggles of Red Gap.* Garden City, N.Y.: Doubleday, Page, 1915.

Winslow, Pete. *A Daisy in the Memory of a Shark.* San Francisco: City Lights Books, 1973.

Wolf, Leonard. *A Dream of Dracula: In Search of the Living Dead.* Boston: Little, Brown, 1972.

Wolf, Leonard, and Wolf, Deborah. *Voices from the Love Generation.* Boston: Little, Brown, 1968.

Woodhull, Victoria. "Tried as by Fire, or, the True and the False Society, an oration delivered 150 consecutive nights." 1874.

Wong, Jade Snow. *Fifth Chinese Daughter.* New York: Harper & Brothers, 1950.

Wood, Charles Erskine Scott. *Heavenly Discourse.* New York: Vanguard Press, 1927.

Wright, William [Dan de Quille, pseud.]. *The Big Bonanza.* New York: A. A. Knopf, 1947.

Yevtushenko, Yevgeni. *Stolen Apples.* Garden City, N.Y.: Doubleday, 1971.

Young, Al. *Sitting Pretty.* New York: Holt, Rinehart, and Winston, 1976.

Young, Al. *Snakes.* New York: Holt, Rinehart, and Winston, 1970.

Photo Credits

By page number:

1, 4, 5 (top, bottom), 6, 7, 8, 9, 11, 13, 15, 27, 33, 34, 37, 43, 45, 47, 49, 52, 53 (top), 56, 57, 58 (bottom), 62, 65, 67, 68 (center), 69, 72, 73, 74, 75, 77, 79, 83, 84, 87, 89, 91, 92, 93, 94, 95, 99, 104 (left), 105, 108, 109, 111, 112, 113, 114, 115, 116, 117, 118, 124, 127 (left), 128, 129, 130, 131, 132, 145, 148 (left), 154. Courtesy, The Bancroft Library, University of California, Berkeley.

10, 19, 41, 44, 51, 71 (top), 90, 102, 104 (right), 106, 146, 151 (left, right), Courtesy, San Francisco Public Library.

16. Courtesy, Doe Library, University of California, Berkeley .

18. Courtesy, California Historical Society.

17, 20, 21, 22, 23, 24, 25 (top, bottom), 26, 28, 30, 31, 38, 39, 61, 76, 81, 85, 125. Courtesy, California State Library, Sacramento.

32, 59. Courtesy, John Howell-Books.

46, 48, 53 (bottom), 55, 58 (top), 68 (top, bottom), 69 (left), 71 (bottom). *The Story of the Files* by Ella Sterling Cummins, 1893.

50, 100, 101, 103, 126. Courtesy, Oakland Public Library.

54, 70, 82, 133, 139, 140, 152. Courtesy, Oscar Lewis.

63. Photograph by Mak Takahashi.

97, 98. *The Coppa Murals* by Warren Unna. Copyright © 1952 by The Book Club of California.

121. Photograph by Pamela Mosher.

127 (right). Courtesy, Sadakichi Hartmann Archive, University of California Library, Riverside.

135, 136, 137, 138. Copyright © 1975 by City Publishing Company and David Fechheimer. (136-138, photographs by Edmund Shea.)

141 (left). Photograph by Raymond Foye.

141 (center). Photograph by Pirkle Jones.

141 (right). Photograph by Barry Jablon.

143. Courtesy, ILWU Library.

147. Photograph by Dave Mitchell.

148 (right), 149 (bottom), 162 (top), 191. Courtesy, Henri Lenoir.

149 (top). Photograph by Sam Cherry.

150. *The San Francisco Book* by Herb Caen. Photograph by Max Yavno. Copyright © 1948 by Houghton, Mifflin & Co.

158. Courtesy, Imogen Cunningham Trust, Berkeley.

159. Courtesy, KPFA.

161, 170, 189, 222 (bottom). Photographs by Gui de Angulo.

162 (bottom). Courtesy, Cavalli & Company.

163, 169, 176 (left), 177, 182, 183, 190, 198, 199, 201, 206, 207, 208, 210, 221. City Lights Archive.

164, 165. Courtesy, Knute Stiles.

166, 167, 168, 171, 173, 175, 187. Courtesy, Ruth Witt-Diamant.

172. Photograph by Jonathan Williams.

174. Photograph by Gerhard Gsheidle.

176 (right). Courtesy, Charles and Janet Richards.

178, 179, 197 (left). Courtesy, Carolyn Cassady.

180. Photograph by Harry Redl. Courtesy, Fantasy Records, Berkeley.

184. Courtesy, Grove Press.

186. Photograph by Jerry Stoll.

188. Courtesy, *Beatitude Magazine.*

192, 193. Photographs by James Oliver Mitchell.

194, 195. Photographs by Larry Keenan, Jr.

196. Courtesy, Michael McClure.

197, 204, 205. Photographs by Christa Fleischmann. Courtesy, Glide Publications.

202. Photograph by Elizabeth Sunflower.

203. Courtesy, The Estate of Alan Watts.

208. Photograph by Michael Zagaris. Courtesy, *After Dark* magazine.

209. Photograph by Walter Chappell. Courtesy, Jerry Kamstra.

211 (left). Courtesy, Kay Boyle.

211 (right). Photograph by Pamela Mosher.

213 (left). Courtesy, Judy Stone.

213 (right). Courtesy, Hartmut Gerdes, Gilbert Shelton (Rip Off Press), and DuMont Buchverlag, Köln.

214. Photograph by James Santana.

215. Photograph by Karen Pataki.

217. Photograph by Pennfield Jensen.

218. Photograph by Lela Januskowsky.

219, 220. Photographs by Bennett Hall.

222 (top). Photograph by Buckminister McBride.

223. Photograph by Mark Green.

224. Photograph by James Oliver Mitchell.

225. Photograph by Philip Buchanan. Courtesy, Ilke Hartmann.

226. Photograph by André Lewis.

227. Photographs by John Clements.

228. Photograph by Mike Vawter.

229. Photograph by Andrée Abecassis.

230. Photograph by Adrian Pugnetti.

231. Photograph by Tim Hildebrand.

232. Courtesy, The Eagle Cafe.

Back cover (left), photograph by Ilke Hartmann;
(right), photograph by Chris Felver.

Index

Abbott, Steve, 186
Adam, Helen, 173
Adams, Alice, 218
Aitken, Robert, 96, 97
Albright, Thomas, 185
Alegria, Fernando, 227
Allen, Donald M., 181, 184, 224, 225
Allen, Florence, 191
Anarchism, 74, 77, 100, 128, 129, 153, 155, 156, 163
Anderson, Margaret, 128, 132
Anderson, Poul, 212
Anderson, Sherwood, 158
Angel Island poems, 63
Angelou, Maya, 218
Angulo, Jaime de, 132, 159, 160, 161
Anthony, Susan B., 51, 83
Antiwar movement, 139, 153, 155-57, 159, 167-69, 175
Anza, Juan Bautista de, 4
Argonaut, 64, 67, 68, 111, 142, 188
Ark, 155-58, 182
Ark II–Moby I, 157
Arnold, Matthew, 54, 59
Arthur, Gavin, 197
Ashton, Dore, 184, 185
Atherton, Gertrude, 9, 44, 67, 85, 86, 117, 124
Auden, W. H., 164, 171
Austin, Mary, 66, 78, 107-10, 117-20, 132, 134
Ayres, Lily, 177

Baker, Edward Dickinson, 33
Baker, Ray Stannard, 117
Baker-Roshi, Richard, 202
Bamford, Frederick Irons, 100
Bancroft, Hubert Howe, *xi*, 16, 20, 49, 56, 141
Barker, Eric. 116
Barlow, Robert, 153
Barrows, George, 153
Bazovsky, Max, Jr., 219
Beach, Mary, 198
Beadle and Adams's dime novels, 55
Beatitude, 188, 223
Bechdolt, Fred, 117-19
Beckwourth, James P., 50
Beecher, Henry Ward, 58
Bell, James Madison, 33
Bell, Philip, 33
Bellamy, Edward, 72, 75, 83
Belson, Jordan, 185
Bender, Albert, 139, 140, 152
Benet, George, 228
Benét, William Rose, 114, 125, 158
Benjamin, Robert Charles O'Hara, 62
Bennett, Raine, 117, 129
Berkeley Renaissance, 153-57, 167, 171, 176
Berkman, Alexander, 129
Berman, Wallace, 185, 196
Berkson, Bill, 224
Berriault, Gina, 218

Berrigan, Ted, 224
Berssenbrugge, Mei-mei, 219, 230
Bierce, Ambrose, 44, 45, 55, 60, 61,64-71, 77, 78, 88, 96, 104, 106, 107, 144
Bierstadt, Albert, 35
Bischoff, Elmer, 185
Bjorkman, Edwin, 128
Black Cat Café, 148, 149
Bladen, Ronald, 157, 185
Blue, Janice, 221
Bohemia, 117, 129, 130
Bohemian Club and Grove, *x*, 70, 92, 93, 104, 105, 107, 112, 115, 123, 125, 130
Bolinas writers, *xi*, 147, 224, 225
Bolton, "Black Bart," 62
Borregaard, Ebbe, 224
Borthwick, J. D., 16
Bosqui, Edward, 52
Bowan, James, 104
Bowen, Michael, 185
Bowman, James, 48
Boyle, Kay, 210, 211
Brannan, Sam, 14, 35
Brautigan, Richard, 186, 190, 191, 224
Brewer, William, 24
Briggs, Robert, 174
Brooks, Van Wyck, 107
Broughton, James, 167, 184
Brown, John, 33, 71
Browne, J. Ross, 22, 23, 28
Browning, Robert and Elizabeth Barrett, 54
Bruce, Lenny, 181, 183
Bruchac, Joe, 230
Bryant, Edwin, 17
Bryant, William Cullen, 45
Buckley, Lord, 181
Bukowski, Charles, 210, 221
Burdick, Eugene, 181
Burgess, Gelett, 88-92, 94, 96, 97, 123, 132
Burroughs, William S., 181, 198, 219
Bynner, Witter, 132
Byron, Lord Gordon George, 19, 38, 39, 53, 71, 73

Cabet, Etienne, 72
Caen, Herb, 150, 151, 186, 211, 217
Caldwell, Erskine, 191, 216, 217
California Star, 14, 19, 45
Californian, 31, 35, 36, 42, 50, 55, 77
Californio literature, 10, 11
Callahan, Robert, 231
Cardenal, Ernesto, 227
Carmel Colony, *xi*, 47, 107-20, 132, 224
Carpenter, Don, 191, 215
Carroll, Jim, 224
Carson, Robert, 228
Cassady, Carolyn, 179
Cassady, Neal, 178, 179
Cather, Willa, 110

Cavalli & Company, 162
The Cellar, 174–77
Cervantes, Saavedra, Miguel de, 3
Chan, Jeffery Paul, 215
Chamisso, Adelbert von, 9
Chaplin, Charles, 21, 123, 163, 166
Cheney, John Vance, 78
Cherkovski, Neeli, 188, 223
Chin, Frank, 215, 216, 230
Choris, Ludovik (Louis), 8, 9
Circle, 153–56, 167, 171
City Lights, 163
City Lights Books, 134, 162, 163, 180–83, 186, 190, 194, 195, 209, 210, 219, 222, 226
City Lights Poets Theater, 172, 207, 208
City of San Francisco, 134–39, 211
Clappe, Louise, 18
Clare, Ada, 37, 52
Clark, Tom, 224
Clemens, Samuel. *See* Twain, Mark
Coblentz, Stanton, 133
Coffield, Glen, 153
Collins, Robert, 62
Compass, 169
Connell, Evan S., 191
Conner, Bruce, 185
Conrad, Barnaby, 151
Contact, 188, 191
Cooke, Grace MacGowan, 114, 118, 119
Coolbrith, Ina, 50, 51, 53, 77, 83, 105, 133, 152
Coppola, Frances Ford, 134, 213
Coppa's Restaurant and Murals, 96–98, 108, 111, 117
Corman, Cid, 157
Corso, Gregory, 134, 176, 184, 219, 222, 223
Counterpoint, 164–66, 172
Coyote (myth), 7
Crane, Clarkson, 132, 141, 152
Crawford, F. Marion, 59
Creekmore, Hubert, 153
Creeley, Robert, 157, 173, 224, 225
Crehan, Hubert, 185
Crews, Judson, 153
cummings, e. e., 153, 157
Cummins (Mighels), Ella Sterling, 46, 56
Cunningham, Imogen, 158

Daggett, Rollin M., 27, 28
Dana, Richard Henry, 12–14, 17, 233
Dawson, Emma Frances, 44, 69, 71, 88
Delano, Alonzo, 21
Dennis, Gene, 230
Derby, George Horatio, 20
Dickens, Charles, 19, 40, 42, 59
DiPrima, Diane, 185, 224
Dixon, Maynard, 123, 130
Dodge, Mabel (Luhan), 110, 124, 160
Dorn, Edward, 225
Doss, Margot Patterson, 224
Douglass, Elisha Perkins, 16
Douglass, Frederick, 33, 58
Doxey, William, 91
Doyle, Arthur Conan, 211, 212
Dreiser, Theodore, 141, 142, 191

Dumas, Alexandre, 17, 19, 40
Duncan, Isadora, 51, 130, 131
Duncan, Joseph, 50
Duncan, Robert, 157, 158, 160, 163, 173, 181, 184, 187, 191, 218
Durrell, Lawrence, 153
Dylan, Bob, 134, 191, 194, 195, 200

Eagle Café, 232–33
Eastman, Max, 115
Eberhart, Richard, 157, 159, 181
Elgee, Jane Francesca, 60
Elwood, Philip, 159
Emerson, Ralph Waldo, 59, 60, 180
Essenin, Sergei, 130, 131
Evergreen Review, 184, 185, 188, 224
Everson, William, 153, 167, 169, 170, 184
Exploration and conquest, literature of, 3–6, 9, 10, 12, 14

Fabilli, Mary, 153
Fagan, Larry, 194
Fantasy fiction, 67–69, 116, 212
Fechheimer, David, 211
Ferling, Lawrence, 166, 172
Ferlinghetti, Lawrence, 163, 168, 180, 181, 182, 184, 185, 191, 194, 200, 207, 208, 219, 235
Ferlinghetti, Selden Kirby-Smith, 163
Field, Sara Bard, 139, 144
Fitch, Anna M. 27, 46, 48
Flanner, Hildegard, 141
Forbes, Kathryn, 150
Forester, C. S., 150
Fourier, Charles, 72, 73, 77
Fowlie, Wallace, 153
Fox, Charles, 224
Foye, Raymond, 188
Fraser, Kathleen, 219, 220
Friedman, Mickey, 215
Frost, Robert, 151, 152, 159, 235
Frémont, Jessie Benton, 42
French, Nora May, 109, 111
Freneau, Philip, 12
Furuseth, Andrew, 233

Gaines, Ernest, 214, 215
Gardner, Leonard, 218
Garlin, Hamlin, 83
Garnett, Porter, 91–93, 96–98, 111
Genthe, Arnold, 107, 111, 119, 120, 123
Gentry, Curt, 191, 218
George, Henry, 19, 44, 62, 72, 75, 76
George, Phil, 230
Gerdes, Hartmut, 213
Ghiselin, Brewster, 153
Gibbs, Mifflin W., 33
Gidlow, Else, 141
Gilman, Charlotte Perkins, 58, 64, 83, 84
Ginsberg, Allen, 141, 175, 176, 180–82, 184, 191, 194, 195, 198, 199, 200–202, 206–08, 216, 225
Gleason, Madeline, 204, 205
Gleason, Ralph J. 159, 184
Goad, 157
Gold, Herbert, 191, 216, 217

Gold Rush, literature of, 16–18
Golden Era, 24, 26–29, 34, 35, 37, 38, 40–42, 50, 53, 55, 57, 58, 96
Golden Goose, 157
Goldman, Emma, 100, 128, 129
Goll, Ivan, 153
Goodman, Joseph T., 28, 29, 46, 48
Goodman, Paul, 157
Goodrow, Gary, 194
Gores, Joe, 212
Gottschalk, Louis Moreau, 37
Graham, Bill, 198, 200, 207
Greeley, Horace, *ix*, 73, 235
Green, Clay, 52
Greer, Maretta, 200, 201
Greist, Nathan, 100
Grieg, Michael, 177, 194, 217
Griffin, Susan, 218
Grogan, Emmett, 200
Gunn, Thom, 219
Gustafson, Jim, 219

Hammett, Dashiell, 123, 135–38, 211, 212
Hardinge, Emma, 57
Harmon, James, 157, 182
Harris, Mark, 218
Harris, Thomas Lake, 73, 74, 77
Hart, James D., 130, 134, 141, 145
Hart, Jerome, 66, 67
Hart, Lawrence, 153
Harte, Bret, 9, 18, 31, 33–36, 42–46, 49, 51–53, 67
Hartmann, Sadakichi, 96, 127, 128
Harrity, Richard, 191
Haskell, Burnette G., 74, 75
Hawkins, Bobbie Louise, 224
Havighurst, Walter, 142
Hearst, William Randolph, 64, 70
Hellman, Lillian, 123, 134
Hennacy, Ammon, 156
Herms, George, 185
Hernandez Cruz, Victor, 230, 231
Heron, Herbert (Peet), 114, 119, 120
Heron, Opal (Peet), 114, 117
Hesperian (1858), 24, 27
Hesperian (1930), 140, 141
Hill, Lewis, 159
Hinckle III, Warren, 134, 139, 169
Hirschman, Jack, 219
Hitchcock, George, 148, 149, 204, 205
"Hobo," 221
Hodes, Ida, 167
Hoffer, Eric, 228, 229
Hogan, William, 159, 181
Hood, Tom, 54, 64
Hopper, James M. (Jimmy) 88, 103, 107, 109, 111, 117–20, 129
Howard, Charles, 153
Howells, William D., 59, 68, 72
Howl trial, 180–82
Hoyem, Andrew, 194
Hsu, Kai-yu, 63
Huggins, Ericka, 202
Hughes, Langston, 115

Human Be-In, 200, 201
Hutchings, J. M., 27

Illiterati, 169
Inada, Lawson, 230
Inferno, 157
Ingersoll, Col. Robert, 58
Irwin, Inez, 88, 117
Irwin, Wallace, 88
Irwin, Will, 88, 117

Jackson, Helen Hunt, 85, 110
Jackson, Joseph Henry, 145, 150, 217
Jacob, Max, 153
Jacobs, Paul, 134
James, William, 110
Jeffers, Robinson, 106, 115, 117, 124, 133, 140, 144, 158, 170
Jenkins, Joyce, 186
Les Jeunes, 89–92, 94, 96
Joans, Ted, 226
Jordan, David Starr, 77, 119

KPFA/FM, 153, 155, 159, 160, 166–68, 202
Kael, Pauline, 159, 163
Kamstra, Jerry, 172, 209
Kandel, Lenore, 174, 181
Kaufman, Bob, 184, 186, 188, 221, 223
Kazin, Alfred, 100, 140
Keeler, Ralph, 68
Kees, Weldon, 153, 176, 177
Kemble, Edward, 45
Kendall, W. A. ("Comet Quirls"), 27, 46
Kerouac, Jack, 147, 176, 178, 179, 184, 185, 191–93, 216, 222, 235
Kesey, Ken, 179
King, Clarence, 78
Kingsbury, Alice, 48
Kingston, Maxine Hong, 216, 218
Kipling, Rudyard, 80, 212
Koller, James, 224
Kroeber, Theodora, 127
Kroeber, A. L., 127, 160
Kuhlman, Walter, 185
Kuo, Alex, 230
Kyger, Joanne, 204, 224

Labor questions, 61–64, 72, 74, 75, 77, 78, 83, 100–102, 114, 115, 142–44, 147, 211, 230
LaVigne, Robert, 194
Lafler, Henry ("Fra"/"Harry"), 97, 111, 119, 120
Laing, R. D., 179
Lamantia, Philip, 153, 157, 163, 167, 184, 189, 191, 226
Lamott, Kenneth, 224
Langton, Daniel, 194
Lark, 89–92, 94, 96, 123, 132
Laughing Horse, 132
Laughlin, James, 156, 181
Lawrence, D. H., 132, 141, 160, 181
Lawrence, Joseph T., 29, 38, 40
Leary, Timothy, 198–200
Leblanc, Peter, 185
Leffland, Ella, 218

Leiber, Fritz, 116, 212
Leigh, Carol, 176
Leite, George, 153, 155
Lenoir, Henri, 148, 149, 151, 191
Letter sheets, 18
Levy, Stella, 194
Lewis, Austin, 100, 107
Lewis, Oscar, 141, 150, 152
Lewis, Sinclair, 114, 115
Lezinsky, David Lesser, 171
Lihn, Enrique, 219
Lipton, Dean, 212
Lipton, Lawrence, 157
Litvak, Leo, 218
Lobeira, Vasco de, 3
London, Charmian, 102, 103, 104
London, Jack, 44, 51, 55, 64, 88, 96, 99–105, 107, 109,
    114, 118, 119, 123, 144, 145, 192, 235
Long, Karl, 144
Lowell, Robert, 159
Lowenthal, Leo, 181
Ludlow, Fitz Hugh, 35
Lundborg, Florence, 91, 117

MacAdams, Lewis, 218, 224
MacAgy, Douglas, 153
MacGowan, Alice, 114, 118, 119
MacIntyre, C. F., 153
MacNaughton, Duncan, 224
McBride, Richard, 163
McCabe, Charles, 139
McClure, Michael, 157, 174, 184, 185, 189, 191, 194–96,
    219, 225
McCracken, Michael, 185
McCrackin, Josephine Clifford, 71
McEwen, Arthur, 29, 48
McGahey, Jeanne, 153
McGettigan, Francisca Vallejo, 9
McHugh, Vincent, 177, 182
McKuen, Rod, 147, 228
McWilliams, Carey, 107, 141
Marcuse, Herbert, 198, 200
Margolis, William, 180, 188
Markham, Edwin, 44, 55, 76–78, 133
Martin, Dick, 176
Martin, Peter D., 163
Martinez, Xavier, 96, 97, 107, 118–20
Marx, Karl, 58, 74, 75, 77, 99, 100, 144, 200
Meltzer, David, 185, 189, 194, 219, 224, 231
Melville, Herman, 22, 169
Mencken, H. L., 101, 107, 132
Menken, Adah Isaacs, 33, 38–40, 57
Meyerzove, Lee, 194
Micheline, Jack, 221
Miles, Josephine, 141, 153, 158, 184, 204, 205
Milhaud, Darius, 153, 159
Miller, Henry, 153–55, 160, 166, 172, 181, 184, 185, 235
Miller, Joaquin, 33, 41, 46, 51–55, 60, 64, 77, 83, 94, 96, 112
Miller, Minnie Myrtle, 53, 55
Millet, Jean François, 78
Millet, Kate, 219, 220
Milne, Robert Duncan, 69
Modjeska, Helena, 72, 73

Moe, David, 221
Monroe, Arthur, 185
Montalvo, Garcí Ordóñez, 3, 4, 7
Montgomery, John, 219
Montgomery Block, 95–98, 128, 129, 189, 213, 233
Mooney, Tom, 114, 129, 141, 142, 213
Moore, Daniel, 197
Moore, Marianne, 158, 159
Moore, Richard, 153, 157
Moore, Rosalie, 153
Morgan, Robin, 219, 220
Mori, Toshio, 216
Morrow, William C., 68, 69, 88
Morris, William, 192
Mother Earth, 100, 128
Muir, John, 60, 78, 79
Mulford, Prentice, 40, 41, 44, 52, 57, 64
Murao, Shigeyoshi, 163, 174, 181, 182, 194
Murieta, Joaquin, 24, 25, 53
Murray, Carol, 220

Nahl, Charles Christian, 21, 24, 25
Nelson, Brian, 228
Newell, Robert Henry ("Orpheus C. Kerr"), 40
Nichols, Luther, 217
Nin, Anaïs, 153
Noguchi, Yone, 55, 91, 94, 96
Norris, Charles, 96, 125
Norris, Frank, *x*, 44, 55, 86–89, 96, 100, 125, 152
Norris, Kathleen, 96, 125
Norse, Harold, 153, 223
Notley, Alice, 224

O'Hara, Frank, 185
Oijer, Bruno, 219
Olsen, Tillie, 218
Olson, Charles, 157, 158, 187, 225
Oppen, George, 204
Oracle, 198–200
Orlovitz, Gil, 153
Orlovsky, Peter, 176, 194
Ortiz, Simon, 219, 228, 231
Overland Monthly, 44, 51–53, 55, 77, 78, 99, 108, 117, 188
Owen, Robert, 72, 73

Palóu, Francisco, 5, 6
Parkinson, Ariel, 141, 167
Parkinson, Thomas, 141, 153, 157, 181
Parsons, Neil, 230
Partch, Harry, 153
Partington, Blanche, 107, 117
Patchen, Kenneth, 153, 156, 169, 174, 181
Paz, Octavio, 158
Peck, George Washington, 17
Peixotto, Ernest, 91, 117
Pelieu, Claude (Washburn), 198
Persky, Stan, 194
Peters, Charles Rollo, 112
Peters (Lamantia), Nancy J., 226
Petit Journal de Refusées, 92
Phelps, Janette "Hagar," 58
Piercy, Marge, 219, 220
Pioneer, 18, 27

Pioneer Bookstore, 19
Pittsinger, Eliza, 33, 48, 57
Platt's Hall speakers, 58–60
Poe, Edgar Allan, 34, 46, 70, 73, 94, 188
Poetry, popular, 27, 45–49, 174–77, 221
Poetry Center, 159, 171–73, 181, 187
Poetry Flash, 186, 216, 218, 219
Poetry Readings, series, 186
Poets' Follies, 176, 177, 222
Polk, Willis, 91
Pollack, Edward, 46
Pommy-Vega, Janine, 202
Porter, Bern, 153, 157
Porter, Bruce, 83, 90, 91, 111
Pound, Ezra, 128, 133, 156, 160, 207, 211, 225
Pronzini, Bill, 212

Quin, Mike, 142

Ramiz, José, 148, 149
Ramparts, 134, 169
Ramsey, Henry, 140, 141
Read, Herbert, 156
Realf, Richard, 71
Reed, Ishmael, 219, 230, 231
Reich, Charles, 218
Religious revival, 195, 197, 198, 202, 203
Revolution, social, 58, 74, 75, 101, 109, 115, 156, 200
Rexroth, Kenneth, 153, 155, 156, 158, 159, 167, 168, 169,
    174, 175, 181, 184, 218
Rezanov, Nicolai, 9
Rhodes, William "Caxton," 46, 62, 68
Rice, Anne, 212
Ridge, John Rollin, 24, 25, 33
Riley, James Whitcomb, 83, 92
Robertson, A. M., 116
Robinson, Alfred, 14
Roethke, Theodore, 158, 159
Rolling Stone, 198, 224
Roman, Anton, 42, 44, 49
Rorty, James, 133, 134
Rosenshine, Annette, 123
Rosetti, Dante Gabriel, 38, 40, 54
Royce, Josiah, 18, 44
Royce, Sarah, 16
Ruggles, Eugene, 221
Rukeyser, Muriel, 158, 224
Rumaker, Michael, 184
Ruskin Club, 100, 112
Russell, Sanders, 157
Ryan, William, 191

Saccaro, James, 185
Sales, Grover, 163, 228
Sampson, Cornelius, 148, 149
San Francisco Athenaeum, 33
San Francisco Chronicle, 31, 59, 60, 80, 86, 104, 139, 145,
    147, 150, 151, 159, 166, 177, 181, 211, 213, 217, 228, 233
San Francisco Examiner, 60, 64, 70, 77, 78, 88, 139,
    140, 215
San Francisco Renaissance, 167, 169, 184
Sanchez, Carol Lee, 219
Sandburg, Carl, 115

Saroyan, Aram, 147, 224
Saroyan, William, 144–47, 150, 216, 217
Satty, Wilfried, 185
Schaff, David, 194
Scheer, Robert, 134, 169
Scheffauer, Herman, 70, 71
Science fiction, 67–69, 212
Schell, Orville, 224
Schenker, Donald, 194
Schliemann, Heinrich, 17
Schneck, Stephen, 218
Schorer, Mark, 114, 141, 158, 181
Shange, Ntozake, 219
Shaw, George Bernard, 76, 110
Shea, Edmund, 136–38
Shinn, Millicent Washburn, 44
Sienkiewicz, Henryk, 73
Sill, Edward Rowland, 44, 46, 55, 77
Simon, Linda, 123
Sinclair, Mary Kimbrough Craig, 112, 113
Sinclair, Upton, 66, 72, 99, 112, 113, 118–20, 132, 158
Slavery, abolition of, 12, 33, 46, 58, 71
Smith, Clark Ashton, 47, 116, 129
Smith, Hassel, 185
Smith, Joseph, 14, 50
Snyder, Gary, 184, 198–202, 204, 225
Socialism, radical, 60, 64, 72–76, 83, 84, 99, 100, 107, 112,
    115, 130, 134, 139, 155, 158, 192
Spicer, Jack, 160, 163, 167, 184, 186, 225
Spiritualism, 41, 57, 72, 212
Stackpole, Ralph, 123, 141
Stanley, Don, 217
Stanton, Elizabeth Cady, 58
Starr, Kevin, 139, 140
Stauffacher, Jack, 148
Stegner, Wallace, 78, 150
Steele, Danielle, 212
Steffens, Lincoln, 110, 115, 117, 142
Stein, Gertrude, 115, 124, 158, 235
Steinbeck, John, 115, 147, 148, 235
Sterling, Carrie, 103, 107, 111
Sterling, George, 55, 71, 96–98, 103–9, 112, 114, 116–20,
    129, 132, 133, 141, 144, 152
Stevenson, Robert Louis, 52, 80–82, 90, 96, 108,
    117, 127
Stewart, Priscilla, 33
Stewart, George, 150
Stiles, Knute, 164
Still, Clyfford, 185
Stock, Robert, 157, 177
Stoddard, Charles Warren, 33, 35, 37, 40, 46, 48, 51, 52,
    57, 67, 77, 80, 94, 96, 112
Stone, Irving, 145
Stone, Judy, 213
Stowe, Harriet Beecher, 19, 53, 83
Strawn-Hamilton, Frank, 100, 101
Strunsky, Anna, 100, 117
Swett, John, 79
Swift, John Franklin, 62
Swinburne, Algernon, 40, 106

Taggard, Genevieve, 132–34
Tagore, Rabindranath, 125, 126

Tavernier, Jules, 96
Taylor, Bayard, 16, 59
Temko, Alan, 159
Thomas, Dylan, 159, 164–66, 175, 191
Thoreau, Henry David, 17, 159
Toklas, Alice B., 115, 123, 124
Tomkins, Juliet Wilbor, 88, 91
Traven, B., 213
Triem, Eva, 167
Trollope, Anthony, 59
Turner, Ethel Duffy, 47, 117
Twain, Mark, *x*, 20, 22, 29–32, 35, 36, 40, 42, 45, 48, 51, 52, 57, 65, 235

Ungaretti, Giuseppi, 153
Unger, Frank, 52
Utopias, 72–76

Vaché, Jacques, 153
Valaoritis, Nanos, 210
Vallejo, Mariano Guadalupe, 11
Varda, Jean, 153, 191, 203
Vesuvio Bar, 151, 162, 163, 191
Victor, Frances Fuller, 44, 55, 56
Vietor, Jack, 218
Virginia City Territorial Enterprise, 28, 29, 32, 48, 49
Voznesensky, Andrei, 9, 206, 207

Waldman, Anne, 219
Walker, Franklin, 21, 35, 64
Ward, Artemus, 29, 31
Warsh, Lewis, 224
Warshall, Peter, 224
Wasp, 60, 64, 66, 69, 88
Waterfront writers, 228
Watson, Burton, 194
Watts, Alan, 159, 198, 199, 202, 203
Wave, 86, 88, 89
Webb, Charles Henry, 33–36, 40
Weeks, James, 185
Weiss, Ruth, 221
Welch, James, 230
Welch, Lew, 147, 194, 204, 205, 225
Wells, Carolyn, 91
Wên-hua-she, Society for the Splendors of Literature, 63

Wentworth, May, 49
Whalen, Philip, 184, 191, 192, 202, 204, 224, 225
What Cheer House Library, 19
Whitaker, Herman (Jim), 55, 100, 107
Whitfield, James M., 33
Whitman, Walt, 14, 34, 37, 52, 59, 130, 132, 180, 181, 190
Whittier, John Greenleaf, 41, 59
Wieners, John, 186, 189
Wierzbicki, Felix, P, 19
Wiggin, Kate Douglas, 44, 83, 84
Wigglesworth, Michael, 57
Wilcox, Collin, 212
Wilde, Oscar, 59, 60, 98
Williams, Michael, 115, 119
Williams, Oscar, 153
Williams, Virgil, 80, 96
Williams, William Carlos, 153, 159
Wilson, Adrian, 169, 176
Wilson, Cecilia, 33
Wilson, Harry Leon, 117
Winter, Ella, 115, 144, 158
Winters, Ivor. 141
Witt-Diamant, Ruth, 153, 159, 166, 168, 171, 181
Wolf, Leonard, 153, 212
Wolf, Thomas, 147, 192
Wolfe, Tom, 179, 215
Women's Emancipation, 46, 57, 58, 83, 84, 86, 110, 123, 129, 220
Wong, Jade Snow, 215, 216
Wong, Nellie, 216
Wong, Shawn, 230, 231
Wood Rat (Costanoan poet), 8
Wood, Charles Erskine Scott, 139, 141, 144
Woodcock, George, 156
Woodhull, Victoria Claflin, 58
Wright, Willard Huntington, 118–20
Wright, William (Dan de Quille), 28

Yat-sen, Sun, 96
Yeats, William Butler, 60, 110, 119, 141
Yevtushenko, Yevgeny, 206–8
Young, Al, 172, 230

Zap comics, 181